YOUTH CULTURES

YOUTH CULTURES

Texts, Images, and Identities

Edited by Kerry Mallan and Sharyn Pearce

Westport, Connecticut
London

Library of Congress Cataloging-in-Publication Data

Youth cultures : texts, images, and identities / edited by Kerry Mallan and Sharyn Pearce.
    p. cm.
    Includes bibliographical references and index.
    ISBN 0–275–97409–X (alk. paper)
    1. Youth. 2. Popular culture. 3. Mass media and youth. 4. Motion pictures and youth.
5. Music and youth. 6. Youth in mass media. 7. Youth in motion pictures. 8. Youth in
literature. I. Mallan, Kerry. II. Pearce, Sharyn.
HQ796.Y59273   2003
305.235—dc21   2002029773

British Library Cataloguing in Publication Data is available.

Library of Congress Catalog Card Number: 2002029773
ISBN: 0–275–97409–X

First published in 2003

Praeger Publishers, 88 Post Road West, Westport, CT 06881
An imprint of Greenwood Publishing Group, Inc.
www.praeger.com

Printed in the United States of America

The paper used in this book complies with the
Permanent Paper Standard issued by the National
Information Standards Organization (Z39.48–1984).

P

To Susan, Kimberley, and Chris

Contents

Introduction:
Tales of Youth in Postmodern Culture

Kerry Mallan and Sharyn Pearce

As a defining age category, "youth" is often regarded as a state of becoming, as a necessary (and often tortuous) pathway to adulthood. The reward of adult status carries with it the mythical virtues of maturity, independence, stability, and above all a secure identity: One which is whole and not troubled by the uncertainties that characterize the transience of youth, especially in these times of profound global economic and social change. By foregrounding the slipperiness of the concept "youth," the various essays in this collection reveal that any attempt to position youth within set parameters is futile. While the age category youth can extend from thirteen years to twenty-five years, categorization is mostly a tool for institutional and policy purposes. As several of the writers in this collection argue, the age continuum for youth extends at both ends. While age is only one dimension, and an unreliable one at that, there are other ways of defining youth which avoid falling into the trap of universalizing the experiences of youth according to psychological, physical, and emotional stages of development; these other ways take into account the social and historical dimensions that affect the experience of being young.

When youth is the subject of a book such as this, there is a tendency to tell tales which rely heavily on "us-versus-them" oppositions. While such oppositional tales may indeed be compelling, they are nevertheless versions of a more complex social phenomenon which refuses simplistic ways of seeing its subject. The images of youth in contemporary societies are diverse: Celebratory, terrifying, and sympathetic. Like adult culture, youth culture is sometimes mistakenly regarded as being monolithic and unidimensional. In a manner similar to the diversity of textual and visual images of youth, youthful identity resists a coherent and stable meaning. The elusiveness of identity is matched by the shifts in self-image. Consequently, how young people are seen and how they see themselves are not straightforward forms of mediation and knowing; thus, the mirroring of youth in a multiplicity of texts can never be seen as mimetic of an anterior world. Like shards of glass from a broken mirror, the image of youth in contemporary western societies is always fragmented. Thus, youth cannot be seen as a fixed, preexisting entity or a unified image. Rather, it is a complex, mercurial signifier offering mixed messages and resisting a single interpretation or positioning.

ISSUES AND APPROACHES

This book does not offer a utopian view of youth. Neither does it offer a dystopian view of universal youth negativity, despair, and apathy. Rather, it attempts to interrogate the cultural spaces that youth occupy and that are represented in the texts produced for them, about them, and, sometimes, by them. The various writers in this collection relate tales from the diverse cultural landscapes of popular literature, film and television, computer games, magazines, pop music and music videos, fashion, journalism, and arts education policy. Instead of telling grand narratives about youth, the writers provide a series of perceptive commentaries on and critical analyses of the intersections between narrative (both fictional and institutional), identity, subjectivity, and agency and the ways these intersections can be viewed from various theoretical positions. Significant among these tales is the unchallengeable fact that young people constitute a highly differentiated group, and any attempts to totalize the identity of youth elide notions of class, gender, and ethnicity or "race," as well as other social, economic, and political factors. In a similar way, to speak of youth "cultures" is to acknowledge the diversity of western societies' artistic, communicative, and entertainment expressions and practices.

In writing *about* youth, one can be accused of speaking on behalf of the subject, thus denying the subject her/his own voice. While an empirical approach was not part of this book's overall intention, the politics of voice is one which emerges in the following chapters through an examination of the textual constructions of youthful identities and their various social, cultural, and historical inscriptions. It is in their theorizing and reading of the textual images and identities of youth that the writers consider the contradictions embedded in these discursive strategies and narrative emplotments, and in doing so they offer useful ways of applying critical ideas and theoretical frameworks to perennial problems and issues that surround youth and the cultures they inhabit. Many of the contributors write from a relatively eclectic standpoint, bringing a richness to their intellectual arguments by drawing on a range of theories derived from critical film and feminist analysis, psychoanalytical criticism, poststructuralism, semiotics, sociology, cultural studies, and literary theory. Such diverse theoretical perspectives help to provide ways of thinking about the issues, texts, and practices that circulate within youth cultures, indicating their underlying tensions and contradictions. It is because these theoretical stories are situated within the writers' own personal predilections and disciplinary traditions that we need to be mindful of the view that "All theories have a story to tell, about social life and an attitude toward it" (McLaren 93). Therefore, the contents of this book provide dialogical contexts for affirming, interrogating, and extending understanding of youthful identities and subjectivities which are constructed in multiple and contradictory ways.

KEY THEMES AND QUESTIONS

The following questions frame the various approaches taken in this collection to the subject of youth cultures and foreground a series of interconnecting themes that run throughout the chapters:

- How are the identities, subjectivities, and desires of young people represented in their texts, electronic media, and social practices?
- How are images of female and male and patterns of gender behavior and intersubjectivity constructed in the texts?
- In what ways do these textual representations of youth appear to resist or conform to the dominant culture at the level of the youthful body?
- What is the impact of government policy, institutional practices, and corporate power on young people's identities, agency, and development of creative self-formation?
- How are class, gender, sexuality, and ethnicity shaped within popular cultural discourses?

The ensuing discussion offers a more detailed thematic overview of the book's contents and conveys a sense of the direction taken by the individual writers. Themes are rarely treated in isolation, and there is also the inevitable cross-linking across chapters which invite juxtaposition of theoretical ideas and interpretation. Discussions of youth are, by necessity, framed within a context of consumerism, popular culture, and corporate cultural politics.

ARE WE HAVING FUN YET? THE PRODUCTION OF PLEASURE WITHIN YOUTH CULTURES

The production of pleasure within youth cultures is tied to the way various modes of desire and subjectivity are embraced. A central resource for eliciting youthful pleasures and desires is the mass media, which communicates most

effectively through the senses and emotions, thus ensuring an affective investment by youth. However, despite the heavy imprints of corporate power on aspects of youth cultures, and popular cultural texts and practices in particular,
youth are both resistant to and embracing of these various cultural expressions.
Channeled through the avenues of popular culture, these youth-centered images and narratives open up spaces of possibility for young people in their efforts to give expression to the meaning of their lives—their desires, dreams,
and fears; they also test the limits of existing pedagogical, moral, and sexual
discourses. Given the push and pull of competing desires and expectations, it is
incumbent upon youth to be sharp and mistrusting of the manipulated imagery and representations disseminated through multimedia channels and proliferated in a world inhabited by spin doctors, image consultants, and predatory
marketers—all of whom offer pleasure as a viable commodity to be purchased,
enjoyed, and repeated.

It is therefore through the sensuous body that youth learn how to experience themselves. Whether such experience can be said to be authentic or simply a simulation manufactured by corporate sponsors and marketers is central
to Karen Brooks's argument ("Nothing Sells like Teen Spirit"). Brooks contends that the conflicting representations of youth across a range of media "reconstruct youth as objects: As sites of spectacle and desire for a mass audience"
(pp. 1). This observation is supported by cultural theorist Peter McLaren, who
sees the interpolation of youth into the postmodern world of electronic and artificially generated images as having prompted the crisis in modernist identity
and given expression to "marketplace identities" (105): Identities which he
considers are being fashioned "around the excesses of the marketing and consumption and the natural social relations of post-industrial capitalism" (2).
Brooks posits the notion of a liminal space as a site where youth, or its subversive and celebratory "teen spirit," can coexist with the dominant culture
while at the same time subverting the latter's hegemonic powers of control
and delineation.

An emerging and successful manifestation of a particular kind of "teen
spirit" is recounted in Kearney's chapter ("Girls Make Movies"). Kearney
considers the problem of "generational dynamics that construct cultural production as an adult-only enterprise" (pp. 24). In her discussion of movies made
by teenage girls, Kearney argues that female youth are capable cultural producers and calls attention to "how ingrained the stereotype of girls as culturally unproductive still is today, particularly in the film industry" (pp. 18). The
extent of some girls' creative endeavors in filmmaking has resulted in their
forming their own production companies. Kearney acknowledges the impact
of feminist youth cultures and "girl power" discourses in inspiring girls to become involved in creative productions. Her chapter also highlights how these
female-produced texts offer new kinds of pleasure to female youth in their attempts to produce films which establish a "girl's gaze" and engage in the contradictory experiences of female youth. In this sense, these girl-made movies

have found their own liminal space for telling their counternarratives. While these texts may not have the same mass circulatory power and distribution of mainstream texts, they nevertheless rupture the grand narrative of females' cultural unproductivity and destabilize the notion of a universal female youth identity.

Another instance of liminal space occurs in the realm of popular music and is particularly located within the visual/aural dimensions of the music video. In her chapter on popular antiromance songs ("Stronger Than Yesterday?"), Clare Bradford draws attention to the multisensory nature of the video clip which relies on the words, melody/voice quality, and visual and performative aspects to give sensory pleasures. She also sees these texts as embodying contradictory ideological messages in their "play of ideas about gender identities and about relations between men and women, realized in lyrics and visual forms characterized by complexity, ambiguity, and inconclusiveness" (pp. 45). Bradford's analysis of the textual and performative elements of music videos draws attention to the ways bodies not only take in sensory elements such as sight and sound, but also language and ideas—words, lexical choices, symbols, and rhythms. Thus the sensuous body is also a knowing one, capable of making meanings from texts which rely on pastiche, nonlinear narratives, and random and autonomous signifiers. By acknowledging the potential for both affective and intellectual investments by young people in popular culture, Bradford challenges the notion that "The plurality of meanings in video clips makes us talk of their senses, not of their sense" (Fiske 75).

Songs have formed part of every generation's pleasure-seeking endeavors. Furthermore, they not only serve a communicative function in retelling human experiences and emotions, but they also play a significant part in the cultural and historical formation of youthful subjectivity. While popular music, music videos, and their accompanying discourses become a rhetorical force for youth's insertion into commodity culture, youth also makes a considerable investment in this symbolic order. Hence, investment implies both appropriation of and identification with the symbols generated and circulated through this form of cultural practice/product. However, identification does not preclude resistance. The free-floating signifiers or polysemy of meaning attached to any symbol are not the only means by which resistance can take place. The body, too, has the ability to take up endless subject positions and to engage with any number of representations in its pursuit of pleasure and search for an elusive identity.

YOUTHFUL BODIES AS SITES OF CULTURAL INSCRIPTION, CONSUMPTION, AND GOVERNANCE

Youth live in a "predatory culture ... of stalkers and victims" where identity is fashioned around the excesses of the marketplace and consumer culture (McLaren 2). John Hartley and Catharine Lumby ("Working Girls or Drop-Dead Gorgeous?") observe that the young girl has been one such targeted "victim" throughout the 1990s. These writers argue that the young girl's "stalkers"—the pedophile, the journalist, the modeling agent, the fashion industry entrepreneur, and the artist—see female youth as a prime target for exploitation and consumption. "Stalkers" also attempt to position her as the enduring object of the male gaze: "Voyeurism shadows the anxious scrutiny of teenage girls in popular discourse," as Hartley and Lumby observe in this volume (pp. 54).

This concept of the youthful female body as a site of cultural inscription and objectification is featured in several of the chapters in this collection (see Stephens, Mallan, Brooks, and Tait). As Hartley and Lumby argue, the concept summons up familiar binaries. The binaries attempt to enforce the dichotomous strategies of categorization which serve the vested interests of phallocentrism and patriarchal order. However, all the writers see this attempt to strip the young girl of agency by restricting her within a limited space of the innocent, sexualized "other" as problematic. This is especially so when it is placed alongside stories of female empowerment circulating through popular culture and evident in the lived experiences of many young women. In popular cultural texts, female youth are represented as investing in their bodies in culturally specific ways which resist the idea of the feminine body as the unspoken, abjected Other. As Hartley and Lumby observe, "girls are the new boys; running the country—or at least its public narrative" (pp. 66).

This last point raises two interesting aspects of the argument: One has to do with the ambivalent processes of cultural inscription and commodification of female bodies in popular discourses; the other concerns the place of male youth in these conflicting tales of female dominance/subjugation. Sharyn Pearce ("As Wholesome As ...") and Gordon Tait ("The Seven Things All Men Love in Bed") take up the notion of governance of the sexed and sexual body. For Pearce, the popular American teen film *American Pie,* is a "manual for self-formation, a means whereby young men can progress relatively smoothly toward adulthood with particular reference to the management of sexual conduct" (pp. 70). In a similar vein, Tait considers how women's magazines can be regarded as "practical manuals which enlist young women to do specific kinds of work on themselves," thus providing female readers with "a significant source of practices and techniques through which particular types of self are shaped" (pp. 82). Both writers see these particular cultural texts as working as contemporary "sex" manuals which are characterized by their open and at times confronting treatment of (hetero)sexuality. In this sense, they serve a pedagogical function for young people through their images, language, and humor which appeal to their targeted audiences. While there are similarities in how these texts function as tools of governance and instruction for young women and young men, the writers offer insights into the different ways femininity and masculinity, sexuality, and gender relations are variously constituted in contemporary western societies.

A consistent thread throughout the chapters is the notion that youth sells; not only the concept of youth, but also the gamut of material and social practices and modes of production that are part of its orbit of consumption and representation. In addition to the pedagogical and governing function of the various cultural discourses discussed thus far, David Buckingham ("Living in a Young Country?") astutely notes the ways in which contemporary policies in the United Kingdom are imbued with a youthful imagery and rhetoric which are appropriate for rallying enthusiasm and commitment to the ideals of a "young country." In an era in which both politicians and academics speak of "New Times," youth is an ideal symbolic and conceptual image to promote and sell to a population characterized by a growing cynicism and weariness about political promises. Buckingham discusses how Britain's "New Labour" policy, particularly in its education and cultural policy relating to youth, is contradictory: In one sense, it espouses "the culturalist rhetoric of access and empowerment, and indeed to the celebration of the 'young country'" (pp. 103), while, in another sense, it offers a disciplinary caveat which warns that leisure time needs to be channeled "in responsibly 'creative' directions" (pp. 104). The situation Buckingham describes is not unlike that in other western societies, wherein government policy and political rhetoric contain contradictions and paradoxes; it would appear that such inherent contradictions are a necessary safety valve without which the tide of reform could pose a real threat to the dominant cultural hegemony. Buckingham offers hope rather than despair, for he sees the new emphasis on youthful creativity as representing an important opportunity, albeit one which needs to be closely monitored from within the arts community and subjected to rigorous self-examination. In his discussion of youthful creativity, there is an interesting cross-cultural linkage with Kearney's chapter on the creative endeavors of girl filmmakers; in the instances Kearney recounts, practice has proceeded largely without policy directives, and in some cases it has contributed to the reformation of policy, with particular reference to media literacy education.

While Buckingham's chapter looks at British cultural policy as a means of ensuring that youthful hands are not idle but are kept busy in appropriately creative endeavors, Claudia Nelson ("The Unheimlich Maneuver") takes a different tack but one which is not unrelated to Buckingham's thesis. Nelson considers the ways in which selected fictional texts, termed "urban waif tales," often operate on "the assumption that the social problem of the homeless teenager is really the domestic problem of the failed parent" (pp. 110). In the real world of social policy and politics, these novels represent the problem of homeless youth and the underlying causes for their circumstances as reasons for government action in terms of policy and structures for youth protection, surveillance, and governance. In the books that Nelson discusses, the body of the homeless youth is one which is abjected, literally cast out of its domestic space; thus, homeless youth become "refugees from monstrous homes" (Nelson pp. 111, in this volume). In reading these texts through the Freudian dual notions of the *heimlich/unheimlich*, the domestic/antidomestic, and the know-able/repressed, Nelson provides accounts of both adults and youth which disrupt social myths of domesticity, family, and parenthood. In the novels, the body of youth is one which is open to criticism, abuse, and resignification. These fictional characters are McLaren's "victims" living in a predatory world of stalkers. Such tales of horror are of course not confined to a writer's creative imagination. Fictional urban waifs have their counterparts in the real world where homeless and other displaced youth inhabit a landscape of terror.

Within these competing discourses of cultural consumption, inscription, and governance which accompany news stories, magazines, film, fiction, and government imperatives, youth are variously demonized, celebrated, victimized, exploited, and "marked as disposable" (Giroux 21)—literally murdered, abjected, replaced.

AGENCY, SUBJECTIVITY, AND DISCOURSES OF POSSIBILITY

An emerging issue implied in the above discussion concerns the extent to which subjectivity can be realized only in a totalizing opposition to otherness (i.e., youth/adult; female/male; stalker/victim) or whether it can be self-reflexive, looking to its own constitutive elements. Embedded in this issue is the notion of difference with respect to social relations, personal knowledges and discursive formations, and cultural experiences. Central to these matters of difference is the question of agency. A view of agency, offered by feminist critic Judith Butler, is that it *"is always and only a political prerogative.* As such, it seems crucial to question the conditions of its possibility, not to take it for granted as an *a priori* guarantee" (13; Butler's italics). For Butler, agency is located in the performativity of signifiers which are repeated, cited, and open to transformation. Within this context of discursive formation, subjectivity must be considered as problematic, and agency as always provisional, since subjects are continually re/produced within and by relations of power and systems of exclusion, alterity, abjection, and erasure.

John Stephens ("I'll Never Be the Same After That Summer") considers how youth in teen film progress from states of abjection to subjective agency: "Teen films are primarily concerned with subjectivity and intersubjectivity and with the social contexts in which these are produced, lost, or denied" (pp. 124). According to Stephens, a key feature of the development of subjective agency lies in the subject's transition from childhood to adulthood, from a state of lesser to greater potentiality. However, in making this transition, agency is only possible for the young protagonists who choose nonconformity and alienation. In the examples Stephens discusses, abjection is viewed as a pivotal point for realizing agency or for descending into a state of dysfunction or total erasure. Like Nelson, Stephens considers the notion of abjection as being rooted in paternal (parental) inadequacy. It is in the specific (and sometimes shared) characteristics of the genres and their narrative strategies that both writers are able to foreground the representation of youthful abjection as productive or denying of subjective agency and intersubjectivity.

Kerry Mallan ("Hitting Below the Belt") continues the discussion of agency, subjectivity, and the notion of abjection. In looking at the development of the action femininity trend evinced in the mainstream television series *Buffy, the Vampire Slayer* and the independent film *Girlfight*, Mallan highlights the ambivalences which surround this image of femininity in popular culture. As she argues, "the 'action girl' persona cannot simply be utilized as a way of rectifying what was excluded or defined as inferior within patriarchal culture and conventional cinema" (pp. 143). It is in their separate treatments of difference that the two texts draw attention to the ways cultural and historical specificities are able to confirm or trouble the complacency of western universalizing notions of female identity, subjectivity, and ethnicity. However, a feature which emerges in accounts of teen film by both Mallan and Stephens is a form of ludic postmodernism that is evident in the films' adoption of self-reflexivity, continual playfulness of signifiers, and frame-breaking strategies. While it can be rightly argued that ludic postmodernism lacks a critical, transformative potential, it nevertheless is a form of representation which is appealing to youth audiences.

Playfulness in its many guises is an element which characterizes the chapters written by Lisa Sainsbury, David Buchbinder, and Roderick McGillis. It is perhaps fitting that this aspect is reserved for the concluding paragraphs of this Introduction, since it also returns to the earlier discussion of pleasure as a significant feature of youth cultures and texts. These chapters too highlight a discourse of possibility which serves to balance the discourse of despair which is apt to characterize many of the debates surrounding youth today. Sainsbury's chapter ("Game On") utilizes Bakhtin's notion of carnival as a playful and potentially empowering space for children to enter when it is applied to postmodern fantasies in the form of elective and compulsive narratives—texts which involve the reader to varying degrees in making choices which affect narrative construction and interactivity between reader and text. The interactive nature of computer-based texts invites reader participation in ways which subvert conventional modes of reading through their challenging multilinear narrative structures, call to play, and strategies of inserting the reader-player as the key protagonist in the adventure. Of the three texts she discusses, it is the electronic narrative form which Sainsbury sees as having the most potential for playing with "the boundaries between author and player-reader, reality and fantasy" (pp. 166).

David Buchbinder's chapter ("The Orangutan in the Library") considers the fantasy world created in Terry Pratchett's popular Discworld series. Like the texts Sainsbury discusses, Pratchett's Discworld series plays with and subverts aspects of traditional narrative and genre form, but it does so in different ways. For instance, the texts that Sainsbury discusses subvert through their playing with both conventional forms of narrative and ways of reading which invite young players to take up the subject position offered by the text/game through direct address. However, the Discworld books play with the inherent features of the genre (imaginary closed universes, archaic language, quest motif, allusion) through processes of inversion, satire, and other forms of comedic play, intertextuality, references to real-world politics, history, sociocultural issues, and popular culture. While the appeal of the series for youth obviously stems from its particular form of ludic textuality, Buchbinder proposes that another feature of its popularity is the "motif of control" of the young by the old that forms a consistent thread throughout the books and which may resonate with adolescent readers, particularly males, who are "still trying to find their own social identities in an eventful world" (pp. 180).

Finally, we come to Roderick McGillis's chapter ("Coprophilia for Kids"). McGillis, like Buchbinder and other writers in the collection, looks at humor in texts for young people. However, the form of humor which he discusses is grossness and its appeal to children. Like the instances of gross humor concentrated on bodily fluids that Pearce discusses in *American Pie*, McGillis makes reference to the "five regrettable fluids" that feature in the "array of the gross and vulgar available for consumption" (pp. 183). Rather than see this as a new trend and further evidence of cultural decline, McGillis correctly points out that vulgarity and grossness have always been part of the culture of childhood. It can also be interpreted as part of Bakhtin's carnival, which "works to contain as much as to release dangerous energies," in McGillis's words. Hence, young people's desire for the undesirable and disgusting is a form of transgression and silent protest against the strictures of adult society with its socially sanctioned forms of behavior and codes of politeness. Nevertheless, McGillis reminds us that these desires are also another avenue of children's play which can be marketed and exploited for profit. Consequently, children, like older members of their generation, exist in the liminal space between pleasure and commodification.

As the various chapters in this book demonstrate, youth's identities are in a continual process of formation and reformation as young people engage with the images, texts, and practices that are available for consumption, appropriation, and reinterpretation. However, one needs to be mindful of the fact that youth are not necessarily passive dupes susceptible to the vagaries of a Machiavellian marketplace. Youth are also savvy consumers, manipulators, and producers capable of subverting, resisting, and transforming the popular images that attempt to fix and define their existence. The texts located in youth cultures are an important part of youth's cultural capital and are thereby significant in terms of historical, social, and political constructions of youth and as a means for understanding the relations of power and identity formations that youth experience, struggle over, and resist.

The editors would like to thank the following people for their helpful comments and support: Raylee Elliott Burns, Barbara Hanna, Lyn Linning, Geraldine Massey, and Kimberley Mallan. Special thanks go to Margaret Miles for her superb formatting of the manuscript and to Helen Horton for expertise in indexing. Financial support was also provided by the Centre for Community and Cross-Cultural Studies, QUT Carseldine, Queensland University of Technology.

WORKS CITED

Butler, Judith. 1992. "Contingent Foundations: Feminism and the Question of Postmodernism." Pp. 3–21 in *Feminists Theorize the Political,* eds. Judith Butler and J. Scott. New York: Routledge.

Fiske, John. 1986. "MTV: Poststructural, Postmodern." *Journal of Communication Inquiry,* 10: 74–79.

Giroux, Henry. 2000. *Stealing Innocence: Corporate Culture's War on Children.* New York: Palgrave.

McLaren, Peter. 1995. *Critical Pedagogy and Predatory Culture.* New York: Routledge.

Nothing Sells like Teen Spirit:
The Commodification of Youth Culture

Karen Brooks

Commodification reifies and fixates the complexity of youth along with the range of possible identities they might assume while simultaneously exploiting them as fodder for the logic of the market.

—Giroux 28

"Youth" has long been a contentious designation in both academic and public discourse facilitating debates about generationalism, ageism, and specificity (Wulff 6–7). The category "youth" is most often used to describe young people when they refuse to model their behavior on what the parent culture considers appropriate (Oswell 38).[1] Young people are frequently represented as "out of control" and as a threat, not only to the hierarchical foundations of society, but most importantly to themselves. As Henry Giroux writes, "the discourse on youth shifts from an emphasis on social failings in the society to questions of individual character, social policy moves from the language of social investment—creating safety nets for children—to the language of containment and blame" (17).

These oppositional classifications of young people as either *dangerous* or *in danger* pathologize youth and youth culture and institutionalize a way of reading "youth" that is reflected in various popular cultural forms (Oswell 38–39). These conflicting representations are evident across a range of media where the images and cultures of youth are appropriated and commodified by mainstream market forces which elide any notion of agency in young people and the youthful "concepts" they sell. Rather, they reconstruct youth as objects: As sites of spectacle and desire for a mass audience (Giroux 21). By capturing and (re)producing contradictory but finite identities for young people, the idea of youth is harnessed and sold as a commodity that is attractive and available to consumers of all ages. The mechanisms of commodification suppress and objectify the liminal nature of teen spirit and create an endorsed and desirable youth market.

This chapter briefly examines this youth market and the forces through which it is endorsed, such as fashion, the media—including television, advertising, and print media—and young celebrity figures such as the fourteen-year-old Australian singer Nikki Webster, who featured in the Sydney 2000 Olympics opening ceremony, and the controversial American rap artist Eminem. It also considers the commodification of youth through the deliberate marketing of products to a consumer group termed "middle youth." Through an examination of the production and consumption of youth music, this chapter attempts to problematize the ways in which young people are complicit in, and resist, the dominant culture's forces of commodification. Also explored are the ways in which the creation/mobilization of a youth identity that is counter to those validated by mainstream culture must also engage with the very hegemonic forces it seeks to resist in order to be circulated. The question that then arises is, Does the authentication of the hegemony render young people's voices invalid? In attempting to answer this question, the notion of a liminal space will be posited: Such a space can subvert adult culture while at the same time representing aspects of youth culture within mainstream adult forms.

THE VOICE(S) OF YOUTH

The category "youth" endlessly shifts and slides between the binary opposites of adult/child, innocence/knowledge, and power/powerlessness, disrupting the essentialism of these psychological and social sites and causing discomfort in adult circles. As David Oswell argues, "'Youth' defines a moment of disturbance: A space *in between*" (38). Instead of being empowered as a liminal site, this "between" space is reconfigured as a "geography of exclusion" (46) where youth are always located as neither/nor and refused a legitimate voice and individual power. Denied any political agency, youth are narrated in social and cultural spheres by voices that turn youth itself into an "empty category inhabited by the desires, fantasies, and interests of the adult world" (Giroux 35). Thus, images of youth are (re)located in a circuit of cultural exchange where they are defined by generational politics and the ideologies of an older generation (Grossberg 484–85; Davis).

When young people's bodies (and minds) enter into a cultural marketplace, they are appropriated, commodified, circulated, and consumed. On the one hand, control over the way in which they are represented appears to lie within what I broadly describe as market forces. This term embraces those authoritarian producers and distributors, such as the media, advertising executives, stylists, public relations officials, managers, and educators, who might attempt to represent the best interests of their youthful clientele while simultaneously seeking to meet the desires of their entire potential audience. The potential audience is, of course, not simply young people, but a range of consumers encompassing diverse ages, classes, cultural backgrounds, and gender who, ironically, desire both heterogeneity *and* homogeneity in their consumer choices. On the other hand, there is evidence to suggest that increasingly young people are wresting power from the producers of these images and reproducing versions of themselves that both conform to and resist stereotypes. Still, to what degree does this reactionary and proactive process empower either the young producer or consumer, or does it rather simply confirm their choices by (re)placing them within a limited range of options which have already been incorporated into the cultural hegemony?

Many television commercials and music videos purporting to be about or for young people serve corporate and public interests by selling back to the predominantly adult market images of youth that confirm the stereotypes disseminated and maintained by a hegemonic cultural pedagogy. The contribution of television to this economic and cultural distribution of "teen spirit" is evident in programs like *Rage, Video Hits, Neighbours, Home and Away, Heartbreak High, Degrassi Junior High, Dawson's Creek, Buffy: The Vampire Slayer, MTV, Beverly Hills 90210,* and *South Park.*[2] In these television shows, youth is a performance, a "repeated ritualization" (Oswell 42) that can be imitated and consumed by audiences of all ages, perpetuating and commodifying what the dominant market forces imagine youth, in all its manifestations, to constitute. The commodification of young people "represent[s] an invigorated referent for a mid-life consciousness aggressively in search of acquiring a more youthful state of mind and lifestyle" (Giroux 36–37). Youth, as a commodity, is the ultimate cultural elixir, transfigured and marketed to an aging population as a panacea for social and psychological disease.

Through particular modes of production and imagery, corporate society harnesses the essence of youth and sells back to the adult culture an antiaging formula. By targeting those euphemistically referred to as the young at heart, a range of products is skewed towards the 25–50-year-old demographic so that they may relive their youth. According to a number of manufacturers such as Sony, Lego, Nokia, and Swatch, the emphasis on various items designed for the entertainment of "kidults"—the aging baby boomer—has substantially increased (Lloyd). Hugh Mackay writes that the reason for this preoccupation with toys and accessories normally associated with young people—such as Playstations, fashionable watches, mobile phones, scooters, and sophisticated Lego goods—is that there is a recognizable body of adult consumers who want to surround themselves with products that advance and maintain the illusion of youth. According to Mackay:

Their apparently "elastic adolescence," stretching all the way into middle age, may not be about to snap, but it's beginning to look pretty thin. Some of them will decide it's time to settle down to the serious business of planning and saving for retirement. Others, with every prospect of earning good money well into their sixties, will embark on a fresh round of spending, especially on recreational and "experiential" pursuits, and on items like sports cars or cosmetic surgery that might sustain the adolescent fantasy for a little longer. (quoted in Lloyd 52)

The obsession with youth and the commodification of a specific period of a subject's life in order to artificially recapture and sustain it can be understood in terms of a "cultural necrophilia" (Peretti 19), that is, a love of a specific temporal period concomitant with attitudes that, for the adult subject, are no longer applicable: They are dead. It is indicative of an aging generation of "adulescents" that continue to blur the distinction between themselves and people half their age by consuming and validating the hip and fashionable and spouting ideologies that are irrelevant to the position and economic power they now hold (Peretti 16). Jacques Peretti refers to these people as "middle youth": That is, those "late-twenties/early thirties middle-income professionals looking back to their youth and forward to middle age at a single glance" (15). Furthermore, according to Peretti, these people now have the power, as the editors, television producers, and "demographics people at ad agencies" to create youth in their own nostalgic image and become fashionable all over again by marketing back to other adolescents and young people fixed notions of youth style (16). In the process, youth and youthfulness are transformed into another form of mass consumption, and the notion of rebellion and opposition to the mainstream into a fad: One that is forever "functional, fashionable and fun" (Lloyd 52) for people of all ages.[3]

HEROIN CHIC AND THE BODY (UN)BEAUTIFUL

When removed from any temporal or spatial verities, the commercial representations of youth acknowledge the contradictions in and ambivalence of this stage of maturation and turn angst, rebellion, and even nihilism into desirable commodities. By mapping these psychological conditions specifically onto a young body, the market forces create what Lawrence Grossberg describes as a "topography of desire" (484); that is, a site from which ideological or political struggle is elided, reducing the body to a purely superficial or external referent. The debate which occurred in the late 1990s surrounding the production of "heroin chic" is an example of the fetishization, trivialization, and commodification of young people's ideologies and fashion choices by a particular market. By reconstructing and exteriorizing the psychosocial complexities of heroin use into a "look," the fashion industry created a desirable and uncomplicated product: Where young people could don a façade without the associated dangers of drug use.[4] This marketing strategy turned antiestablishment behavior and possible drug addiction into a maligned fashion statement and, in the process, commodified the debates surrounding youth, drug use, and the fears of older generations. The binary oppositions of right/wrong, good/bad, and young/old were played out not as ethical or moral debates about addiction and potential social consequences, but as commodified ideologies. Once again, the binary oppositions that uphold establishment practices and relegate youth beyond the margins were reaffirmed.

In Foucauldian terminology, heroin chic was an instance of use value being submerged into appearance value (Finkelstein 112). If young people looked as if they were on drugs, then the logical conclusion was that they were, because, as Joanne Finkelstein argues, appearances are fashioned and seem to reveal the political and social positions of those who adopt a particular "look" (105–12). Nonetheless, the flexibility of expressing the self through a look like heroin chic was denied to youth: First, it was a created phenomenon, appearing as though it emerged from the margins, and second, because of the panic it aroused.[5] Heroin chic was condemned by the U.S. president of the time, Bill Clinton, who said that "you do not have to glamorize addiction to sell clothes" (quoted in Blanchard 2), linking the look with the behavior and implying that by moderating one you will control the other. Needless to say, the fashion houses found another look to exploit.

One of the ironies extant in the youth market and its associated products is that while young people may think they are resisting the dominant culture by adopting a particular mien or lifestyle, they are, in effect, sustaining the commercial viability of the commodification of teen spirit. This contradiction is evident in nearly all youth commodities—even when the young people are producers of the representations themselves. On the one hand, young people take an active role in the production and distribution of "youth" (through the creation and successful marketing of music, theater, and film) while, on the other, they purchase and consume the images that both mainstream and alternative markets create. When *attempts* are made to realistically represent young people's voices and diversity, they are tolerated to some extent by the dominant culture. However, hegemonic forces ensure that these alternative models of representation and modes of discourse are contained within their own liminal spaces—alternative music scenes, 'zines, and, more recently, cyberspace (Giroux 35).

YOUNG PEOPLE'S BODIES AND THE MEDIA

Commonly, many representations of young people are placed in contexts that popularize notions of youth, thus reconfirming establishment ideologies surrounding the (in)appropriate policing and control of young people. Word associations are automatically deployed to justify and indeed reify the adult culture's attitudes to young people. Binaries such as youth and crime, youth and drugs, youth and unemployment, and youth and gangs are frequently employed by the media to arouse an acute psychosocial antipathy toward young people that is difficult to invalidate. The specificity of these terms develops and excludes other age groups, despite the fact that social phenomena such as unemployment, drugs, gangs, and crime are not exclusive to young people. By limiting the scope of these terms through their unproblematic association with youth, adult culture is identified as part of the "solution," not the "problem." The linking of youth to negative social phenomena or undesirable behaviors, as Stuart Hitchings explains, "whip[s] up fear and distrust of young people [which] is central to the onslaught of repressive legislation aimed at youth" (78). This polarization of youth and adult once more legitimates young people's inability/prohibition to access any knowledge or power that can potentially disrupt these fundamentally capricious sociocultural boundaries.

Instead of empowering youth, mainstream culture, arm in arm with corporate interests, seeks to commodify and privatize youth. As Phillip Adams notes, "marketers exploit a kid's impatience to grow up, ruthlessly accelerating the process, abbreviating the few short years of wonderment" for economic exploitation. Giroux too considers the economic exploitation of youth, noting that within "the slick world of advertising, teenage bodies are sought after for the exchange value (or profit) generated through the marketing of adolescent sexuality, which offers a marginal exoticism and ample pleasures for the largely male consumer" (28). Contemporary magazines, Internet sites, television series, films, and music videos abound with sexualized images of young people.[6]

In the June 2000 issue of *FHM* magazine, for example, the "delectable" actress, Holly Valance from the Australian soap opera *Neighbours,* is featured on the cover and in an eight-page spread (Bastick 92–99). *FHM* deliberately markets itself as a "guy" magazine, in that it unapologetically relies on sex to sell, so the appearance of Valance as a sexually desirable object appearing in a series of provocative poses in underwear, sleepwear, and swimsuit is not out of character for this publication. Valance is deliberately marketed to appeal to (male) adult drives and desires. The article commences with the announcement that readers are about to see the actress "minus her Erinsborough pinafore [school uniform]" (93), thus foregrounding its intentions to play on the stereotypical male fantasy of the sexually active *enfante terrible*. Valance is sixteen years old and her age is mentioned twice very early in the article, thus simultaneously drawing attention to her youth, her sexuality, and the apparent lack of artifice surrounding both. Arguably, the images are erotic: She is posing provocatively, presenting a sexual aesthetic which positions her as an object of the male gaze. Unable to drive, not legally able to drink or vote, Valance becomes part of an ongoing mainstream rhetoric that fails to legitimate the youthful body except as a site of desire and possibility. The article accompanying the photographs, however, while suitably trite, states that Valance offered a "terse, yet polite 'no comment' to FHM's prying sex-orientated questions" (95): Questions designed to remind the reader that although young, Valance is also a sexual subject. By refusing to reveal her sexual activity and attitudes, Valance opens a liminal space wherein the forbidden and desired collide and unravel. In presenting *herself* concurrently as object (to be gazed upon) and subject (through silence), she bestows agency upon *herself* controlling, to a degree, her representation. When read in this context, the contrasting visual and verbal representations enable a negotiation between viewer/reader and Valance regarding youthful sexuality and its boundaries of desire.

This Lolita-esque depiction is becoming more frequent in mainstream media, where a permissible soft-porn (and imaginative hard-core) and the sexualization of the young body become naturalized. In 2001 tiny Nikki Webster released a pop single and accompanying video entitled "Strawberry Kisses." Not only do the lyrics play on Webster's "sexy yearning for a missing boyfriend" (Nolan 8), but the film clip features her in a midriff top and tight, hip-hugging pants, gyrating and pouting to an animated and asexual cartoon costar as well as her implied audience. Whereas, Webster's costar may be asexual, she clearly is not—her prepubescent body is on display, complete with cowboy hat, prompting some journalists to refer to her as a "mini Madonna" (Whiting), thus alluding to the sexual provocativeness of her entire ensemble. While Gotham records manager, Ross Fraser, declares that Webster's look was appropriate for her age (Whiting), journalist Jessica Rudd laments Webster's (and other young stars') precociousness and cites her recent signing to the Jäger makeup line as proof of the loss of youth that marketing forces and peer pressure generate. Rudd writes that "For 10-year-olds, the modern alternative to the enchanting world of Narnia is literally only a wardrobe away, as simple as sliding on a pair of stilettos, smearing on some foundation and singing songs of exploitative relationships. Suddenly you're transformed into Britney or Claudia or another deliciously naughty taboo."

Rudd draws attention to the ways in which commodification can, from the nostalgic perspective of adult culture, limit young people's subjectivity by (re)positioning them within a full-grown world where their agency is read as mere play. But Webster herself is more than satisfied with the image she projects and works cooperatively with her mother and stylist to construct a look she is comfortable with (Whiting). In short, the "deliciously naughty taboo" that Webster and her peers represent is consciously commodified; sex sells, even when the subject is below the age of legal consent. While Webster may remain charmingly innocent of the desires her image stimulates (Whiting), she nonetheless continues to arouse them, her mimesis of sexual urges and loss providing capital for herself and the market. Thus, as a willing young producer, her agency positions her within a liminal site where, like Valance, the threshold between taboo and inclusion is continually elided.

In this corporatized and media age, it is easy to overlook the fact that historically, youthful identities have always been shaped by a range of spheres: Family, peers, and, increasingly, popular culture. These work in a psychological and social tandem to mold young people and encourage them to engage in a type of cultural relativism whereby their own identities are formed and discarded according to current social trends and dominant forms. Popular culture, for example, teaches young people to gaze inwardly at the body as a stylized fashionscape, an aesthetic spectacle, a commodified sexual object, or as "a repository of desires that menace, disrupt and undermine public life through acts of violence or predatory sexuality" (Giroux 32). But are these choices any different for older subjects in a world where the cult of celebrity and the adage "fifteen minutes of fame" are also modes of self-validation?

Certainly, not all young people are passive consumers or remain silent about the limited representations of youth that are distributed within culture. Often, their cultural literacy and political savvy are more than adequate to allow them to negotiate the broad terrain of mainstream culture and associated marketing forces and be active producers as well as critical consumers. Valance and Webster are not the only young performers to open up a liminal site through their performances and the corporate distribution of their images. According to the September 2001 issue of *Smash Hits*, it appears that many young people, ranging in age from the early teenage years to the twenties, such as Anna Kournikova, Christina Aguilera, Aaron Carter, Mandy Moore, Billy Piper, and young Australian pop singers Tali and Hayley, have input into the way their images are constructed and circulated. Furthermore, these young people are vocal about and participate in the marketing of their images, brokering lucrative deals in the process.

There is even a self-referentialism surrounding the production and distribution of young celebrities that, ironically, appears to exclude the adult culture which maintains and celebrates their success. An example of this can be seen with the recent publicity surrounding Torah Bright, a fourteen-year-old Australian who won a bronze medal in the half-pipe event at the junior world snowboarding championships in 2000. Bright is currently being touted as the Anna Kournikova of the ski slopes (Ludlow 36). On the one hand, this comparison sexualizes and objectifies the young sportswoman, turning her into a commodity for which a market already exists. On the other hand, it empowers her as a young social and political subject by placing her within a recognizable and successful schema of corporate forces in which self-representation must play a role.

The question that arises, however, is the extent to which Bright, or any other of the above-mentioned young people, can narrate themselves. To deny these young people *any* agency in their public representation is to participate in the cultural forces that seek to silence young people generally or, at least, limit them access to political, economic, and other social modes of address. There is a great deal of ambivalence and contradiction surrounding the production and reception of the images of these successful teens that circulate in popular culture. Superficially, these representations may attract criticism for reinforcing the notion of young women as objects within patriarchal society who can enact a range of limited roles (including sexual ones) but only with the endorsement of adult culture. However, there is also a sense in which these same depictions allow young people creative choice as producers and consumers of popular culture. After all, young consumers will not support models of youth identity that they cannot relate to or that fail to enact aspects of their developing selves—whether it is as a sexualized young performer or as an aggressive and defiant rock artist like Eminem. It is easy to discredit these images as part of a corporate landscape, but it is important to realize that the diverse and sometimes hedonistic representations of young people are not merely about the dissemination of a hip aesthetic. They also have the power to transform attitudes and present different modes of being by recovering, for the young consumers, a meaningful discourse that empowers teens as political subjects with legitimate voices in a global market.

Conversely, a circle of consumption is created and a form of cannibalism ensues. Young people are the primary subjects of these images as well as the principal consumers. As such, through a cultural feasting, they are invited to devour themselves. Thus, young people and consumers as a whole are recognized as "aspects of the one digestive system. This is a system which eats indiscriminately, one that cannot process what it has consumed" (Gibbs 77). In their production and consumption, young celebrities such as Webster and Bright signify not only their roles as cultural commodities, but the very different and complex subjectivities that young people adopt as consumers and producers.

WALKING THE LIMEN: THE VERVE

The production and consumption of pop/rock music and the surrounding pop music culture can be seen as other sites whereat youth can actively seek out and celebrate states of resistance and liminality. Musicians, however, do not necessarily lose their validity or authenticity for youth when they become commodified. Some young artists, instead of identifying their space as one of oppression and silence, embrace the unlimited potential of liminal space as a site of disruption and as a medium for change. The now defunct British group The Verve produced an album called *Urban Hymns* from which the single "Bitter Sweet Symphony" received a great deal of airplay, and the film clip was shown repeatedly on commercial stations in Australia and overseas. The Verve used the auditory and visual material of their song to both resist and acknowledge various forms of cultural imperialism; thus signifying, through their music and the film clip, an internalization of the standards of commodification (Best 21).

As a cultural commodity, "Bitter Sweet Symphony" has resonances that allow it to circulate within a broad (primarily western) market and over a wide cultural terrain (Straw 495). Its subsequent appeal, however, comes from a youth market that, like the "star" of the video, resists the various pedagogies that dictate that the behaviors and desires be recognized as nonconformist. The protagonist in the clip walks against the flow of pedestrians, unmindful of those he disturbs, uncaring of whose space he invades. And yet, like the contradiction in the title, his words subvert his aggressive actions. Whilst walking against the mainstream, he acknowledges his desire to be the same and to transform himself into a socially acceptable subject. The clip is a representation of not only liminal space (caught between the binary oppositions of conformity and difference), but of the contradictory nature of popular culture as well, wherein the gap between popularity and high art is exposed. In theory, the young man in the film clip desires the embrace of the dominant culture, to be successful and acknowledged as a legitimate subject, but through the processes of commodification he is simply in his mode *performing* youth for the consumption of the audience. The combination of symphonic melodies and popular rock to create an "urban hymn" also opens a liminal space, as does the title of the song: It is bitter and sweet at the same time, thus acknowledging new sensations, new sites from which to speak. In being contradictory, the band actually enables subjectivity by forcing a slippage of meaning or an opening up of liminal space where meanings are, ultimately, irreducible (Spivak 274–75). Richard Ashcroft, the lead singer and songwriter of the group, states that

The thing about this business is, they want rock & roll, but when they get it, when they get the real true essence of someone they shit themselves.... [T]his business is about placing real people and real life forces among this ordered crap and telling them to perform—who the fuck are you to get me here today to do this for you? Fuck you! I don't want to end up a Kurt Cobain. (quoted in Gordon 23)

In light of Ashcroft's response, it is easy to read "Bitter Sweet Symphony" as a self-conscious text that manifests an awareness of its own production and its role as a popular commodity. This awareness, depending on the cultural terrain through which it is circulated, invests the song, finally, with the potential for resistance.

CELEBRATING LIMINALITY

The Australian group silverchair and their song "Freak" also offer their audiences a model of resistance through incorporation and commodification. Despite clever marketing strategies on the part of silverchair's record label Murmur, the band, though acknowledged as successful in terms of sales and public approval, were/are still identified as "the kids from Newcastle" (Humphrey 19). The categorization, "kids," locates the band in a subordinate position on the adult/child social binary and reduces the band's accomplishments to mere play. This type of reduction is further emphasized in the ridiculing of the band's name and, by association, their performance. In the popular press, silverchair were referred to as "nirvana-in-pyjamas" or "silver(high)chair" (Jinman 17–18). The gesture to the successful Australian preschool programs, *Playschool* and its spin-off, *Bananas in Pyjamas,* locates the band as either imitators of their American superiors or as babes in an adult industry. The notion that a group of then-fourteen- and fifteen-year-olds could have something "critical" to say about youth and society in general was not taken seriously. Yet silverchair proved that adolescents working in the fundamentally adult-dominated music industry could achieve economic success and often critical commentary. The group produced two successful albums, and the first single off their second album, *Freakshow,* challenged the boundaries between the dominant and primarily economic world that had brought them success.

The combination of lyrics and visuals in the song "Freak" can be read in numerous ways. The position of the "freak" in the film clip is multiple and shifting, depending on audience context and response. The *mise en scène,* however, reveals that the young men are quite clearly being exploited by corporate powers (represented by the two adult and "human" figures in the clip). The sweat of the band's labors is being transformed into a tonic that is readily consumed by an old woman who, it first appears, is trying to recapture her lost youth. Giroux argues that youth and the various images of youth are often used to revitalize and please the mass market. This scene concurs with Giroux's argument that young people's allure is often used to revitalize and please an adult mass market and also to indulge a youthful narcissism.

The "Freak" film clip ultimately parodies the notion of the allure of a youthful self and surface by turning the happy recipient of the young people's bodily products into an alien or freak. The alien is delighted with her transfiguration from old woman to freak: A process that has been aided through the literal ingestion of youth. The reconfigured woman, like the youth whose "spirit" she has paid for, is now an Other site of youthful display and desire. In its production and reception this film clip opens up a liminal space as it foregrounds the position of the freak, the marginalized and powerless in society, and uses the dominant discourse, the commodifiers and marketers of teen spirit, to reposition and thus legitimate youth as a viable product. The hegemony may try to insist upon an essentialist category of youth, but silverchair refuse this specificity and the social formations of youth that are constructed for them. It can be posited that silverchair use their song to explore liminal space creating, in the process, a freak or alien. This alien figure, because it has been constructed within the realms of mainstream culture and under the control of the commercial powers, is endorsed (the signature on the check) and thus given currency within the circuits of cultural exchange. In exchanging the "alien" look for money, the concept of the "freak" is legitimated, reinstating youth (the real freaks) within public discourse. The young people, like Kurt Cobain, may clock in and out and serve their time working for the system,[7] but this is *served* time, signaling the potential threat they pose as disruptive presences.

Many mainstream songs created by and for young people, such as those performed by rap artist Eminem, the Offspring, Wheatus and even Britney Spears, reveal youth to be a complex identity fraught with social dangers and the possibility of rejection from not only adult culture, but from a range of heterogeneous youth cultures as well, thus highlighting the liminal nature of teen spirit as something either/or. Offspring's hit singles, "Pretty Fly (for a White Guy)" and "Get a Job" from the album *Americana*, explore this conundrum very well. In the accompanying video clips, a range of youth identities is offered for viewer recognition and positive and negative association. Subcultural identities such as street gangs, hip-hop culture, car culture, and ethnic subjectivities are proffered as is a primary and alienated subject—the youthful reject who seeks to belong but is ultimately rejected from all spheres. The only place for this alien youth identity (who appears across both clips in his inappropriate and "wannabe" vehicle) is, like the song, within mainstream pop culture. *Americana* sold more than 10 million albums worldwide (Yorke 61), placing it firmly within a highly successful and privileged domain that is admired by adult culture: Financial rewards equate with achievement and acceptance. Yet, Offspring's music also "speaks" to young people who may find in the group's lyrics an empowering message—or one which, despite financial success, still manages to alarm parents, who accuse the group of poisoning their children (Dwyer 58). Perhaps it is this opposition from the adult culture that will ensure Offspring's continued success long after they themselves have moved out of their "youth."[8]

Rap artist Marshall Mathers III (otherwise known as Eminem) is a contentious voice in the mainstream music scene. Controversy surrounds Eminem's songs, which, despite the lack of direct evidence to support this, are understood to incite homophobia, misogyny, and violence. The national secretary of the Australian Family Association, Richard Muelenberg, along with some prominent politicians such as Peter Slipper, federal member for the Sunshine Coast region in Queensland, Australia, sought to have Eminem's application for a visa to Australia in 2001 rejected on the grounds that he was "an equal opportunity offender," and he was likened to the offensive Holocaust historian, David Irving (Apter 15). In October 2000 a women's group in Canada tried to prevent Eminem from entering the country and, in November 2000, university students in Illinois petitioned to have his show canceled (Buck 24). There is a sense in which the popular press and mainstream's reaction to Eminem represents a deliberate demonization of youth and youth culture in order to assert control and create what Davis refers to as a "false sense of community among a predominantly middle-aged constituency, by appealing to a shared enemy" (quoted in Hitching 79). Nonetheless, in interviews Eminem continues to express surprise and consternation at what he feels is a deliberate blurring of his identity with that of the characters he creates in his music.

People think they know me from my music, but they don't.... Some of my views that come across in my music aren't the same as in real life. A lot of my personal life is reflected in my music and a lot of it is just to get under people's skin—and it's worked so far. The kids get me. People in their teens and 20s understand where I'm coming from. (Buck 23)

Eminem and his music promote moral outrage in the adult culture and prompt media claims of obscenity. Ironically, his target demographic can relate to and identify with his songs and place his lyrics within a context of ongoing sociocultural debate about racism, sexism, youth, drugs, fame, and identity. It seems that if a young person is to be "educated" about the serious issues affecting all aspects of their world, then her/his education can only occur with a great deal of censorship and the approval of adult culture. In the older generation's eyes, Eminem, as a pedagogical tool of instruction and growth, does not qualify.

Recognition of the conflicting social, sexual, and psychological forces that construct young people and their transformation into commodities has meant that, during the 1990s and in the new millennium, "youth" and youth culture have become large and commercially viable markets. While young people such as Bright, Valance, Webster, Ashcroft, and Eminem often participate in the production and dissemination of themselves as products, indulging in a cultural and psychological cannibalism, they also seek, in different ways and to varying degrees, to resist those forces that essentialize and homogenize teen spirit. Through their active participation in, and control of, their image, popular cultural forms such as television, magazines, films, and radio can become productive sites of pedagogy and negotiation. There is within the audiences that these media seek to include (and exclude) a sense of intervention as well as a passive and critical consumption occurring. Beverly Best argues that "individuals are *unconsciously* bound to discourses that oppress them, such as patriarchy or consumerism. Subjects [even youthful subjects] choose negotiated positions, strategically, just as they choose to grant or withhold allegiance to particular discourses" (24).

Young people may willingly consume various images of themselves, but to suggest that the consumption is uncritical is incorrect; it may be indiscriminate, but young people are more than capable of offering opinions and critiques of the ways in which they are represented. As young filmmaker Daniel Marsden states, "I think that most people have their heads screwed on properly, even if they're told every night by *A Current Affair* that they don't. They still have a sense of self. But it can't be healthy to have them continually portrayed as 'lost youth' (quoted in Jackman).

CONCLUSION

Popular culture is a continually shifting territory where identities are fashioned and refashioned accordingly. Because of their apparent lack of political agency, young people are most often reduced to objects in this process: They are commodified and marketed back to themselves, stripped of any history, individual identity, or power (Giroux 73). The commodification of youth and youth culture presents young people as important only when they are either products or consumers as opposed to critical, social subjects (Giroux 73). Yet it is important to remember that youth are often discerning consumers; they are also increasingly becoming intelligent producers in control, to a degree, of their own representations, and they are capable of self-investment in cultural products.

Teen spirit is a valuable commodity: The adult market has long recognized its commercial attractiveness and harnessed its multiple forms, continuing to sell it for profitable returns. But in recognizing the significance and desirability of youth as a commodity, in all its complex psychosocial manifestations, and choosing to manufacture versions of it themselves, young people are able to take control of the ways in which they are represented. They are able to promote more agential images which run counter to the other cultural forms that render them victims, scapegoats, in danger, and dangerous. Youth are able to appropriate *themselves* as cultural products, position *themselves* within the circuits of consumption and so resist, challenge, and even, in a subversive gesture, celebrate the ideological imperialism that (re)creates young people as commodities instead of recognizing their potential as liminal subjects.

NOTES

1. See, for example, the newspaper reports surrounding the death of James Bulger in Britain (Oswell, 1998: 38–39).

2. Nostalgic and morally appropriate interpretations of young people are evidenced in programs like *Happy Days* and *The Brady Bunch*, which contrast strongly with films produced around the same period, like *Quadrophenia, Hair, Tommy*, and *Animal House*.

3. Television shows like *Ally McBeal, Sex and the City, Dawson's Creek*, and *Melrose Place* fuel these ideas of rejecting aging.

4. See Tamsin Blanchard, "A Smack in the Face for Gurus of Heroin Chic," *Independent International*, May–June 1997, pp. 2, 14, for discussions on heroin chic and lesbian chic.

5. The look was also fetishized and displaced from any serious social consideration by being paraded on European catwalks and appearing in photographs in glamorous magazines. Fundamentally, the "look" was financially unavailable to the majority of youth. Not only that, but "heroin chic" represented a version of youth that was constructed by the mainstream and functioned primarily to promote establishment hysteria.

6. See for example, *Ralph, FHM, Dolly, Cleo, Cosmopolitan, Dawson's Creek, Go!*, and *American Pie*. It is a case of putting old heads on young shoulders, literally and figuratively.

7. In his suicide note, Kurt Cobain wrote, "I feel I should have a punch-in clock before I walk out on stage.... [I need to be] slightly numb in order to regain the enthusiasm I once had as a child" (quoted in Thompson 8).

8. "Pretty Fly (for a White Guy)" was the biggest-selling single in Australia (Yorke 61).

WORKS CITED

Adams, Phillip. "Preying Games." *Weekend Australian*, 27–28 Apr. 1996, "Weekend Review," 2.

Apter, Jeff. "No Visa for Eminem?" *Rolling Stone*, Aug. 2001, 15.

Ashcroft, Richard. "Bitter Sweet Symphony." The Verve. *Urban Hymns*. Hut Records, 1997.

Bastick, John. "Ramsay's Treat." *FHM*, June 2000, 93–99.

Best, Beverly. "Over the Counter-Culture: Retheorizing Resistance in Popular Culture." Pp. 18–35 in *The Clubcultures Reader*, ed. Steve Redhead, Derek Wynne, and Justin O'Connor. Oxford: Blackwell, 1997.

Blanchard, Tamsin. "A Smack in the Face for Gurus of Heroin Chic." *Independent International*, May–June 1997, 12.

Bradiotti, Rosa. *Nomadic Subjects*. New York: Columbia University Press, 1994.

Buck, Robbie. "People Don't Know Me: Eminem." *Smash Hits*, Sept. 2001, 22–24.

Davis, Mark. *Gangland*. Sydney, Austral.: Allen and Unwin, 1997.

Dwyer, Michael. "King of the Hill: Dexter Holland, the Offspring." *Rolling Stone Yearbook 1999/2000*, 54–58.

Finkelstein, Joanne. *After a Fashion*. Melbourne, Austral.: Melbourne University Press, 1996.

Gibbs, Anna. "Eaten Alive/Dead Meat: Consumption and Modern Cannibalism." *Planet Diana: Cultural Studies and Global Mourning*, ed. Ien Ang, Ruth Barcan, Helen Grace, Elaine Lally, Justine Lloyd, and Zoë Sofoulis. Nepean, Austral.: Research Centre in Intercommunal Studies, 1997, 75–80.

Giroux, Henry A. *Channel Surfing: Race Talk and the Destruction of Today's Youth*. Houndsmill, Eng.: Macmillan, 1997.

Goodman, Fred. "Courtney Love vs. the Music Biz." *Rolling Stone*, Aug. 2001, 14–16.

Gordon, Jade. "Choir-Starter." *Juice*, Dec. 1997, 22–23.

Grossberg, Lawrence. "Another Boring Day in Paradise: Rock and Roll and the Empowerment of Everyday Life." *The Subcultures Reader*, ed. Ken Gelder and Sarah Thornton. London: Routledge, 1997, 477–93.

Hitchings, Stuart. "War on Youth." *Juice*, Feb. 2000, 74–79.

Holland, Dexter. "Get a Job" and "Pretty Fly (for a White Guy)." Perf. *The Offspring. Americana*. Columbia Records, 1998.

Humphrey, Andrew. " ... Days in the Sun: silverchair." *Rolling Stone*, Feb. 1997, 30–37.

Jackman, Christine. "Dumb Struck." *Brisbane Courier Mail*, 14 Feb. 1998, 28.

Jinman, Richard. "Sells like Teen Spirit." *Weekend Australian*, 23–24 Mar. 1996, "Weekend Magazine," 12–18.

Johns, Daniel. "Freak." Silverchair. *Freakshow*. Murmur Records, 1997.

Lloyd, Simon. "Big Kids, Big Money." *Business Review Weekly*, 28 Jan. 2000, 50–57.

Ludlow, Mark. "Snow Princess." *Sunday Mail*, 29 July 2001, 36.

Nolan, Katie. "This Is Just Embarrassing." *Brisbane Courier Mail*, 23 June 2001, "Magazine," 8.

Oswell, David. "A Question of Belonging: Television, Youth and the Domestic." *Cool Places: Geographies of Youth Cultures*, ed. Tracey Skelton and Gill Valentine. London: Routledge, 1998, 35–49.

Peretti, Jacques. "Middle Youth Ate My Culture." *Modern Review* 5 (Mar. 1998): 15–19.

Rudd, Jessica. "Oops ... Childhood's Vanished." *Brisbane Courier Mail*, 26 Mar. 2001, 11.

Spivak, Gayatri Chakravorty. "Can the Subaltern Speak?" *Marxism and the Interpretation of Culture*, ed. Cary Nelson and Lawrence Grossberg. London: Macmillan, 1988, 271–313.

Straw, Will. "Communities and Scenes in Popular Music." *The Subcultures Reader,* ed.
    Ken Gelder and Sarah Thornton. London: Routledge, 1997, 494–505.
"Strawberry Kisses." Nikki Webster. Gotham Records, 2001.
Thompson, Dave. *Never Fade Away: The Kurt Cobain Story.* London: Pan Macmillan,
    1994.
Udo, Tommy. "From Despair to Nowhere: The Sad and Lonely Death of Kurt Cobain."
    New Musical Express, 18 Apr. 1994, 6.
Whiting, Frances. "Moppet Madonna 'Not Too Sexy.'" *Sunday Mail,* 24 June 2001, 41.
Wulff, Helena. "Introducing Youth Culture in Its Own Right: The State of the Art and
    the New Possibilities." *Youth Cultures: A Cross-Cultural Perspective,* ed. Vered
    Amit-talai and Helena Wulff. London: Routledge, 1995, 1–18.
Yorke, Ritchie. "Punks Are Feeling Lucky." *Sunday Mail,* 18 Feb. 2001, 61.

2

Girls Make Movies

Mary Celeste Kearney

To me the great hope is that now these little 8mm video recorders are around, and people who normally wouldn't make movies are going to be making them. And suddenly, one day some little fat girl in Ohio is going to be the new Mozart and make a beautiful film with her father's camcorder, and for once the so-called professionalism about movies will be destroyed forever, and it will really become an art form.
—Francis Ford Coppola, *Hearts of Darkness*

We didn't need Hollywood; we *were* Hollywood.
—Sadie Benning, *It Wasn't Love*

In 1998 a series of commercials was released to promote the new Independent Film Channel (IFC), a U.S. cable television enterprise devoted to broadcasting non-Hollywood fare. IFC's first advertising campaign, "Break the Rules," featured actor Hallie Eisenberg as a brilliant new independent film director named Christie. Though much of the humor in the Christie series is due to the commercials' foregrounding of the immature behavior often attributed to directors, the promotions are also amusing because their presentation of a young female director is so at odds with our preconceived notions of filmmakers as adult males and of girls as culturally unproductive. Nevertheless, in order to make sense of, and find humor in, IFC's promotional discourse, the viewer is encouraged to reference those very stereotypes.

For example, at the beginning of the first commercial in the Christie campaign, well-known film actors and industry executives speak reverentially about Christie, such as Bingham Ray, who refers to her as "a phenomenon", and Matt Damon, who says she has "amazing, raw, real talent."[1] Despite the typical use of Christie as a name for females rather than males, in the absence of Christie's visual representation when this dialogue is heard, the viewer is encouraged to recall the stereotypical image of a film director: A man. When Christie finally appears, humor is created not only through the dissonance caused by the director stereotype in the viewer's mind converging with the image of a young girl on the screen, but also through the excessively stereotypical construction of Christie as a female child. The title of her new film, *Horses Are Pretty*, is mentioned repeatedly in the commercials, which also feature scenes of adult actors rehearsing Christie's puerile dialogue: "You shut up," "No, *you* shut up," "I said it first," "No you didn't. *I* said it first."

My reason for focusing on the Christie commercials is not to denounce IFC for its sexist and ageist discursive strategies, but rather to call attention to how ingrained the stereotype of girls as culturally unproductive still is today, particularly in the film industry. Indeed, the advertisements promoting IFC not only rely on but reproduce a popular understanding of girls as not engaged in the world of cultural creativity. Thus, the Christie commercials are most amusing if the viewer believes that no girl filmmakers exist, even within the "rule-breaking" realm of independent cinema. Nonetheless, the increased involvement of female youth as cultural producers over the last decade proves such a belief false. In fact, contemporary American girls are perhaps more involved in cultural production than at any other point in history, and they are creating cultural texts in virtually every form of medium possible, including films and videos. Some girl filmmakers have become so creatively prolific that they have formed their own production companies.[2]

In this chapter, I explore the rise of American girls' moviemaking in relation to the broader context of the increase in girls' activity in cultural production. As I argue, both these phenomena have been inspired by several other developments in the last two decades, including the widespread accessibility of inexpensive forms of media technology, the emergence of production-oriented female youth cultures, the rise of girls' advocacy in response to reports of female adolescents' problems with self-esteem, the popularization of a "girl power" ethos, and the formation of adult-run media education programs organized specifically for female youth. In addition, I analyze several movies created by female youth in order to explore the various ways in which girls use audiovisual media to negotiate the ideologies of gender and generation circulating in popular discourse.

REVOLUTIONIZING MEDIA EDUCATION: TEACHING YOUTH MEDIA PRODUCTION

There is little doubt that the recent rise in girls' cultural productivity is due in part to the emergence of inexpensive, user-friendly forms of media technology that make the creation of cultural texts easier, faster, and cheaper than ever before. The effects of such technological advancements are perhaps most evident in the world of filmmaking, which was revolutionized in the 1980s by the development of amateur video camcorders, and again in the 1990s by the introduction of digital editing systems. In turn, the phenomenal expansion of the World Wide Web over the last few years has created new venues for the exhibition of girl-made cultural texts, as well as new avenues for much broader distribution of such creations.

In addition to these technological developments, other social forces, such as media literacy initiatives, have contributed significantly to the greater involvement of female youth in the realm of cultural production. Although the media literacy movement has a thirty-year history in the United States, since the early 1990s there has been a tremendous increase in media education classes for American youth, due in part to the reemergence of concern about the media's cultural dominance and their allegedly dangerous effects on young people. Many advocates for media literacy, particularly those associated with religious organizations, focus primarily on teaching critical skills to young people so that they can decode the various messages imposed by the mass media, a form of media pedagogy Kathleen Tyner labels *protectionist*, and other scholars argue is both apolitical and theoretically antiquated (Hobbs). Additionally, media literacy curricula often are criticized for ignoring the media savvy of most young people before they have attended media education workshops, especially disenfranchised youth, whose lack of representation or misrepresentation in the mainstream media typically elicits their development of a critical, and in many cases oppositional, gaze (hooks).

Despite the continued dominance of the protectionist approach in many media literacy programs in the United States, since the mid-1990s an increasing number of media educators and scholars, such as the United Kingdom's David Buckingham, have been calling for students' education in media production also. In contrast to media literacy advocates' protectionist perspective on teaching media to youth, these media educators have what might be called a *promotionist* approach which is grounded in not only a different understanding of young people and their abilities, but also in a different perspective on the mass media. For example, rather than understanding the media as directly reflective of and influential on society, media educators, many of whom have been trained in critical media theory, approach the media as social constructs which contain multiple and often contradictory messages and thus elicit multiple and often contradictory responses. In turn, rather than approaching youth as ignorant, endangered victims, media educators acknowledge and respect young people as intelligent, engaged members of society who have the ability to become further empowered through media education and practice. Thus, instead of positioning themselves as the saviors of media-infected youth, media educators see their role as one of facilitating, supporting, and promoting young people's critical and creative media abilities.

CREATING BETTER WOMEN: GIRLS' ADVOCACY AND MEDIA LITERACY CURRICULA FOR FEMALE YOUTH

A unique element in the current U.S. media literacy revolution is the development of several media workshops for female youth. This phenomenon can be linked not only to the popularization of feminist ideologies since the 1960s, but also to an increase in girls' advocacy in recent years. With roots as old as the social reform movements of the early 1800s, contemporary girls' advocacy initiatives blossomed in the early 1980s largely as the result of the publication of Carol Gilligan's *In a Different Voice,* which countered traditional theories of developmental psychology by arguing that adolescence is especially difficult for girls who, unlike most boys, struggle between contradictory social messages that encourage them to attach to and separate from others. Girls' advocacy experienced another resurgence in the early 1990s with the publication of the American Association of University Women's report, *Shortchanging Girls, Shortchanging America,* and Mary Pipher's best-seller, *Reviving Ophelia: Saving the Selves of Adolescent Girls,* both of which reported that girls' self-esteem is "at risk" once female youth enter adolescence. Although these studies are important and necessary in that they expose the many difficulties related to growing up female in a male-dominated society, it is disturbing that they have been accompanied by more calls for adult intervention in the lives of adolescent girls which in turn have contributed to the popular construction of girls as disempowered victims and adults, especially women, as girls' saviors.

Many media education workshops developed for girls demonstrate the strong influence both the protectionist media literacy movement and the interventionist girls' advocacy movement have had on the media education of female youth. For example, "Girls Re-Cast TV," the media literacy curriculum developed by Girls Inc., an advocacy organization for disadvantaged female youth, appears to have been developed from the belief that television represents females in stereotypical ways that are dangerous to girls' self-esteem. For example, as part of the "Action Kit" used in this program, girls are asked to "watch TV, look closely at people's eyes, hair, clothes and skin. Listen to their tone of voice and how they respond to each other. Notice what they do, where they live and where they go to school. Does it look like your life?"

While Girls Inc.'s attempts to help female youth develop as discerning media consumers are to be commended, the questions its curriculum poses suggest an outdated understanding of media representations as direct reflections of (and thus influences on) reality. Moreover, despite its construction of media representations as unrealistic and therefore dangerous, the Girls Inc. curriculum does not encourage female youth to produce their own media texts, an activity which might challenge such disturbing mainstream representations.

Similarly, the media literacy curricula developed by the Girl Scouts, the largest American organization dedicated to improving girls' "media know-how," focus primarily on developing critical abilities and provide minimal information on media technology and even less in the way of hands-on media experience, especially for younger girls.[3] To my knowledge, the only encouragement for female youth to produce their own media texts appears in a guidebook published in 1999 for Cadette and Senior Girl Scouts. Unfortunately, however, the book's limited suggestions on how to make a magazine, Web site, or television show do not provide girls with enough information to effectively start, much less complete, such projects.

GIRL POWER: RIOT GRRRL AND MEDIA PRODUCTION WORKSHOPS FOR FEMALE YOUTH

Many girls who have become engaged in cultural production in the last decade have been inspired to do so by Riot Grrrl, a noncentralized feminist youth culture which emerged in the United States during the early 1990s. The original Riot Grrrls came together as a result of the misogyny they experienced in their allegedly radical communities and, calling for "Revolution Girl-Style Now," encouraged other girls to speak out about the unique strengths of female youth. Riot Grrrls refuse the protectionist approach of media literacy educators and the interventionist perspective of girls' advocates by demonstrating that female youth are empowered cultural producers as well as engaged political and social agents. Indeed, Riot Grrrls began spreading their message of "girl power" long before the Spice Girls depoliticized that phrase for commercial purposes, and girl advocates seized upon it as their motto. Fully embracing the DIY (Do It Yourself) ideology associated with both punks and leftist activists, Riot Grrrls create the cultural texts they consume and thus signal an important broadening of female youth culture beyond the conventional realm of girls' consumer-oriented "bedroom culture."

Although the majority of Riot Grrrls' cultural creations have appeared in inexpensive and technologically uncomplicated forms, such as 'zines and music, many female youth influenced by this community are involved in film and video projects also. For example, Sadie Benning, the *wunderkind* of 1990s video art, has indicated that the inspiration for many of her videos came from her contact with Riot Grrrl bands and 'zines:

[W]hen I heard Bikini Kill and when I read these zines, it was so much what I had wanted when I was in high school. It really creates a break in the chain, you know, being able to have words to put upon things that are happening to you and knowing that we all exist and [can find] one another. (quoted in Phoenix 41–42)

In 1989 fifteen-year-old Benning began making videos in her bedroom with a Fisher-Price Pixelvision camera she received from her father for Christmas. Living at that time with her mother in Milwaukee, Wisconsin, Benning effectively became the midwestern girl director who Coppola predicted would materialize as a result of the camcorder's wide dispersion. Indeed, Benning's videos began to be screened publicly in 1990, and in less than a year she was being hyped as the "auteur of adolescence" (Masters D1).

Benning's videos, most of which she produced in her room, are clearly from a teenager's perspective, yet they debunk the stereotypical notion of girls' "bedroom culture" as a cheerful space of heterosexual awakening and commercial consumption. Instead, Benning presents herself as both a lesbian and an active cultural producer who is anxious about the alienating and often violent society in which she lives. Similar to Riot Grrrl 'zines, her autobiographical and inexpensively produced videos freely appropriate texts from mainstream media culture yet relocate them in order to tell her own story of growing up lesbian. For example, in *It Wasn't Love* (1992), Benning cleverly mixes the visual images from the prototypical bad-girl movie, *The Bad Seed* (1956), with Prince's song "I Wanna Be Your Lover" (1979), to produce a lesbian coming-of-age text that resonates with Riot Grrrl-like affirmations of female youth: "We didn't need Hollywood, we *were* Hollywood." With more than thirty articles written about her by 1994, Benning and her widely circulated videos motivated many other girls to get involved in filmmaking practices.

Influenced by girl filmmakers like Benning, the "girl power" ethos of the Riot Grrrl movement, and the push to include production in media education curricula, several media workshops for female youth have been developed in recent years to facilitate girls' critical media skills, as well as their engagement with media technologies and production practices. For example, in 1997, Street-Level Youth Media, an organization devoted to promoting young people's knowledge and use of the media, developed a ten-week-long "Girls Only" program. This curriculum focused on improving girls' assertiveness and self-confidence, as well as placing a heavy emphasis on the development of the participant's media literacy, including facilitating girls' confidence and competence in expressing their own voices and opinions through media.

In addition to Street-Level Youth Media's girls-only class, several other workshops have emerged which are similarly devoted to improving both girls' critical abilities and their knowledge and use of media technology. One such class, "Girls Making Headlines," was designed in 2000 by three graduate students as part of a joint venture in youth media education organized by the Austin Museum of Art and the Department of Radio-Television-Film at the University of Texas.[4] As described by one of the instructors "the goal of the class was to teach [female youth] to analyze how girls are represented in the mainstream media....As a corollary to this, the production skills we were teaching them were geared to providing them with the tools to counter those representations they didn't like with work of their own" (Ross).

Thus, in addition to instructing girls in critical analyses of the media, particularly representations of girls and women, the instructors developed a component of the workshop which entails the students' production of a television news magazine devoted to issues of importance to girls.

For female youth who have no access to media workshops, in 2001 Andrea Richards wrote *Girl Director*, the first guidebook for aspiring young filmmakers. The publication of this text by Girl Press (a company devoted to printing "slightly dangerous books for girl mavericks") demonstrates a shift in the predominantly male-oriented discourse of most guidebooks directed to young media producers. Moreover, *Girl Director's* publication at this particular moment demonstrates that an increasing number of adults, especially young women,[5] understand the importance of educating girls in not only the analytic skills involved in media criticism, but also the technical and creative practices of media production. Like many of the other young women who are involved in media education for girls, Richards believes that learning about women directors, being educated in the tools and practices of filmmaking, and making movies can be significant steps to girls' empowerment:

Part of what I wanted to do with the book was to demystify the process of filmmaking in general, to make it extremely accessible by encouraging girls to make films by any means necessary.... Filmmaking doesn't have to be a huge production that is limited to an elite group of artists or Hollywood moguls. It can be just as easy as putting out a 'zine. Which led me to wonder why girls aren't doing more of it—especially today's girls, who are far more comfortable with technology and have easier access to tools—than girls of my generation did. So from the beginning, the book was about empowering girls to pick up cameras and have both the know-how and the confidence to call the shots. (e-mail 23 June 2001)

In true girl power spirit, Richards acknowledges that her writing of *Girl Director* was about taking direct action and encouraging girls to do the same. As the introduction to her book states:

Yeah, you ought to be in pictures—MAKING THEM, that is.... So are you going to be a couch potato your whole life, watching OTHER people's stories, or are you ready to take charge and put something of YOUR OWN on the screen? By making a movie, you can show your perspective on a story, a song, an idea, the world, whatever. SO, GIRL DIRECTOR, WHY NOT TAKE YOUR PLACE ON THE SET? We're all waiting. (3)

PROBLEMATIZING THE EMPOWERMENT DISCOURSE OF MEDIA EDUCATION

Despite Richards' and other instructors' arguments for the further empowerment of girls through education in media technology and production practices, several scholars have challenged the utopian rhetoric that often permeates such discourse. For example, Tyner questions the resiliency of any empowerment gained through such programs:

At best, the esteem accrued through media production is a result of completing a project from beginning to end with adults who care. At its worst, the good feeling produced by working in an endeavor that approximates broadcast media simply is a borrowed esteem that defers true empowerment in order to keep students busy in activities that are self-absorbing and that keep them out of trouble in class. True self-esteem that enables students to give back to their communities, grows out of a mastery of skills, but also out of identifying, analyzing and overcoming the daily erosion of human dignity in an unjust society.

While Tyner is wise to question the ability of media production to fully empower youth, I would argue that when gender and generational identities are understood as significant influences on the degree to which a person has access to power, a different perspective on the potential for growth through media education emerges. For instance, because media technologies have been gendered masculine and men have been overwhelmingly privileged in the film and television industries, it can be argued that learning about and using filmmaking equipment, and thus becoming part of productive media culture, are far more liberating experiences for females than they are for males. While the issue of patriarchy has been much discussed by women trying to enter this "boys' club," very little attention has been paid to the generational dynamics that construct cultural production as an adults-only enterprise. Yet because the media industries have been dominated also by older individuals, participation in filmmaking practices is bound to be more empowering for youth than for adults. Given that girls are both young and female, and thus have at least a doubly deprivileged status because of their age and sex, their education in and use of media technologies are potentially more liberating than they are for either boys or women. The empowerment boost gained from engaging in media production is perhaps even more substantial for female youth whose racial, ethnic, class, or sexual identity marks them as disadvantaged.

Unfortunately, the skewed gendering and generationalizing of media technologies and practices have contributed significantly to most girls' minimal interest in media production. As Richards points out via e-mail, "I think it honestly doesn't occur to girls that they can be a film director—the possibility has never even been planted in their heads, because it's so off limits through cultural and gender stereotypes." In addition, the male and adult dominance of the mass media has influenced girls' lack of confidence and, in some cases, competence when using such tools. These problems often are magnified for *teenage* girls, for whom confidence and self-esteem become increasingly difficult to maintain once they enter adolescence. While I want to avoid labeling such girls "victims," I do think it is necessary to acknowledge that, unlike many male adolescents, teenage girls often have special needs when learning how to use media technology that should be addressed by their instructors.

In interviews I conducted with various media educators who had taught female youth, several noted that many girls have no problem approaching and using media technology, particularly those female youth who are already familiar with photography, acting, or writing, skills which are necessary for filmmaking also. However, other instructors noted how some girls' problems with self-confidence can negatively affect their self-perceptions as being technically competent. For example, one instructor who has worked with both female and male youth in media education programs reported

Dealing with ... self-esteem issues is something I find mostly in girls, rather than boys: boys just do it without considering that they can't, but girls sometimes lack the confidence to think they're capable. I don't want to generalize, because there are plenty of girls who go at it fearlessly, but the ones who have fear [about using media technology] have always been girls.... Fighting the prejudices they already hold about women and technology is always a challenge. (Zander)

Other instructors echoed this particular challenge, noting that "getting them to believe they can do it" is the most difficult part of teaching girls about the tools and techniques of media production (Soe).

One instructor suggested that the gender dynamics in co-ed workshops can also affect girls' confidence with media technology and mentioned that "fighting boys for access" is one of the biggest problem female youth face in such classes (Soe). Another instructor reiterated this point:

The boys seemed to be more controlling from the start. They wanted to operate the cameras and always know what was going on.... The girls seemed to be reluctant at first to take over responsibility, but once they started doing things, they were just as verbal about wanting to operate the cameras and came up with great suggestions. (Fleishman)

Because of many girls' hesitancy and lack of confidence in using technology, particularly when boys are present, most media educators working with female youth understand the need to take extra measures to provide girls with a supportive environment that facilitates their assertiveness as well as their creativity. For example, one instructor who noted boys' dominance in media workshops argued that girls need "initial information that they are also very talented and that they can also do all of these wonderful things just as well as the boys" (Fleishman).

Another strategy often used to create a nurturing, noncompetitive environment for female youth learning about media is to exclude males from, and privilege female-oriented issues in, such workshops. As the instructor of one such program told me, "Working with girls [alone] provided a safe space to address the specific gender issues they encounter, which clearly isn't possible when boys are around" (Zander). Another instructor reiterated this point: "Creating a girls-only space seemed critical to making [a] space that was open to thinking about being a girl and expressing it" (Lotz). Girls' greater levels of comfort and confidence in girls-only classes are substantiated by some of the female youth who enroll in such workshops. For example, when asked whether she would prefer a girls-only or co-ed media workshop, one ten-year-old girl stated, "I would probably take a girls' class because I'm more comfortable working with girls, but I might take a co-ed class for the variety."[6] Another girl responded that her favorite part of the workshop was that no boys were involved. When asked whether their girls-only workshop would have been different had boys been included, all students who responded to this question answered in the affirmative, and the majority noted that it would be have been more difficult to include female-centered subjects because male youth are not interested in or care about such topics.

Virtually all the instructors whom I interviewed reported that girls' education in filmmaking strengthens their self-confidence, particularly in relation to seeing themselves as cultural producers. As one instructor stated, "It was rewarding for them to know that THEY made this cool video, practically by themselves" (Moore). Another instructor noted, "they learned how to DO things. The finished product was something you could tell they were proud of!" (Ross). Other instructors noted a general increase in assertiveness which was not specifically related to media production: "I saw girls who were afraid to open their mouths begin to question and think critically" (Lewis). Indeed, one eleven-year-old girl who participated in a media workshop was aware of her own rise in self-esteem simply through her contact with media technology, and noted that, for her, the best part of the class was simply "Walking around campus with a tripod on my shoulder. It made me feel important."[7]

These reports from workshop instructors and attendees make problematic Tyner's assertions that the self-esteem disadvantaged youth get from their involvement in media production is "borrowed" and thus a deferment of their true empowerment. While it is extremely difficult to discern the longevity of the self-esteem boost gained by youth through filmmaking, girls' active engagement with tools and practices traditionally dominated by adult males is, at the very least, one of the small steps they can take in becoming comfortable with technology, engaging actively with culture, asserting their perspectives in a new way, and feeling self-confident and proud of their accomplishments.

WHAT ARE "GIRLS' MOVIES"? THE IDENTITY–AUTHORSHIP CONNECTION

So how do girls express themselves through audiovisual media, and what forms do those expressions take? One of the questions that has dogged my research of cultural artifacts produced by female youth is if and how these texts can be differentiated from those produced by other cultural agents, particularly individuals with whom girls share the same generational status—boys—and those with whom girls share the same sex identity—women. In other words, I am curious about whether the modifier girl is a legitimate and useful signifier that can differentiate the various artifacts female youth create from those produced by other people. Despite the extreme difficulty if not impossibility of answering this question, the relationship of identity and authorship in girls' films is one that needs further exploration.

Questions about the effects of identity on the creation of cultural texts have vexed cultural scholars for many years now, particularly those who study texts produced by members of marginalized groups. For example, feminist scholars studying films produced by women have been hesitant to place all such texts into the category of "women's films" for fear of reproducing an essentialist understanding of female identity, dismissing crucial differences among women, and suggesting that women filmmakers can and do function in a place outside the male-dominated film industry. At the same time, however, feminist film theorists have been reluctant to let go of sexual and gender differences as influences on authorship because to do so may risk the elision of certain features apparent in women-made films that suggest relations to their creators' biological, psychological, and social constitutions. This conundrum has made feminist criticism of women-produced movies a difficult task, as Lucy Fisher notes:

[T]he feminist critic who focuses on the creations of female artists must ... decide how to position them.... [T]he theorist confronts a fork in the road, a critical choice. Shall the work of women artists be situated within the preexistent male discourse? Or should it be constituted as a separate province, an alternate heritage? (4)

Fisher's solution is to read women's films intertextually alongside those produced by men. Borrowing from her approach, we might analyze girls' movies in relation to films produced by boys.

Speaking to the question of the relationship of marginalized identity and film authorship, Richard Dyer argues that analyses of the effects of an author's identity on the texts s/he produces are "haunted" by the dubious figures of both the author, whose status as the master meaning-maker has been thoroughly debunked, as well as the marginalized subject, whose deprivileged and essentialized identity has been constructed by those with the privilege of individuality (185–86). Refusing to let go of either of these problematic figures, Dyer attempts to resolve this haunting by arguing that "it still matters who specifically made a film, whose performance a film is, though this is neither all-determining nor having any assumable relationship to the person's life or consciousness. What is significant is the authors' material social position in relation to discourse, the access to discourses they have on account of who they are" (188).

In addition, Dyer notes that the concept of authority cannot be tossed to the wind when considering texts produced by disenfranchised individuals, for whom the ability to speak authoritatively in public about themselves and their communities is precisely what is at stake: "The idea of authority implied in that of authorship, the feeling that it is a way of claiming legitimacy and power for a text's meanings and affects, is indeed what is at issue" in texts produced by marginalized groups. "They are about claiming the right to speak, ... claiming a special authority for their image" (196).

Using Dyer's argument, then, we might theorize that the films and videos produced by female youth can be understood as "girls' movies" because they reveal not only their creators' access to and negotiations of discourses of girl-hood, but also their insistence on speaking authoritatively from a particular form of deprivileged subjectivity that is related to both their sex and their age. Before using Dyer's approach to analyze girls' movies, I will first explore Fisher's strategy and read girls' films alongside those produced by boys.

THE FISHER APPROACH: READING GIRLS' AND BOYS' FILMS INTERTEXTUALLY

Although I recognize the problems associated with making generalized com-ments about girls' movies since this risks dismissing significant differences be-tween such texts, some common characteristics can be found across a number of girls' films which differentiate them from movies made by boys. For exam-ple, female youth tend to occupy all the important crew roles during the mak-ing of girls' movies, from director to cinematographer to editor. In addition, these films typically feature female youth as primary cast members. This fem-inizing of girls' moviemaking practices and narratives demonstrates a desire to establish what might be called the "girl's gaze" which explores the various modes and meanings of girlhood. In contrast, boys' films tend to privilege male youth in both cast and crew positions, which reveals their investment in estab-lishing the "boy's gaze" and negotiating youthful masculinity.

Another obvious point of difference between boys' and girls' films is related to genre and modes of representation. From my analysis of more than a hun-dred youth-produced films, I have found that a significant number of narrative movies produced by boys, especially middle-class younger teens, adhere to the conventions for the action/adventure genre and thus typically include repre-sentations of violence which their creators often spectacularize through fake blood, explosions, and sound effects.[8] Several instructors of youth-oriented media workshops have noticed this gendered difference of content as well. For example, one instructor who has taught many media shops to both boys and girls remarks, "Boys are just so into blowing things up, having strange army or violent things going on in their videos" (Ponczek). In contrast, I have found very few films produced by girls that contain images of violence, and even fewer that present such imagery in the same way boys' films do. Indeed, girls' movies that include acts of aggression often demonstrate their filmmakers' re-fusal to employ the representational strategies typically used to sensationalize violence. For example, Gina Podesta's 3 Bitches (1997) and Erica Shapiro's Twin Tales (1999) both depict girls being hit by their boyfriends; however, neither of these films spectacularizes violence. Instead, such scenes are used to construct a critical commentary on the larger social problem of male-against-female abuse.

There is little doubt that girls' and boys' choices for film content and modes of representation are related less to their chromosomal composition than to their gendered enculturation. Therefore, I am not arguing that boys are naturally drawn to cultural texts that feature violence, but rather that, as Dyer suggests, male youth are encouraged to understand such discourse as "theirs" and thus reproduce it in their own films. Girls, by contrast, are typically discouraged from engaging with texts that include violence and instead are urged to identify with "wholesome," melodramatic narratives that foreground relationships. As Barbara Hudson has argued, because the generational stage of adolescence has been gendered masculine, boys are allowed to act upon both their gendered and generational status without reproach; however, a girl's femininity is potentially compromised by any displays of behavior that might be read as adolescent.

Connecting these conflicting ideologies to representations of adolescence and femininity in popular culture, Hudson notes that whereas adolescence is constructed through male-dominated images of "the restless, searching youth, ... the sower of wild oats, the tester of growing powers" (35), by contrast femininity is portrayed as "involving the skill to make lasting relationships, with the ability to care very deeply for very few people" (47). Hudson's argument is substantiated by my own research: Boys' films often demonstrate restlessness, rebellion, and a desire to test boundaries and limits, while girls' movies often focus on the development of interpersonal relationships.

THE DYER APPROACH: NEGOTIATIONS OF GENDER AND GENERATION DISCOURSES IN GIRLS' MOVIES

While Fisher's intertextual approach advocates analyzing films by marginalized individuals alongside those produced by members of dominant groups, Dyer's intratextual approach suggests looking within individual film texts to examine filmmakers' negotiations of discourses to which they have access. Using Dyer's strategy, the label of "girls' movie" can be applied to those films which reflect girls' engagements with discourses of gender and generation. Interestingly, such cinematic negotiation of these two discourses does not appear in films created by younger girls but is readily apparent in those produced by older female youth.

Many teen girls' narrative films focus on dating, which is not surprising given that, as noted above, female youth are encouraged to privilege interpersonal relations, and the emergence of a sexualized identity is perhaps the most significant marker of adolescence. While, at first glance, girls' dating films appear at risk of reproducing traditional sexual and gender politics, they rarely mimic the "happily ever after" stories made for girls by the mainstream media industries and instead demonstrate an active negotiation of and, at times, resistance to both heterosexual and patriarchal ideologies. For example, Alison Pipen's *Angel Face* (1999) opens with scenes of romantic bliss between two teen lovers yet has as its narrative center the grief a girl faces upon the death of her boyfriend. Similarly, *The Party* (1998), by Kimberly Po, pulls in the viewer through what appears to be a typical heterosexual dating experience; yet the film's main objective is to explore the controversial issue of date rape, not romance.

While Pipen and Po use melodramatic conventions to portray and then complicate romance narratives, other girl directors have used humor to poke fun at heterosexual dating and gender relations. For example, Carley Steiner's *Nightcrawlers* (1998) first appears to be a conventional story about a girl obsessed with finding a boyfriend in order to achieve happiness. However, the video's use of comedic editing strategies, which allow for multiple potential boyfriends to come knocking at her door in quick succession only to be rejected, suggests the impossibility of finding the perfect mate, as well as the frustration that ensues when one makes romance the primary criterion for happiness.

Another narrative film that uses humor to foreground the difficulties associated with heterosexual dating is Tricia Grashaw's *Ultimate Guide to Flirting* (1996), which uses parody to illustrate the ludicrousness of dating rituals and traditional modes of femininity. In the film, two girls happen upon a guide for flirting in a teen magazine and begin practicing each of the steps described in order to improve their attractiveness to the opposite sex. Despite much practice, when the girls try out their new flirting skills on a group of boys, they are rejected immediately as annoying. The parodic, exaggerated, and somewhat unruly facial expressions and body movements of the two characters, not to mention the nonnormative appearance of the actors playing them, demonstrate an active resistance to the heterosexualized discourse of teen magazines that encourages girls to manipulate their bodies and behavior in order to be seen as attractive by boys.

As Grashaw's film demonstrates, many movies made by teenage girls reveal their creators' active negotiations of discourses of gender; however, very few teen girls' films reveal such levels of engagement with discourses of generation, especially outside a heterosexualized context. Indeed, other than dating, issues related to the generational uniqueness of female adolescence typically remain unexplored in girls' movies. This avoidance of generational discourse by many girl filmmakers can be understood in part as a result of what Hudson argues is the traditional subversion of femininity by adolescence which for decades has discouraged teenage girls from fully occupying their generational identity.

Nevertheless, Shapiro's *Twin Tales* reveals that some teenage girls are reclaiming an adolescent identity as a means of resisting traditional gender roles and behaviors. The films created by such girls demonstrate how the rebelliousness of adolescence may be useful in liberating female youth. In the clever twinning of her sound and image tracks, Shapiro connects teenage girls' rebelliousness directly to the emergence of feminist consciousness. On the sound track, we hear a young woman talking about her early experiences in the pink world of ballet class, where she revels in the risqué stories told by older girls. As the narrator tells her tale, the viewer sees a young woman running down the street away from a possible stalker and then becoming absorbed in Simone de Beauvoir's *Second Sex*, as well as other influential feminist texts. While the film's images continue to explore the girl's growing awareness of patriarchy and misogyny, the soundtrack suggests her understanding of the greater need for both female independence and female solidarity in the face of such difficulties.

PUTTING IT OUT THERE: THE EXHIBITION AND DISTRIBUTION OF GIRLS' MOVIES

While many movies made by girls demonstrate a different perspective from films made for girls, it is disturbing that such films are typically seen only by the filmmakers and their instructors, friends, and family members. Fortunately, the girl power ethos has moved well beyond the Riot Grrrl community during the last decade, thus contributing to an increasing number of avenues for the exhibition and distribution of girls' movies. For example, since the early 1990s several local, national, and international film festivals devoted to youth-made movies have emerged, including the National Children's Film Festival. In turn, many larger, adult-oriented festivals, such as the Chicago International Film Festival, now include screenings of films produced by youth. Many films shown at these festivals are picked up by the HBO Family channel, which features youth-made movies on *30 x 30: Kid Flicks*, or by PBS, whose *Zoom* also shows films created by young people.

To my knowledge, only two film festivals have included programs devoted specifically to girls' movies, Women in the Director's Chair (WIDC) and the DocSide Short Film Festival. While WIDC has packaged its girls' films in a traveling program called the Media Girls Tour, DocSide's program of girls' movies was screened only once.[9] Fortunately, however, fifteen documentaries of DocSide's girl program were compiled into one video, *Smashing the Myth (or Not Just White, Rich, and Dangerously Thin)* (2001), which is distributed by Listen Up!, a network of more than thirty youth media organizations.[10]

Another organization that distributes the work of girl filmmakers is Big Miss Moviola, which compiles such movies into video "chainletters" of which it has to date produced twelve. Big Miss Moviola, formed in 1996 by performance artist Miranda July, provides a unique service for girl directors whose films rarely have the opportunity to enter the mainstream systems of distribution and exhibition. In an effort to promote better networking among girl filmmakers, each Big Miss Moviola chainletter is accompanied by a paper 'zine, which includes contact information for the filmmakers. Not to be left behind by the digital revolution, July also recently launched a Web site that serves as an alternate market place for the selling of the Big Miss Moviola chainletters, as well as a public forum for communication between the girl filmmakers and those inexperienced in media production.[11]

CONCLUSION

As the work of July, Richards, and other young women attests, an enormous amount of activity is taking place today in the United States in order to facilitate girls' involvement in media education and filmmaking, as well as to promote and distribute girls' movies. As I have demonstrated, such activity is linked to a variety of social, political, and technological transformations which have occurred in only the past two decades. In addition to being part of the much broader phenomenon of an increase in female youth's cultural productivity, the rise of girls' media education is the result of greater accessibility to less expensive and more user-friendly media technologies, as well as the explosion of media literacy initiatives and the incorporation of production in media education curricula. In turn, the increase in girls-only media workshops is related to the resurgence of girls' advocacy and, perhaps more significantly, the emergence of the Riot Grrrl movement and its privileging of "girl power" as an ideological framework for the political, social, and cultural promotion and activity of female youth.

As a result of these various phenomena, more girls are taking classes in media criticism and production than ever before, and more female youth are producing their own films and managing their own production companies. Yet, rather than mimicking the representation and discursive strategies of the mainstream film industry, these girls are creating movies that demonstrate attempts not only to establish a "girl's gaze," but also to engage directly with the ideologies of gender and generation prevalent in popular culture and contradictorily experienced by female youth. While we have yet to see a "girl Mozart" whose films destroy the professionalism attributed to contemporary filmmaking, the female youth who are picking up film and video cameras and recording their stories are, at the very least, revolutionizing female youth culture. If we would like a better understanding of this phenomenon, we would do well to watch the movies girls make.

NOTES

This article is dedicated to girl directors everywhere.

1. This commercial was produced on 25 Feb. 1998 by Rainbow Media.

2. For example, Ashli and Callie Pfeiffer (fourteen and fifteen years old today) formed YaYa Productions in 1998. Alyssa Buecker, now seventeen, also recently formed her own production company, Milbo Productions.

3. In 1999 the Girl Scouts of America introduced the Media Savvy Interest Patch and published three *Media Know-How* books, one each for the Daisy/Brownie levels, the Junior level, and the Cadette/Senior levels.

4. Amanda Lotz and Sharon Ross designed the "Girls Making Headlines" class in spring 2000. Upon Lotz's relocation, Diane Zander stepped in as the workshop's co-

instructor for the summer 2000 class. Elizabeth Sikes taught the class in summer 2001. Clarissa Moore served as a teaching assistant for both classes.

5. With the exception of one teacher who is over fifty years old, the average age of the media workshop instructors I interviewed for this essay is twenty-eight.

6. "Girls Making Headlines" student survey (18 June 2001).

7. "Girls Making Headlines" student survey (15 June 2001).

8. For example, see Rusty Kelley's *New American Dream*, Trey Pool's *Beware of the Dog*, Brandon Bryant and Will McCord's *Demons of the Darkness*.

9. The DocSide Short Film Festival screened its girl film program in fall 2000 in San Antonio, Texas. See http://www.listenup.org/grrrl.

10. *Smashing the Myth (or Not Just White, Rich, and Dangerously Thin)*, Listen Up!, 2001. This was curated by Lauren Dowdall, Tamara Garcia, Emily Green, Christen Marquez, Rhea Mokund, Natalie Neptune, Claire Steinberg, Iriane Todd, and Miyo Tubridy. The Project Facilitator was Austin Haeberle.

11. The Big Miss Moviola Web site may be accessed at http://www.joanie4jackie.com.

WORKS CITED

American Association of University Women. *Shortchanging Girls, Shortchanging America*. Washington, DC: American Association of University Women, 1991.

Beauvoir, Simone de. *The Second Sex*, trans. H. M. Parshley. New York, Vintage, 1989.

Buckingham, David, and Julian Sefton-Green. *Cultural Studies Goes to School Reading and Teaching Popular Media*. Bristol, Eng.: Taylor & Francis, 1994.

Dyer, Richard. "Believing in Fairies: The Author and the Homosexual." *Inside Out*, ed. Diana Fuss. New York: Routledge, 1991. 185–201.

Fisher, Lucy. *Shot/Countershot: Film Tradition and Women's Cinema*. Princeton, NJ: Princeton University Press, 1989.

Fleishman, Jeremy. E-mail response to author's questionnaire, 25 Apr. 2001.

Gilligan, Carol. *In a Different Voice: Psychological Theory and Women's Development*. Cambridge, MA.: Harvard University Press, 1982.

Girl Scouts of the USA. *Media Know-How for Cadette and Senior Girl Scouts*. New York: Girl Scouts of the U.S.A., 1999.

Girls Inc. "Girls Re-Cast TV Action Kit." http://www.girlsinc.org/PROGRAMS.html.

Hearts of Darkness: A Filmmaker's Apocalypse. Dir. Fax Bahr, George Hickenlooper, Eleanor Coppola. Triton, 1991.

Hobbs, Renee. "The Seven Great Debates in the Media Literacy Movement." http://www.medialit.org/ReadingRoom/keyarticles/sevengreat.htm. 5 May 2001.

hooks, bell. "The Oppositional Gaze." *Black Looks: Race and Representation*. Boston: South End, 1992.

Hudson, Barbara. "Femininity and Adolescence." *Gender and Generation*, ed. Angela McRobbie and Mica Nava. London: Macmillan, 1984. 31–53.

It Wasn't Love. Dir. Sadie Benning. 1992.

LeRoy, Mervyn. *The Bad Seed*. Dir. Warner Brothers, 1956.

Lewis, Anne. E-mail response to author's questionnaire, 20 Apr. 2001.

Lotz, Amanda. E-mail correspondence with the author, 21 June 2001.

Masters, Kim. "Auteur of Adolescence: Sadie Benning, Talking to the Camera." *Washington Post*, 17 Oct. 1992, D1–D2.

Moore, Clarissa. E-mail response to author's questionnaire, 22 Apr. 2001.

Phoenix, Val C. "From Womyn to Grrrls: Finding Sisterhood in Girl Style Revolution." *Deneuve* (Jan./Feb. 1994): 41–42.

Pipher, Mary. *Reviving Ophelia: Saving the Selves of Adolescent Girls.* New York: Pantheon, 1994.

Ponczek, Tasha. E-mail response to author's questionnaire, 10 May 2001.

Prince. "I Wanna Be Your Lover." Prince. Warner Bros., 1979.

Richards, Andrea. *Girl Director: A How to Guide for the First Time Flat Broke Filmmaker (and Videomaker).* Los Angeles: Girl Press, 2001.

———. E-mail correspondence with the author, 23 June 2001.

Ross, Sharon. E-mail response to author's questionnaire, 30 Apr. 2001.

Street-Level Youth Media. "Girls Only Pilot Program: Background." http://www.streetlevel.iit.edu/outhprojects/chikweb/Programs/o.html. 6 May 2001.

Soe, Valerie. E-mail response to author's questionnaire, 29 May 2001.

Tyner, Kathleen. "The Media Education Elephant." http://www.interact.uoregon.edu/MediaLit/FA/mltyner/elephant.html. 5 May 2001.

Zander, Diane. E-mail response to author's questionnaire, 20 Apr. 2001.

3

Stronger Than Yesterday?
Romance and Antiromance in Popular Music

Clare Bradford

Britney Spears's 1999 song "Baby One More Time" involves a narrative in which the female narrator complains about her loneliness, which is occasioned by her lover's failure to page her. In Spears's "Stronger," produced a year later, a playful allusion is made to the earlier song with the assertion that the narrator is "stronger than yesterday," no longer dependent on the presence of her lover for her sense of self. This "stronger" stance is replicated in a number of contemporary Top 40 songs sung by women vocalists and groups, including Britney Spears, Pink, All Saints, 3LW, Destiny's Child, TLC, Jennifer Lopez, and Christina Aguilera, and is informed by a discursive strand which I will refer to as "antiromance," realized in song lyrics and the performative and textual strategies of music videos. The young audiences implied by these texts are engaged in processes of identity-formation involving interactions between self and others in social environments marked for gender, ethnicity, and class. Musical texts serve as demarcation signs between groups and subgroups within youth culture at the same time that they construct meanings about individual agency and identity, and my reading of antiromance texts focuses on how they position young audiences in regard to gendered identities.

I do not want to imply that the texts I consider constitute a univocal body of songs. They are diverse and often contradictory, coexisting with pop songs located firmly within conventional paradigms of romance; indeed, almost all singers perform both antiromance and romantic songs. To various extents, antiromance songs contest the naturalized ideologies which cluster around western traditions of romantic love, namely those built on patriarchal binaries which distinguish the feminine from the masculine, such as that men are active and women passive; that men are rational and women emotional; that men initiate and end relationships while women wait and suffer. At one end of the anti-romance spectrum are songs such as Jennifer Lopez's "Love Don't Cost a Thing" and Christina Aguilera's "Genie in a Bottle," which fold back into romance while claiming for women a right to sexual pleasure. At the other end of the spectrum are texts which deploy strategies of parody, black humor, and slapstick: For instance, in Sunshine Anderson's video version of the song "Heard It All Before," the female protagonist produces a remote control and "shuts down" her former lover; and in Pink's "There You Go," the protagonist grabs the attention of her boyfriend by driving a motorcycle through the window of the room where he sits absorbed in his PlayStation. My sources include lyrics and music videos performed by various female singers and a televised concert by Britney Spears, described in the introduction to this 2001 concert as a "sexy nineteen-year-old pop music teen queen."

The "teen queen" genre of pop music is directed particularly at a female audience, from the prepubescent girls who constitute most of the audience at the Britney Spears concert, to the adolescents and young adults implied by the Destiny's Child song "Independent Women," which features in the soundtrack of the film *Charlie's Angels*.[1] The musicologist David Brackett observes that to discuss pop music only in relation to "the music itself"—the sounds, their production, their relations to one another, their effects—is to ignore the fact that "musical meaning is *socially* constructed—even the type of musical meaning that seems to derive from internal musical relationships" (xii). The pop songs which I discuss are produced within the globalized economies of the pop music and media industries. Their linguistic and performative features are shaped by the genres and styles of popular music, which tend toward the replication of cultural ideologies of romantic love; at the same time, they are informed by meanings consonant with feminist principles concerning female agency, though in ambiguous and ambivalent ways.

Notions of authorship are notoriously slippery in regard to pop music, since, as David Hesmondhalgh notes, the production of popular music is inescapably "multitextual" (208). The songs performed by teen queens are typically attributed to a list of songwriters, occasionally including the singers; for instance, Beyonce Knowles of Destiny's Child is listed along with Samuel J. Barnes, Jean Claude Olivier, and Cory Rooney as one of the writers of the song "Independent Women." While the "I" of the song is performatively appropriated by the female singer, questions of style and delivery are negotiated within production processes typically controlled by men: A survey of the CD covers of teen queen albums shows that their songs tend to be written, produced, and recorded by men. Additionally, television programs on the making of teen queen video clips show that the producers, choreographers, and designers of these videos are predominantly male. Teen queen songs are thus developed in contexts where women are performers and backing vocalists and men cultural producers. It would be rash to assume that the woman singer is merely a *tabula rasa* on which male producers inscribe their versions of the feminine; nevertheless, the singer's identification with the "I" of lyrics is highly unstable, just as the gender ideologies of antiromance songs are informed by a range of discursive strands.

Pop songs are consumed by listeners who sing along with them and memorize them; but this does not mean that the song is constituted by the words; indeed, it is often claimed that for their consumers the words of a pop song are far less significant than melody and voice quality (Mills 151). Another set of signifying practices is constituted by the visual and performative strategies mobilized in the video clip genre, which has developed, from its beginnings as a way of merely promoting a song, into what Simon Frith describes as "a source of income in itself, perhaps a more important source of income, indeed, than the music it is supposedly selling" (97). The actions performed by singers in music videos are imitated by listeners; as the final credits roll in the Britney Spears concert, the camera lingers on the faces and bodies of young girls as they perform Spears's movements.

At the center of all these signifying practices is the figure of the teen queen herself, produced through Web sites, fan clubs, magazines, and promotional material as an identity at once transparently readable and immeasurably remote. For instance, the Britney Spears concert is followed by Spears speaking directly from the screen about her life in a small town in Louisiana and then by a series of interviews featuring her mother, her first dance instructor, her teachers, her dentist, and her friends, concluding with Spears's longing for home which connects her persona with that of Dorothy in *The Wizard of Oz*, and thus lays claim both to a middle-American demographic and to a global culture permeated by American cultural products. Spears's production as a combination of teen queen and small-town girl is symbolized by the juxtaposition of images in the concert video and the promotional material which follows it. In the concert, for instance, her stature as diva is represented spatially, when she is lifted by crane to a point far above her audience, and when, in another sequence, she stands on top of a giant staircase. In contrast, the downplayed intimacy of the interview sequence is presented as a series of family photographs and home videos. Both representations of Spears are, of course, media constructs, designed to attract female audiences and to ensure their loyalty to the teen queen, who must be both like and unlike her subjects—a girl like them, with similar interests and aspirations; and a pop star who is the object of identificatory fantasies.

The character constructed through first-person narration in the lyrics of "Stronger" seems to be a young woman both sexually experienced (since the song implies a previous romantic relationship) and resistant to the power of romantic love over identity-formation, a woman who is not to be defined by a male partner. Like many antiromance songs, "Stronger" is sung to a male addressee, a former partner, and the lyrics insist that the narrator is not the property of any male with whom she is romantically involved. The language of the song engages its female listeners in a drama in which they are positioned to align themselves with the narrator as she admonishes her former partner and asserts her status as an independent woman. The discursive features of "Stronger" accord with Richard Middleton's model of words/music relationships in popular music, where he identifies three categories: "Affect," in which words and melody merge as "intoned feeling"; "story," where the words determine rhythm and harmonies to produce narrative; and "gesture," in which the voice is deployed more or less as an instrument (quoted in Brackett 30). In "Stronger," the words/music relationship hovers between affect and story. The verses, sung toward the lower register of Spears's voice, allude to a story briefly sketched, and specifically to the narrator's determination to escape from a relationship represented as controlling and limiting, while the chorus falls more clearly within the category of "affect," giving the impression of an emotional and buoyant mood, its rhythm accentuating the word *stronger*, and its vocal range suggesting an expansiveness not present in the limited (and lower) vocal line of the verses.

But such a formalist account of music and words goes only so far in identifying the meanings produced by the song. When the performative aspects of "Stronger" are considered—Spears's production of the teen queen persona, her actions, and the settings in which they occur—more complex significations can be observed. The video version begins with several elements of story: A setting, which includes a scene at a party; three characters—the protagonist (the Spears character), a young man and another young woman; and a series of events involving the protagonist's discovery of a liaison between the other two characters, her argument with the man, and her departure from the party. At one point, Spears strides across a room, followed by the man, who trips over a piece of furniture and scrambles to his feet. Shortly after this, he attempts to pursue her as she leaves but is unable to evade the clutching hand of the other woman. In both cases, the effect is to emphasize the powerfulness and active physicality of the Spears character and the bumbling ineptitude of the young man, in a parodic inversion of stereotypes of romance—the decisive, action-oriented male and the fluttering, emotional female. In the sequence which follows, the Spears character drives alone in the dark through a storm; the car slews around, and Spears is seen standing in the rain; next, through the rapid editing characteristic of music videos, she is shown spinning acrobatically on top of a pile of metal chairs (an allusion to a similar move in a Janet Jackson video), dancing as she holds a walking stick (like a Fred Astaire without top hat and tails), then back at the scene of the dark road, where she walks toward viewers across a bridge.

Throughout this collage of images, the Spears character is masculinized, represented in contexts which evoke stereotypes of masculinity: The car she drives and the walking stick she holds constitute displacements of the male phallus; in the party scene she seems to be associated with a (possibly) violent incident in which her rival falls or is pushed from a chair; she walks and drives alone in the dark, apparently oblivious of danger. Simultaneously, her sexualized body is the object of specular attention, always central to the scenes, dance sequences, and narrative fragments of the video and, in the final moments of the video, subjected to the dismembering effect by which the camera focuses on components of her body: Face, breasts, midriff, legs.

It is exactly this blending of the masculinized and sexualized body of the teen queen that complicates the question of how antiromance texts position female audiences. Feminist film criticism offers some suggestions about how to approach the visual components of antiromance texts, since while the social functions of music videos are quite different from those of film, their production is informed by cinematic references and strategies within an entertainment scene where musical and film performances increasingly converge (Tasker 181–87), and their production and reception raise issues about female audiences and popular genres similar to those which arise in film criticism. As Christine Gledhill observes, "the theoretical convergence of psychoanalysis and cinema has been problematic for feminism in that it has been theorized largely from the perspective of masculinity and its constructions" (166–67), so that female spectatorship is represented within paradigms which suggest "colonized, alienated or masochistic positions of identification" (168). An added problem is the tendency for the notion of the "female spectator" to elide distinctions between the spectator constructed by the text—and identified through strategies of deconstruction—and the actual female audience; specifically, in this discussion, the girls and young women who sing along to pop songs, imitate the moves performed in videos, and attend concerts.

Gledhill suggests that the notion of negotiation allows for a model of meaning production in which "meaning is neither imposed, nor passively imbibed, but arises out of a struggle or negotiation between competing frames of reference, motivation and experience" (169). Central to this model of negotiation is Antonio Gramsci's concept of hegemony, which refers to the shifting play of political, social, and ideological forces, reliant for their potency not on force but on persuasion. The operations of negotiation in meaning production can be examined in relation to institutions, texts, and audiences, while allowing space for "the subjectivities, identities and pleasures" (173) which shape and are shaped by the social practices involved in the reception of texts by their audiences.

The institutional forces most evident in the production of Spears as teen queen are the global economies of record and television companies, for whom the singer and her persona are commodities capable of attracting an audience which will purchase music and watch music videos—the latter interspersed on MTV with advertisements deploying many of the same strategies as the videos, thus further blurring the line between the singer and her commodification. As I have noted, pop music is centrally concerned with the figure of the teen queen and with conventional versions of romantic love, which are at odds with feminist values circulating, even if in diluted forms, within western culture. The antiromance meanings which inform "Stronger" can thus be seen to relate to a negotiation between institutional and cultural purposes and agendas and to unresolved contradictions surrounding versions of the feminine. In regard to textual negotiations, there are obvious tensions between lyrics which construct the female protagonist as autonomous and agential and visual representations which show her as a "bad" girl, seductively clothed and sexually available. As she stands in front of her car, her rain-soaked clothes clinging to her body, the Spears character summons up countless similar cinematic images in which the bodies of women are objectified by a masculine gaze. Yet immediately following this textual moment, she is seen performing acrobatic feats in which her body is encoded as strong and in control. The textual meanings produced by the video are very far from fixed, but it is certain that they cannot be contained within the patriarchal binary which opposes the passive "good" girl to the active "bad" one.

The third level of media analysis suggested by Gledhill's model focuses on reception, which she describes as "the most radical moment of negotiation, because the most variable and unpredictable" (173), complicated by the fact that the audiences of antiromance songs are sometimes individual but often are groups engaged in the diverse social practices of friendship groups and video and film audiences. It is outside the scope of this discussion to consider the "real" audiences of antiromance songs; nevertheless, it is important that textual analysis should take into account the contexts in which reception occurs. Spears's concert performance of "Stronger" is, for instance, quite different from the video version, and although it is impossible to know from viewing the concert what meanings the song has for those who attend, it is clear that setting and audience are influential in determining modes and styles of performance. The concert version dampens down the "bad girl" interpretation of the song, relying rather on Spears's ensemble work with a group of male dancers. Here the Spears character is produced as a blend of pop diva and lead participant in an exercise class. The hints of violence and danger present in the video version are reduced to muted and playful moves; for instance, at one point Spears points at one of the dancers, who simulates a fall; and at another, two of the dancers briefly hold her as she appears to fall. The concert version includes an allusion to the video when a screen behind the dancers shows Spears running along a dark street, but the predominant representation is of the teen queen surrounded by adoring males. This safer, bouncier version seems calculated to appeal to the young audience at the concert, its antiromance lyrics effectively negated by a choreography which produces Spears as romantic love object.

In her essay "Women's Genres: Melodrama, Soap Opera and Theory," Annette Kuhn considers how to theorize the interplay between text and context; in particular, how notions of spectator-text relations might distinguish between the subject positions implied by texts and the actual audiences who consume women's genres of popular production. She invokes Charlotte Brunsdon's formulation of a distinction between "subject positions proposed by texts and a 'social subject' who may or may not take up these positions" (153). As Kuhn notes, Brunsdon's treatment of this distinction maintains a privileging of context, in that "spectator-text relations are...regarded virtually as an effect of socio-cultural contexts" (153). Christine Gledhill's notion of negotiations between individual and cultural meanings can usefully be aligned with Kuhn's invocation of discourse theory. For if, as Kuhn suggests, "both spectators and social audience may...be regarded as discursive constructs," the interplay between texts and their audiences can be seen within the context of a network of negotiations between discursive formations, with "certain discourses possessing greater constitutive authority at specific moments than others" (154). Such a view of popular cultural texts allows for reading strategies which go beyond simplistic oppositions between texts which are complicit with the domination of capitalism and those which resist dominant ideologies, recognizing the "contradictory nature of cultural products, [which] can be the site of both hegemonic *and* counterhegemonic ideological production depending on the context of their reception or production" (Best 19).

A pervasive theme in antiromance lyrics, and one which overlaps with the commodification of music and singers in the global industry of popular music, is a concern with connections between romance and commodification. Pink's "Most Girls," from *Can't Take Me Home,* draws on hip-hop inflexions to construct a persona indifferent to romantic conventions which measure love by gifts of flowers or jewels, like the "fly girl" whose version of romance is focused on the diamond ring she is given. The persona distinguishes herself from women whose dreams are bounded by their desire for material gain, enumerating the signs of her independence: Her job, her car, her rent payments. Female autonomy is thus defined as financial autonomy, a move which leaves space for a version of love uncontaminated by the obligation which a woman might have for a man who gives her material goods. Similarly, the TLC song "Silly Ho" describes the narrator as a woman who has never relied on her partner to buy her what she wants. Indeed, the narrator describes how she has bought her own rings, so overturning the conventional associations of rings with romance. Such a position of autonomy is compared with the sexual obligation incurred by the "silly ho" who will do whatever is required by her man.

Financial transactions such as buying clothes, paying telephone bills, maintaining vehicles, and keeping up rent payments figure prominently in the lyrics of the group Destiny's Child, notably in their hit single "Independent Women," where these transactions figure exchanges of an emotional and relational kind. Thus, the woman who "fronts" or brags about the money she receives from her partner is seen to represent herself as the recipient of male patronage; it would be far better, the lyric suggests, for her to brag about her own money and, by implication, about an autonomous selfhood. To be an independent woman, then, is a matter not merely of paying one's way but of being an equal partner in relational terms, one who pays her way.

The Destiny's Child single "Bills, Bills, Bills" traces the disintegration of a relationship through a series of scenarios relating to financial transactions. The persona, addressing her estranged lover, reminds him how the reciprocity of their early relationship changes when he asks to use her car, drives it, and fails to fill it with fuel before returning it to her. The deterioration of the relationship is further identified with his propensity for going on shopping sprees to the mall, using her mobile phone, and then, when it is time to pay the telephone bill, disavowing any responsibility. The bridge between verses and chorus throughout the song complicates this narrative of relational breakdown, introducing episodes of introspection when the persona laments her inability to make a break with her feckless lover and wonders why she has not found a partner who will support her through times of financial and emotional difficulty. Here two versions of the feminine clash: The independent woman who pays her way and maintains her selfhood within a romantic and sexual relationship and the victim of romance who tolerates her partner's weakness and subordinates her autonomy to her need. These textual negotiations identify antiromance as a site of struggle between women's internalization of cultural discourses which persuade them that they need and desire to be dominated and narratives which celebrate female agency. If the song concludes with an emphatic declaration that their relationship is over, the repetition of the bridging sequence also enforces the sense that gender identity is achieved not once and for all, but in Judith Butler's terms, through "sustained social performances" (141).

The video clip of the song "Survivor" affords a telling example of a conjuncture of textual and cultural discourses. The song's lyrics, like those off "Independent Women" and "Bills, Bills, Bills," draw upon metaphors of financial exchange to assert female independence. The addressee of the song is a male partner from whom she has separated, and the female persona formulates her "survival"—that is, her capacity to withstand the cultural imperatives which promote romantic love as the ideal relational mode—in relation to a set of expectations which are contradicted one by one: Instead of being weak without her partner she is strong; instead of being poverty-stricken she is rich; and instead of being sad she is happy. These expectations, attributed to the departed lover, inscribe a masculine discourse of threats and warnings, while the persona's claims—that she is stronger, richer, and happier without her partner—assert female agency and anticipate a future in which she will continue not merely to survive but to thrive.

The "Survivor" video clip, drawing on the imagery of the "reality" television series of the same name, deploys the setting of a tropical island and sketches an analepsis involving shipwreck and escape in a lifeboat. At the beginning of the video, the three singers emerge from the sea or crawl across the sand, dressed in clothing artfully designed to refer to the fantasy of shipwreck while drawing on the eroticism of female bodies partially concealed. The act of looking is central to this video—the three women gaze about them, while male characters are glimpsed observing the women as they explore the island. More than this, the camera assumes the role of voyeur, pursuing the women as they run and focusing on parts of their bodies exposed by strategically placed rips and holes in their clothing. At one point a male figure is seen on the top of a bluff; at another the camera looks down on the women as they climb up the steep face of a cliff, and these points of view suggest surveillance and control. The lover absent from the song is reinscribed through the male presence of the camera, and thus what is unequivocal in the lyrics—the persona's proclamation of her self-sufficiency—is rendered contingent and uncertain. At the same time, the women's actions as they explore the island are plotted onto stereotypes of male explorers for whom the land is a feminine space to be penetrated by masculine desire. The sense of female transgression and of the appropriation of masculine discourses by the women is especially noticeable in a scene in which one of the women threatens an unseen intruder with a spear; a moment later another of the women places her hand in front of the camera as if to block its gaze.

The island scene cuts abruptly to a cityscape set against a dramatic sky, then back and forth between island and city. The city is coded as a masculine space, its sharp outlines and hard surfaces sharply distinguished from the verdant, luxurious appearance of the island. In cutting between cityscape and island, the video treats the island setting not as fantasy so much as a metaphor for the quotidian world of the city, so that the notion of women as survivors is strengthened rather than undercut by the island sequences. Nevertheless, the presence of the camera and its lingering gaze on bodies and parts of bodies is a powerful discursive strategy which works against the notion of female self-determination by suggesting a panoptic surveillance. It is perhaps a sign of the video clip's function as commodity that it so strenuously reasserts the power of the male gaze in the face of lyrics which clearly promote female autonomy.

Toward the end of "Survivor," the persona lists the ways in which she will resist the temptations of retaliation and revenge: She will not criticize her former partner on the radio, gossip about his family, compromise her Christian principles, or insult him on the Internet. The image of the three women in "Survivor" holding hands as they run toward the rescue helicopter and running together through the sand is echoed in the video versions of many antiromance songs, sometimes in situations where women are represented as protecting themselves from attack. In their focus on the female body subjected to extremes of emotion or sensation, these texts relate to the field of melodrama, which according to Linda Williams's formulation includes pornography, horror, and the women's film or "weepie" (269). In its location within popular music and as a genre designed for female consumption, the antiromance song evades the extremes of bodily excess manifested in pornography and horror, but in its foregrounding of the spectacular female body and its susceptibility to the possibilities of attack it alludes to these more extreme genres.

These allusions are rendered explicit in the video version of the song "All Hooked Up," by All Saints, which plays with signifiers of danger and sexuality within a broadly parodic frame. The four women in the group are seen at the beginning of the video in an ambiguously coded setting whose rich, dark furnishings and dim lighting evoke brothel scenes within cinematic genres such as the western, where they typically incorporate clichés relating to the whore with the heart of gold. The song, in first person address to a male addressee, incorporates spoken male voices which interject against the melodic line. These vocal interventions into the song are cognate with interventions of a physical sort as four dimly glimpsed men enter the building and hide in various places: Behind a curtain, in a cupboard, behind an armchair, behind a vent. Each of the women is viewed through the eyes of these intruders, with the camera playing on what the men see. Thus, the man hiding behind a vent sees through its slats a midriff, breasts, buttocks, observed in a way which isolates body parts from bodies. As this narration of surveillance and danger builds up, each of the women is viewed separately, occupying a distinct space within the setting and with the camera lingering on sensuous details through shots such as those of hands running over rich fabrics or embossed wall coverings; in another instance, one of the women tracing the contours of her breasts. As the song proceeds, each of the women engages in a moment of physical action when she uncovers the man who is observing her and ejects him. The four men, having been tossed to the floor and thrown through walls, are seen clambering to their feet and escaping, although one is caught as though in the stocks, his head through a hole in the wall. This strenuous activity, which is accompanied by scenes of lamps breaking and walls crumbling, is made strange by the contrast between the women's faces, which do not lose their composure, and the panic and alarm shown by the intruders.

The excessiveness of the physical action, allied with camera shots which disclose the fact that the male figures tossed about are in fact dummies, foregrounds the constructedness of the narrative, and, by implication, of gendered identities. Thus, the setting, with its rich furnishings and fabrics, is dissociated from the stereotypes of cinematic brothel scenes and reinterpreted as a space where women exercise autonomy and power; the woman's hands moving over her breasts signify her pleasure in her body as much as the erotic charge afforded the viewer. In writing of horror films such as *Halloween*, which feature female characters initially victimized but ultimately powerful, Carol Clover argues that viewers are positioned to engage in cross-gender identification, siding first with the male killer and then with the androgynous "Final Girl" who is triumphant at the end. The video of "All Hooked Up" incorporates a parodic take on this cinematic genre: The women are anything but androgynous; the male attackers are incompetent and cowardly; and in any case the male figures tossed about are dummies and not "real" men. The viewers of the video are never invited to align themselves with the male intruders, but at the same time its textual reflexivity precludes a full-blown identification with the women characters. Rather, its playfulness invites a distanced and amused response to the narrative, interrogating representational practices as much as gender ideologies.

The antiromance songs and videos which I have discussed support Frith and Savage's claim that popular culture engages with questions of value and meaning as "an expressive tool for people otherwise excluded from the public voice"

(15). Specifically, they position young audiences engaged in processes of identity formation. Many of these texts produce strong arguments for female autonomy, at the same time that they themselves constitute commodities within the global economies of record and media companies. They are thus simultaneously progressive and complicit with global capitalism; at once sites of resistance and dependent on the maintenance of structures of power. Self-conscious texts such as the video version of "All Hooked Up" make explicit what is observable across the gamut of antiromance: The play of ideas about gender identities and about relations between men and women, realized in lyrics and visual forms characterized by complexity, ambiguity, and inconclusiveness.

NOTE

1. I do not mean to imply that teen queens such as Britney Spears do not have male followings. A scan of teen queen Web sites suggests that male interests relate to specularity rather than to music, whereas female audiences respond to a "package" comprising music, lyrics, and presentation.

WORKS CITED

Aguilera, Christina. "Genie in a Bottle." Christina Aguilera. RCA, 1999.

All Saints. "All Hooked Up." Saints and Sinners. London, 2000.

Anderson, Sunshine. "Heard It All Before." Your Woman. Soulife, 2001.

Best, Beverly. "Over-the-Counter-Culture: Retheorizing Resistance in Popular Culture." The Clubcultures Reader: Readings in Popular Cultural Studies. Ed. Steve Redhead. Oxford: Blackwell, 1997. 18–35.

Brackett, David. Interpreting Popular Music. Cambridge, Eng.: Cambridge University Press, 1995.

Britney Spears Lands Concert Special. Dir. Marty Callner. Hollywood, 2001.

Butler, Judith. Gender Trouble: Feminism and Subversion of Identity. New York: Routledge, 1990.

Clover, Carol J. "Her Body, Himself: Gender in the Slasher Film." Feminist Film Theory: A Reader, ed. Sue Thornham. New York: New York University Press, 1999. 234–50.

Destiny's Child. "Bills, Bills, Bills." The Writing's on the Wall. Columbia, 1999.

———. "Independent Women." Charlie's Angels Soundtrack. Columbia, 2000.

———. "Survivor." Survivor. Columbia, 2001.

Frith, Simon, ed. Facing the Music: Essays on Pop, Rock and Culture. New York: Pantheon, 1988.

Frith, Simon, and Jon Savage. "Pearls and Swine: Intellectuals and the Mass Media." The Clubcultures Reader: Readings in Popular Cultural Studies, ed. Steve Redhead. Oxford, Eng.: Blackwell, 1997. 7–17.

Gledhill, Christine. "Pleasurable Negotiations." Feminist Film Theory: A Reader, ed. Sue Thornham. New York: New York University Press, 1999. 166–79.

Gramsci, Antonio. *Selections from the Prison Notebooks*. London: Lawrence & Wishart, 1971.

Hesmondhalgh, David. "Rethinking Popular Music After Rock and Soul." *Cultural Studies and Communications*, ed. James Curran, David Morley, and Valerie Walkerdine. London: Arnold, 1996. 195–212.

Kuhn, Annette. "Women's Genres: Melodrama, Soap Opera and Theory." *Feminist Film Theory: A Reader*, ed. Sue Thornham. New York: New York University Press, 1999. 146–56.

Lopez, Jennifer. "Love Don't Cost a Thing." J. Lo. Epic, 2001.

Mills, Sara. *Feminist Stylistics*. London: Routledge, 1995.

Pink. "Most Girls." *Can't Take Me Home*. LaFace, 2000.

———. "There You Go." *Can't Take Me Home*. LaFace, 2000.

Spears, Britney. "Baby One More Time." *Baby One More Time*. Jive, 1999.

———. "Stronger." *Oops! I Did It Again*. Jive, 2000.

Tasker, Yvonne. *Working Girls: Gender and Sexuality in Popular Cinema*. London: Routledge, 1998.

TLC. "Silly Ho." *Fanmail*. LaFace, 1999.

Williams, Linda. "Film Bodies: Gender, Genre and Excess." *Feminist Film Theory: A Reader*, ed. Sue Thornham. New York: New York University Press, 1999. 267–81.

4

Working Girls or Drop-Dead Gorgeous?
Young Girls in Fashion and News

John Hartley and Catharine Lumby

Cultural studies frequently disavows binary oppositions for failing to acknowledge the logocentric interdependence of supposed opposites, such as that whiteness depends for its sense of self on blackness, for example. But binaries are good to think with and good to tinker with, like any form of inclusion and exclusion.

> Toby Miller,
> "What It Is and What It Isn't. Introducing ... Cultural Studies"

BRING BACK BINARISM

Thank G—well, thank something—for Osama bin Laden. Single-handedly—well, with the help of "perpetrators"—this invisible man, millionaire son of a Yemenese builder who had done well out of Middle-Eastern potentates' love of grandiosity, this damn-near carpenter's son restored order to the world. With order, returned truth, goodness, and therefore hope. They returned because bin Laden restored absolute opposites to the embattled Western imaginary. No more messy relativism.

Commentators such as Brendan O'Leary (on openDemocracy.net) noted at the time that the atrocities of 11 September 2001 were not accompanied by the usual explanatory text: No demands were made or manifestos issued. The perpetrators' complete silence and the absence of word from their organization, either on the day or afterward, meant that the destruction of three thousand lives, four passenger planes, both World Trade Center towers, the Pentagon building, and the perpetrators themselves was not an instrumental message. It was an absolute act. 11 September soon came to be coded across the world in a language that mimicked its own terrifying breakdown of communication, its content reduced to a number: "Nine Eleven" or even "Nine One One." For the first hours and for all the participants—perpetrators, victims, and an equally invisible global huddle of bystanders—meaningfulness was nowhere to be found.

The event was soon made to be meaningful. Many found in it meanings that spoke to their own agendas. For some the atrocities signaled the (apparently eagerly awaited) "death" of postmodernism. Among the cheering squad for that event was the unlikely combination of a senior writer with the *Australian* newspaper and the Anglican archbishop of Sydney. For the journalist, Nine One One brought the "end of postmodern relativism" because it restored truth. Apparently "pomo media critics" could no longer deny that such events had occurred or were merely "superfilms."

[Stanley] Fish cautions against invoking the "abstract notions of justice and truth" in our cause. More than 5000 people died on September 11 as a result of terrorist attacks in New York and Washington. True or false? ... The postmodern move is to problematize truth and justice (and other so-called universals) out of existence....

One of the problems that postmodernism gets into is the cul-de-sac called irrealism—the idea that there is no world outside of, or independent of, language.... There are a number of consequences of this for postmodern writers, such as the confusion of images—film, television—with reality. (Slattery 30)

For the archbishop, 11 September signaled the "death" of postmodernism because it restored "absolute evil":

September 11th was one of those days when the world changed.... Without wishing to be alarmist I have to say that if such a deed can be perpetrated, there is no reason whatever why far worse and more horrible things may not be done. Indeed the faces of the innocent in Afghanistan are beginning to haunt us also as terror begets terror. On that day, surely, postmodernism died and we had to readmit the words "absolute evil" to the language. (Jensen)

In short, bin Laden and the perpetrators had restored binarism. Apparently this was a consummation devoutly to be wished, bringing back the lost certainties of a tradition of "adversarial universalism" that went back to modern journalism's own origins in the eighteenth century (Hartley, *Politics* 164). Adversarial universalism achieved a kind of perfection in the rhetoric and public policy of the Cold War, where each side claimed its own ideology and actions to be universal but only comprehensible in opposition to those of the other side. It was a "we" versus "them" world, and many people in public life, up to and including American presidents, seemed all too well aware that the Hebrew word for "opposite" was *satan*.

The connection between news and religion is rarely mentioned these days. But among the founding principles sustaining journalism's everyday practice has been a Judeo-Christian cosmology that saw truth in this post-lapsarian world as the end result of conflict between "absolute truth" (which in that cosmology was divine) and "absolute evil" (the work of the devil). Truth has been binary ever since the days of John Milton, who was not only the great poet of universal-adversarial cosmology (*Paradise Lost*), but also the great champion of press freedom in the pursuit of truth (*Areopagitica*). It could even be argued that modern journalism is the secularization of this once-religious binarism. For several centuries in the West journalism has organized its narration of the limits of organized and bureaucratic public life by binary means—looking for conflict and for "both sides" of a story. Indeed, it is this very characteristic that is said to distinguish journalism from other kinds of public rhetoric such as public relations, propaganda, publicity, and spin. It is therefore no surprise that the journalist and the archbishop should speak the same language and that both were intellectually relieved at the restoration of "absolute" binarism by Osama bin Laden. Talk of "crusades" proved irresistible to both sides of the ensuing "war against terror," in spite of the obvious policy imperative for western governments to steer clear of such language.

DEMONS AND DEATH WISHES

The end of the Cold War has been precisely dated by Mikhail Gorbachev. It occurred at the summit meeting held in Malta, between himself and George Bush Sr., on board the Soviet passenger liner *Maksim Gorky* (510–16). The date was 2–4 December 1989. In the dozen years between then and 11 September 2001, there was no "evil empire" to oppose to journalism's "we-dom." Strange things began to happen. You could sense public discourse casting about for candidates; not directly for another satanic opponent (apart from Saddam Hussein), but more mundanely for something that could fit the existing conflict-based storytelling format. In fact, there seemed to be a great need to sustain the format of universal-adversarial truth telling, well after the Cold War ur-text itself had been abandoned. But the times weren't all that propitious for binary demonism. The remaining "rogue nations"—Cuba, North Korea, Burma—were barely worthy adversaries. You couldn't be "against" any of them in quite that toe-to-toe way that had been possible for those who opposed the USSR.

The times seemed more suited to inward-looking death wish. The great public issues of the period—HIV/AIDS, bioscience and genetic engineering, globalization—did not easily fit binary logic but did bespeak a fascination with human self-harm. Different countries came up with different candidates to replace the "evil empire," but there was a general turn from "enemies without" to "enemies within."

The most striking new emblem of "absolute evil" that emerged in journalism during the period 1989–2001 was the pedophile. This figure was itself a kind of binary opposite to the Soviet Union. Instead of an alien state, ideology, and society, here were anonymous, private, ordinary, like-us individuals, although the Soviet Union was reputed to take that form, with spies and "reds under the bed." As has been well documented, the demonization of the pedophile was conducted across many fronts, including popular (tabloid) and serious (broadsheet) journalism, community activism, and state legislation (see, for instance, Califia, Guilliatt, Lumby, Redfern). Interestingly, very few movies or television dramas dealt with this new "folk devil"; he remained an object of public policy, rather than dramatic identification. The movies stayed with spies and aliens to express "they" opponents.

There was clearly more to the demonization of the pedophile than the need to make the Internet safe for commercialization. His hyperbolized existence was also a guarantee of the existence of his binary opposite, namely innocence. During the 1990s—certainly in the United Kingdom and Australia (see Hartley, "When Your Child")—children in general and young girls in particular were recruited to news discourse to occupy the "we" and the "innocent" poles in a new form of universal adversarialism, where she played opposite the monster. It wasn't exactly the Cold War, but it would do—our innocent children up against the pedophile.

Since the late twentieth century, pedophiles have come to be regarded as subhuman. They have been portrayed as monsters who live beyond the boundaries of civilized society. They were the prisoners that "ordinary" violent criminals despised. And the popular claim that they can't change—a claim that is not supported by many of the psychiatrists and others who work with offenders—confirmed their demonic status. Theirs is an "absolute" evil that is supposedly rooted in the soul. Throughout the 1990s the media constantly warned that it was coming to a suburb near us (Lumby).

"We love children." As an abstract statement about any community, such a comment is banal and unremarkable. But it is also widely acknowledged that love takes many forms, among the most potent of which is eroticization. But putting sex into the context of the "innocent" young girl was absolutely taboo. The shameful overlap between the idea that "we love children" and the person who took that affection too far was projected onto the pedophile himself. He was not so much "absolute evil" as absolute scapegoat—the figure who took on the sinfulness of the community so that it could be excluded from their midst along with him. Meanwhile, and conversely, in order to represent purity, the iconic figure of our love for children, the innocent young girl, had to be dead.

WHAT'S THE USE OF YOUNG GIRLS?

In fashion, young girls are agents—they do something. Models, for instance, who commonly begin their careers as teenagers (legally children), act in the world as self-determining agents. Their career is independent in the same way that many adults are self-determining: They work, they travel, they confront the vicissitudes of freelance casual employment in a highly structured industry, and some achieve both celebrity and material rewards. Some have less glamorous experiences and soon leave the industry. Other young girls intersect with fashion in other ways, as consumers and fans, and as workers in the design, manufacturing, and retail parts of the trade. These activities are secular, modern, commercial, routine, ordinary. In news, conversely, girls rarely appear for what they do—they appear for what they are (taken or made to be); for being, not doing. The young girl usually makes it to the front page only when something very bad has been done to her.

This young girl is by convention a national phenomenon, since abduction or murder stories rarely cross national boundaries. Each country has its own archive and folk memory of its own innocent victims. In unsolved cases, the same photograph of the same girls will intermittently resurface, sometimes decades later. The "young girl as news" differs from the "young girl as model" in this respect too, then, since young models' names can become well known in all countries where fashion glossies and gossip media circulate. The names of celebrity victims mean little to those outside their country of origin (or national readership), apart from rare cases like JonBenet Ramsey, whose picture and story were circulated globally as part of public colloquy about issues raised by her murder.

The more innocent a girl is or looks, the more likely her image is to appear on the front page. Innocence in this context favors the pretty white girl, who appears not even as herself, but as a type—an icon in the religious sense of that word. She is used, in fact, as an aid toward communal meditation on suffering, love, and death. News itself is a secular, modern, commercial institution. But the young girl appears in it for religious purposes.

Following Toby Miller's advice that "binaries are good to think with and good to tinker with, like any form of inclusion and exclusion" (7), it is possible to make a list of how the young girl figures in the news, compared with how they appear in fashion. "Tinkering" with binaries doesn't mean that each opposition is always perfectly reproduced in news and its surrounding discourses, but it does bring into analytical focus how everyday concepts rarely occur without an actual or implied opposite that governs what they mean:

The Young Girl in Journalism

News : Fashion
being : doing
innocence : experience
"looks" : work
appearing : acting
icon : body
death : agency
"at peace" : "in danger"
"we" : "they"
national : global

This list does suggest that the work of the reader in making sense of pictures of young girls in news media includes negotiating such binaries whether they're explicit or not, and the same applies to the reading of girls in fashion. There's a kind of linguistic structure whose default setting automatically associates the world of experience, work, the body, agency, and doing with danger and profanity—which are certainly attributes of fashion in journalistic discourse. Conversely, innocence, "looks," iconic status, and death are hard to dissociate from sacred and religious connotations, even when deployed in everyday journalism.

MODELING AGENCY

It's late, and the Milan nightclub is packed with models letting off steam after the fashion shows. Older, well-off, well-dressed men hover at their margins—in New York they'd be known as "modelizers." But unbeknownst to them or the young women who are the focus of their gaze, there's an intruder in their midst. A man with a mission and a hidden camera. A man posing as a fashion photographer whose real quarries are those he believes prey on the innocence of young women.

The results of British journalist Donal MacIntyre's investigations were the subject of a television documentary that focused on the allegedly deleterious effects modeling has on the physical and psychological health of the young teenage girls who are drawn into it—on the impact of dieting, drug-taking, and predatory men. Key sections consisted of grainy footage shot by the reporter using a camera he concealed beneath his jacket to record casual conversations with fashion industry players and their "prey"—the same technique used by the BBC's *Panorama* to investigate truly dangerous situations such as Afghanistan under the Taliban. Throughout his tone was one of grave moral concern for the young models, a concern that he seemed to assume his audience shared. Certainly when the BBC documentary, called *MacIntyre Undercover,* was first screened in 1999 (in the United Kingdom, Australia, and other markets), it prompted a flurry of media stories around the world about the dark side of the modeling industry and the consequent (alleged) sacking of a number of senior executives (Williamson & Temple).

Modeling has become one of the hottest topics in Australian teen girls' magazines like *Dolly, Girlfriend, Cosmopolitan,* and *Cleo* and teen magazines around the world. The magazines routinely feature stories on individual models and articles on how to get into the industry, and they run or promote modeling contests that readers can enter. The fascination teenage girls have for modeling has spawned a concomitant popular discourse around the risks this fascination poses to adolescent females.

In *Reviving Ophelia,* a bestselling North American book subtitled "Saving the Selves of Adolescent Girls," Mary Pipher sums up a common fear about the impact of models on teenage girls:

As real women grow heavier, models and beautiful women are portrayed as thinner.... Girls compare their own bodies to our cultural ideals and find them wanting. Dieting and dissatisfaction with bodies have become normal reactions to puberty. Girls developed eating disorders when our culture developed a standard of beauty that they couldn't obtain by being healthy. When unnatural thinness became attractive, girls did unnatural things to be thin. (184)

Other popular concerns circulate around the dangers of promoting sexual precocity in teenage girls through exposure to the presumably adult world of fashion, drugs, sex, and celebrity. In 1997, for instance, a furor erupted over a cover girl contest run by Australia's long-running *Dolly* magazine. New South Wales state politician Marlene Goldsmith sparked the debate by claiming that *Dolly* encouraged "children to see themselves as sexual objects" and allowed "paedophiles to get a sense that their activities are legitimate." A range of state and federal ministers and child protection advocates joined Goldsmith in her campaign against the use of young models (Corbett & Symons).

As Goldsmith's comment illustrates, fears that young models encourage young girls to be sexually precocious merge with fears that young-looking models encourage adults to sexualize children. A classic illustration of this double-edged concern is a *Who Weekly* cover story titled "Too Young" and subtitled "High Fashion or Kiddie Porn—How Little Girls Are Used to Sell Glamour" (12 May 1997). The story that follows suggests that allowing young teenage girls to model is tantamount to child abuse, quoting Michael Gross, the author of a book condemning the modeling industry:

Modeling has produced tragic life after tragic life. It is an adult existence; one of drinking in bars, painting your face and wearing an adult costume. Any child paid to dress up as a woman is being placed under enormous psychological pressure. (quoted in Casey 48)

At the heart of these anxieties that circulate around adolescent girls and their attraction to the world of modeling is a belief (or more accurately a wish) that teenage girls are naturally innocent—that in both social and sexual terms they are devoid of agency or, more particularly, desire. It's a conviction that is so deep-rooted that it is repeated mantralike in the face of explicit evidence to the contrary. In *MacIntyre Undercover*, for instance, Donal MacIntyre talks earnestly about the naïveté of young models partying, over footage of the same girls drinking, dancing, and flirting with men—exercising and exploring their sexual power. The effect is almost comic, and his documentary is often compelling viewing for reasons that cut directly across the reporter's intentions: For the voyeurism which shadows his earnest investigations and grainy footage; for his failure to openly address the ethical dilemmas posed by his duplicity; and for his failure to consider that his own probings and presence may at times be implicated in producing the very attitudes and behaviors he wants to expose and denounce.

Again and again, MacIntyre feels compelled to remind us that the young models he's secretly filming are the innocent dupes of the sleazy men who run and feed off the modeling industry—that they're unaware that their beauty is a form of sexual currency. Ironically, in order to prove his thesis—that the modeling industry is really a form of legalized prostitution and corruption of young women—MacIntyre is forced to paint young models as so naïve that they border on stupidity.

If he was to allow a level of knowingness to his subjects, he might have to rethink the moral framework—he might be forced to consider that power relations in the modeling game are slightly more complicated than his moralistic stance suggests. More important, he might be required to question the deeper roots of his own desire to attribute such extreme innocence to postpubescent girls who are discovering their sexual power.

What is ultimately revealed in MacIntyre's documentary is something far more taboo than any of the overt activities he chronicles: That is, the relationship between the desire to watch and to watch over, the latent sexual component of the caretaking gaze. The investigative reporter is by no means exempt from what he seeks to criticize in others. Voyeurism shadows the anxious scrutiny of teenage girls in popular discourse. This is something about which teenage girls themselves can hardly fail to be aware—and the pervasive denial of such desire is surely the flipside of the need to attribute an exaggerated "innocence" to its object.

The attribution of passivity to young women breathes life into the most pessimistic (and simplistic) constructions of the male gaze, portraying it as a force that strips women of all agency and condemns them to perpetual objecthood. Henry Giroux exemplifies this position when he condemns the modern secular commercial world as it applies to young people:

In the profit-driven world of advertising and fashion, the image and culture of youth are appropriated and exploited as a site of spectacle and objectification, where youthful allure and sexual titillation are marked and consumed by teens and adults who want to indulge a stylized narcissism and coddle a self that is all surface. (21)

All that being said, young girls can hardly fail to be aware that the realm of appearances is one where they can exercise one of the few forms of power legally available to them. For this reason, it's hardly surprising that they're fascinated by glimpses into the world of modeling. Teenaged models use the realm of appearances to slip into the adult world and begin openly to indulge in activities the average teenager can only experience covertly or secretly desire—they drink, take drugs, and have casual sex, as well as travel and earn vast sums of money. Models, in short, are icons of agency, not passivity, to young teenage girls.

LOOKS COULD KILL

Fashion exhibits rather than taboos the spectacle of the social fascination with youth, beauty, sex and death, and it does so self-consciously, especially in high-end photographic visualizations from the best photographers. The darker aspects of that fascination, which we argue below were present in medieval meditations on the lives and deaths of saints and martyrs, is explicit in fashion iconography. But it is literally unspeakable in news, although pictures of girls may convey what cannot be said.

There are various rules that govern the selection and representation of stories and pictures in news media. These are a long way from the traditional or classic news values of conflict, recency, coverage of elite persons, and the like. The British journalist Rachel Johnson has written about informal rules that govern whether and how women appear in news photographs in UK news culture. Simply, they have to look right for the newspaper as well as having a story to tell. The *Daily Mail* leads the way in this regard, dispatching a stylist as well as a photographer for news stories featuring women. Johnson writes

What matters, of course, is shifting copies, and, as the broadsheets and the tabloids are now competing not only against each other but also against *Hello!* and OKTV, it matters very much what the people in the photographs look like. If the subjects of the article are female, it helps if they have ... a Beauty Quotient.... If the subjects don't have a high Beauty Quotient already—I mean, we don't all look like Nigella Lawson, or the late Princess of Wales ... —well, our quotient must be upped by whatever means possible.... All this confirms—if any confirmation were needed—that our newspapers are more troubled by how women look than by what we do, think, or say. (14)

Johnson comments that "all the newspapers have [rules] of some description.... The *Times* ... has become noted for carrying at least one photo of a child, an animal or an attractive young female on every page. Let's call it the Pet or Totty Rule."

Such rules would seem to apply strictly to the living; they're in the province of human interest stories. But the *Times*'s "Pet or Totty Rule" applies equally to hard news, front-page stories featuring suffering and death. Here, what appears to be a general, possibly universal, editorial assistant's rule is in operation: If a color photograph of a young girl is published with headline treatment, then she is either missing (believed sexually assaulted/murdered) or dead.

Even these girls are covered by the Beauty Quotient. The more beautiful they are—which is to say, white, thin, attractive, making eye contact with the camera—the more likely their picture is to appear and their story to be covered. Rachel Johnson's weary conclusion about newsworthy women, that "our newspapers are more troubled by how women look than by what we do, think, or say" (14), applies not only to women but also to girls, and not only to people who are alive but also *post mortem*.

Sometimes the newspapers themselves draw attention to the terrible tension between their fascination with desirable teenagers' looks and their newsworthiness, which is ostensibly the fact that they've been murdered. Thirteen-year-old English girl Caroline Dickinson was sexually abused and murdered on a school trip to France—in a dormitory full of her sleeping peers.

The British press ran numerous pictures of her that had been taken by a family friend, where she was artlessly but charmingly modeling teenage fashions in the garden. The *Express* ran several of these pictures on its front and inside news pages. The reporter commented

Any 13-year-old girl is on that uneasy precipice between childhood and womanhood.... These pictures of Caroline Dickinson show it all too clearly, too poignantly. They show a child on the edge of adulthood, like the ancient god Janus looking both ways.... Caroline was a 13-year-old like yours, like mine.... There is no knowingness in the look of her eyes. She's no Lolita, no catwalk nymphet. (*Express*, 21 Sept. 1996, 12)

Images of girls whose beauty, youth, and death are used to stimulate "poignant" meditation among the community of a national press and its readers by now are so familiar and iterative that they constitute an informal genre of journalism. But the attempt to separate the "knowingness" of Lolita and the "catwalk nymphet" (i.e., young fashion models) from the "child" murder victim serves only to connect them. As Miller has pointed out about binaries, that's the "interdependence of supposed opposites" (7).

At first glance that connection may look like just another example of banal—but in this context ghoulish—male "perving." In the case of radically under-age sex-murder victims like six-year-old JonBenet Ramsey, concerns about such perversion are displaced from the press and its readers to the children's careers. Parents are criticized for posing and presenting children in ways that are inappropriately eroticized, but the pictures are printed anyway, and doubtless many readers find them compelling (see, for example, *Who Weekly*, 20 Jan. 1997). Such pictures are invariably published to propose and police the boundaries of the social (Hartley, "When Your Child" 17), the limits of "the gaze."

NEWS SAINTS

The connections among beauty, youth, sex, and death are not fully explained by reference to the gaze. Here also is religion, which is especially potent where social prohibition and taboo require that some connections cannot be admitted. Journalism has always been fascinated by those moments where the unspeakable may be glimpsed; where everyday positives reveal their binary opposites.

News has continued a medieval tradition of using saints as icons of love and suffering, innocence and loss, beauty and death. So rarely do they get into the news as other than attractive victims, typically of sexual violence, that it is hard not to conclude that this association is indeed their *use* in news. That's the part they play in the dramatization of democracy. Their role is a modernization of a medieval binary.

The Young Girl and Religious Rhetoric

News : Fashion
saint : sinner
dead : alive
sacred : profane
religious : secular
medieval : modern

The "news-saint" is cast as the visualization of the human cost of modernization. She is non-American or Third World, abused, unruly, missing or dead. She is the tear-streaked witness to Columbine High. She is the eleven-year-old heroin addict, the thirteen-year-old boxer, underage prostitute, the big-eyed Afghan refugee. She is the entombed victim of pedophiles in Belgium, a toddler dying of famine in the Sudan, war-weary schoolgirl in the Balkans, the picture of poverty in urban ghettos around the world. Sometimes she's been given her own docu-soap, like the teenager in *Maternity* (BBC, 1999)—whose hope died along with her baby. Murder victims like British Caroline Dickinson, Australian Samantha Knight, or American JonBenet Ramsey become celebrity news-saints, not only because their murderers remained at large, but also because color photographs are available to prove they were young and beautiful.

Conversely, real saints—those of medieval Christendom—were material for the news media of their era. The "legends" or hagiographies of virgins and martyrs were popular best-sellers, in both visual and verbal form—painting, sculpture, story, and song. And the stories were often sanguinary in the extreme. The faithful were invited to meditate upon the agonies and torments suffered by innocent virgins and holy martyrs. The events depicted in scenes from the lives of saints teemed with heroes and heroines, villains, victims, and fools. They served the same narrative purpose as contemporary news stories; separating a "we" community from its "others." Outsiders included both mortal enemies of Christendom and supernatural forces of evil, but such is often also the case in contemporary news narrative about sexual violence and murder.

Interestingly, this aspect of medieval iconography has not gone unnoticed in today's media. *Vogue* (Paris), for example, devoted a color feature to the publication of a modern translation of the medieval *Legenda sanctorum*, about the lives, pain, and death of virgins and martyrs. That book was described by *Vogue* (in a highlighted text panel as well as in the story) as "after the Bible, the best-seller of all medieval Christianity, the daily paper of the epoch" (Paulino-Neto 70). Two half-page pictures accompanied the story. One showed a 1498 painting by Ludovico Brea of scenes from the life of Saint Margaret. She is shown stripped to the waist, facing out, her upstretched arms tied to a pillar, while two men set about beating her bare-breasted torso with multithonged whips. As a saint should, she gazes impassively into the middle distance, but her mouth is slightly open. Over the page another painting, this one by Jacques Durandi of Saint Agatha, from around 1450. The saint stands clothed and cloaked, her hands elegantly posed, but her top is open to expose her breasts, both of which have been sliced through, with blood welling from gaping wounds. Both saints are painted as young, nubile, and beautiful. Sado-masochistic desire mixed with religious devotion produced images that were sacralized and sexualized in equal measure. As if the connection was not sufficiently established by the pictures, the feature story opens thus:

C'est à Syracuse, une jeune fille que son refus de sacrifier aux dieux conduit aux pro-xénètes. «Invitez tout le peuple à jouir de cette femme, et qu'on use de son corps jusqu'à ce que mort s'ensuive», commande-t-on. (69)

[There was in Syracuse a young maiden whose refusal to offer sacrifices to the gods led her to the brothel-owners. "Invite all the people to take pleasure with this woman, and may her body be made use of until death ensues" was the command.]

Medieval devotion, art, fashion and journalism can easily converge. In 1999 the British *Observer* newspaper ran a picture on the cover of its weekly magazine that purported to illustrate "modern icons, and the search for belief in a secular world" (28 Nov. 1999). The cover girl is Croydon model Kate Moss, but this is also an artwork by Russian artist Olga Tobreluts, based on a 1476 painting of the *Virgin of the Annunciation* by Antonello da Messina. Moss's face has artfully replaced the virgin's, and her mouth is slightly open. She is discovered reading her book of devotions, but the page we can glimpse shows the word "Calvin" (not the Reformation Protestant, we can safely assume), and her eyes, unlike those of Messina's virgin, are fixed not on the page but on the viewer.

The story inside, which also shows Tobreluts's reworking of Leonardo Di-Caprio as Saint Sebastian and Linda Evangelista as Elizabeth of Austria, explains:

They are double whammies of perfection: As if to say, Kate Moss is so celebrated she is our end-of-century Virgin Mary. Or, the Virgin Mary was as beautiful as Kate Moss, if only we knew how to see her that way. (Wood 30)

The article "Idol worship" includes an explanation of the artist's method and intent:

Tobreluts makes changes which play games with the viewer's mind. She creates new works of art which are also critical tools, ways of understanding the paintings they are based on. In one Antonello da Messina portrait, she has inserted Kate Moss's face, and changed the direction of her gaze, so she is looking directly at us (a digitalized Mona Lisa). She has added a bee on one finger. A bee symbolizes virginity, and draws you, fearing a sting, into the centre of the picture. It involves you in the painting with its strangeness. (30)

Tobreluts is quoted as saying that when art embraced abstraction at the beginning of the twentieth century, "fashion and cinematography took over the theme of beauty, together with the hearts of many fans." The journalist comments: "If art has lost us, then the icons we have now can bring us back to it" (33).

Art doubtless still plays a major role in popular meditation, as is attested by the runaway success of ventures like the Tate Modern Gallery in London or the Guggenheim in Bilbao. But it can only do so in concert with the other means of semiotic distribution in contemporary entertainment culture, including cinema and television, fashion, and journalism itself. Indeed, the feature about Olga Tobreluts in the *Observer* was a publicity story for an art exhibition at the Liverpool Tate and an accompanying book, both called *Heaven* (see Harten).

In the catalogue, *Heaven*'s curator, Doreet LeVitte Harten, comments that "children, in a state of assumed innocence, are regarded as mediators, either angels or devils, no longer are they the small mature persons they used to be in the past" (11). The catalogue also contains essays, one by Jean-Luc Nancy that "speaks of the image's gift of love and death" (48). Another by Thierry de Duve puts the relationship between religion and the Enlightenment on a philosophical and historical footing (that liberty, equality, and fraternity are political and secular versions of faith, hope, and love). But today's media demonstrate "the congruence of present-day religiousness and what the Situationists called the society of the spectacle."

On the one hand, it just so happens, the society of the spectacle nowadays encompasses the public sphere (with all due respect to the heirs of the Enlightenment), so it is illusory to pigeonhole religiousness in the private sphere. We are living more than ever in a state of confusion between the political and the religious. On the other hand, religiousness is extremely hard to avoid once you wish to testify to death from within the society of the spectacle (75).

WATCHING US WATCHING THEM

Of all the supermodels who rose to prominence in the late twentieth century, Kate Moss was the figure whose image fuelled the greatest public debate. Moss became famous because she looked as though she were transgressing the boundary between childlike innocence and adult knowing, a position that produced a very interesting reading of her in the popular media. If looked at as a child, then she was too knowing and was accused of encouraging pedophilia; if looked at as a woman, then she was too skinny and was accused of encouraging anorexia. Naturally, because she straddled the boundaries, she was accused of both. Popular anxieties over images of young or young-looking models frequently turn on questions of knowledge, on questions of what they know: Of the adult world, of adult pleasures, of adult desires. In a "knowledge economy," this sort of "knowingness" is nevertheless seen as inappropriate.

An infamous case in point was a 1995 advertising campaign for fashion designer Calvin Klein shot by top fashion photographer Steven Meisel. It ran in a
variety of media and featured young-looking models variously wearing jeans,
tank tops, denim vests, and visible underwear, posed casually against a backdrop
of cheap wood paneling and purple carpet. On television the ads were accompanied by a voice-over in which an off-camera man gave the models directions
such as "Take your jacket off. Let's check out the results" and "Do you take direction well? Do you like to be directed?"

Complaints about the campaign were immediate. Critics included U.S. president Bill Clinton, child welfare groups, religious organizations, retailers, politicians, and New York's *Daily News*. Claims that the ads amounted to child
pornography were grounded in a range of concerns: That the models were
themselves children directed to affect erotic poses for the camera; that the ads
constituted a blatant appeal to pedophilic instincts in adult consumers; and that
the campaign's aesthetic deliberately imitated the amateur look common in
early 1970s porn magazines.

Henry Giroux added scholarly weight to public opinion by reading Miesel's
images as iconic of a growing tendency to commodify youthful sexuality and to
stereotype young people as "sexually decadent, drug-crazed, pathological and
criminal" (29). The images resonate, he argues, with a cultural perception of the
sexuality of poor, white, urban youth, portraying kids who are "perhaps forced
to negotiate their sexuality as the only currency they have to exchange for
profit or the promise of glamour" (22). He concludes that Meisel invites "the
most intrusive of gazes" (30).

There is, however, a radically different way of understanding these images
and the trouble they've provoked—a perspective which is implicit in an explanation Calvin Klein himself gave for the campaign's rationale in a full-page ad
in the *New York Times*. His statement read in part: "[We are] conveying the idea
that glamour is an inner quality that can be found in regular people in the most
ordinary setting; it is not something exclusive to models and movie stars" (A5).

Klein is characterizing an aesthetic here that can be traced back, in the first
instance, to Andy Warhol's films, movies such as *Heat* and *Chelsea Girls*.
Warhol's aesthetic (which in turn owes a range of debts to popular cultural
sources, in particular 1960s underground gay cinema) is characterized by a continual sliding between the everyday and the stylized, the banal and the strange.
He frequently produces this effect by inverting the relationship between emotional responses and actions. For example, characters might display inappropriate elation over routine tasks or conversations and exhibit boredom when
confronted with something ordinarily exciting. Characters engaging in explicit
sexual activity in his films are frequently depicted as tired and indifferent. The
effect on the viewer is potentially less alienating than dislocating—Warhol's
films do not actively discourage emotional projection on the part of the viewer,
but they also act as a slippery surface to which it's hard to make anything stick.
This aesthetic of dislocation was taken up in the 1980s by U.S. artist Cindy

Sherman in her early self-portraits, in which the artist positions herself in ambiguous locations and situations, depicting moments which may be snapshots of everyday existence or stills from forgotten movies. Both Warhol and Sherman use a heightened contrast between the amateur and the professional to achieve their aesthetic ends.

Steven Miesel's 1995 campaign for Calvin Klein owes a debt to both artists which is, at the very least, indirect. The models in his images fix the camera with looks that range from indifference to insolence—what's striking about all their poses is the strong sense that they know that someone (someone they hold in evident contempt) wants to watch them—and this is arguably part of the photographer's aesthetic purpose and broader cultural point. Their poses are a marked contrast to their clothing and their surroundings, which all suggest an indifference to the presence of a photographer. There's no surrender to the camera—just a series of weary, clichéd poses that might have been culled from an amateur photography magazine of the 1950s. In one image, a young man and woman lean against a ladder. The boy is bare-chested and wears jeans slung around his hips to reveal the top of his white underpants. The girl is wearing a scrappy singlet and faded jeans. Both fix the camera with a sullen, defiant, world-weary look—a look that almost every parent of teenage children will surely recognize.

One possible reading of the Klein campaign, then, relies on discerning the tension between the apparently coercive context in which the models are situated and the response the photographer has directed them to project. The "amateur" studio backdrop and, in the context of the television ads, the intrusive off-camera direction, act as a mirror of the social and marketing context in which the ads will eventually be consumed. The buying power behind the CK jeans division of Calvin Klein, Inc., for which the ads were produced, doesn't belong to the teenage boys and girls who wear the garments in ads, but to older, wealthier consumers who can afford the upmarket range—even if they wind up buying items for their teenage offspring. Viewed in this light, it's not the models in Miesel's photographs who look like puppets but the potential consumers of these images. The campaign, in other words, anticipates the dislocation between the models used to sell its product and the consumers it seeks.

The above reading suggests an alternative source for some of the anxiety that greeted the campaign. The United States—a country with the highest rate of teen pregnancy in the western world, where the provision of sex education and contraceptives to teenagers is hotly disputed—supports a culture that is notable for the plethora of sexualized images of children and teenagers. By posing young-looking models in suggestive poses and skimpy outfits, Steven Meisel did nothing new in the U.S. advertising context. Where Klein's ad campaign genuinely breaks the mold is in its foregrounding of the models' response to being sexualized for the gaze of adults. The gaze of these "teenagers" (all models used in the actual campaign were over the age of eighteen) is ambiguous—and hence unsettling—because it simultaneously acknowledges and refuses the gaze of its intended audience.

"PRINTS OF DARKNESS"

Thierry de Duve comments

Fashion offers angelic creatures with androgynous sexuality as models to be imitated—the same models, incidentally, that a seductive Satan hijacks to his own advantage. In a word, entertainment has replaced religion, and the "cathodic church" has replaced the "Catholic Church," but religiousness is still there. (74)

The overlap between "angelic creatures" and "seductive Satan" is what attracts journalism to this scene. Confusion between opposites is an offence to binary logic; policing such offenses is core business for adversarial-universal journalism.

Art is fertile ground for any attempt to maintain the purity of binaries, precisely because art explores the border zones between opposites. Hence art is frequently used as a pretext for journalism's own campaigns.

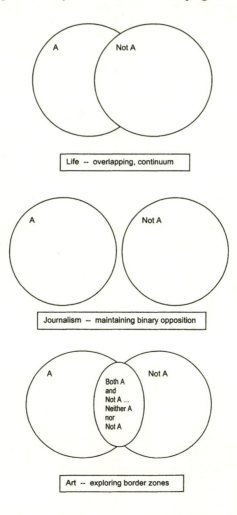

Life -- overlapping, continuum

Journalism -- maintaining binary opposition

Art -- exploring border zones

One such was a furor, which itself attracted global news coverage, about an exhibition called *I am a Camera* at the Saatchi Gallery in London in March 2001. It featured photographs by Tierney Gearon and Nan Goldin. Among the 300 pictures were three that showed naked children, two of them Gearon's own. The newsworthy angle, at first glance, was that the police had visited the gallery and reportedly "threatened to seize some of the photographs" (Karen Mulliner in the *Brisbane Courier Mail*, 17 Mar. 2001) or warned the curator to "take down the photographs or they would seek a court order to have them removed" (Jamie Walker in the *Weekend Australian*, 17–18 Mar. 2001).

Of course, the issue was pedophilia. But the story was not directly about that, nor even about photographers, art, or the police. It turned out to be about journalism. It transpired that a sponsor of the exhibition was the broadsheet newspaper the *Independent on Sunday* (editor, Janet Street Porter, long-time youth-media innovator). Meanwhile, Britain's biggest-selling newspaper, the *News of the World* (editor, Rebekah Wade, at thirty-two the country's youngest) had been conducting a populist campaign against pedophiles, including a controversial naming-and-shaming series that outed men with child-sex convictions, following the murder of eight-year-old Sarah Payne in late 1999 (and see the coverage of Sarah Payne's killer's conviction in the *News of the World* on 16 December 2001, where more men were named, this time as absconded pedophiles). Among the many critics of this campaign had been the *Independent on Sunday*.

Suspicion arose that the *News of the World* may have had a hand in the police raid on the exhibition; officers cited complaints from "sections of the press" when they arrived:

Although Wade has denied directing police to the Saatchi gallery, her paper didn't mince words, denouncing what was otherwise a well-reviewed exhibition by thundering "While the *News of the World* defends the nation's kids ... the *Independent on Sunday*'s bosses are busy backing a revolting exhibition of perversion under the guise of art" (Walker).

The *Courier Mail* added a further quotation from the *News of the World*, in its account of the same story: "Upper crust 'art lovers' are paying £5 to ogle degrading snaps of naked children," screamed the first paragraph of the paper's report. Accompanying it were some of the photos from the exhibition, cropped and doctored to conceal the children's faces and genitals (Milliner 29).

Here then were two Australian newspapers commenting on the antics of two British ones. In a small world it's perhaps no surprise that the *News of the World*, the *Courier Mail*, and the *Australian* are all Murdoch papers, although there was nothing in common between their coverage, apart from the fact that all of them ran the "offending image." This episode shows that the urge to keep binaries pure, to separate childhood innocence from adult sexuality, comes most strongly from journalism itself. The *News of the World* sought to restore "absolute" opposition to this area, and seemed quite prepared to make news in pursuit of this goal.

But there was more to the coverage than that. The *Courier Mail*, in particular, used the occasion to think about a popular politics of reading. It quoted the photographer Tierney Gearon (not directly—this too came secondhand from a British newspaper, the *Guardian*): "I think that the pictures are incredibly innocent and totally unsexual. I don't see sex in any of those prints, and if someone else reads that into them, then surely that is their issue, not mine" (quoted in Milliner).

In what amounted to a seminar on reading practices, the *Courier Mail* went on to interview an array of local quote-worthy luminaries. They included a lecturer in art history, the director of a trust for abused children, a lecturer in art, the director of an art gallery, and a lecturer in public health. Each offered their own take on how the pictures should be read and their own reaction to them, and each lecturer was from a different university, as if to ensure a fair spread of opinion. Here in fact was a sensible public discussion of a serious issue, conducted by journalism, on the grounds of art, by means of an issue that was largely provoked by journalism, using the picture of a naked seven-year-old girl on a beach as an aid to meditation. To make this popular pedagogy of reading more palatable to the casual reader, the relevant pictures were reproduced, and some helpful editorial assistant had decided that all this would be improved by a headline that self-consciously invoked Satan: "Prints of Darkness."

The painful pun of an editorial assistant was no joke to the Anglican archbishop of Sydney, however. His attack on postmodern relativism was in fact based on his own politics of reading. The stakes were high, because he wanted people to read the Bible literally:

The undoubted fact that reading requires a reader, has been turned into the determinative fact for the establishment of meaning. At the extreme . . . it says unabashedly, "the reader is the Author"; when you get to that point you are in a contest with God, to establish who owns his text, for he claims to be the ultimate Author. (Jensen)

Reading, once a matter of "plain teaching of the text," has become instead, and as a direct result of postmodernism and university education, the road to hell:

It is precisely the question of how we should read which is on the agenda of the schools and universities of our nation. Teachers and students are adjudicating between the rights of the reader and the rights of the author to establish what texts mean. . . .

It is not as though we can isolate ourselves from the world. The children of Christian families may well be better equipped and better guarded against the world, but they can never be made invulnerable to it. They, too, are being taught new, subjective ways of reading texts. The state of the culture remains of high significance to us whether we like it or not. Secularism damages the nation and fills the halls of hell.

BRING BACK MESSY RELATIVISM

The Cold War was more than just a prestige television series of the same name. And it hasn't gone away. Its collective paranoia about control, technology, and survival has merely turned inward. The focus for fear of the future—

fear of death—is no longer the spy or the alien. It is the young girl. Like spies and aliens, she is a threshold figure: Sometimes the hope for the future, sometimes evidence or victim of the enemy within. The young girl takes public imagining to the new interactive media generation, supplanting the two great obsessions of broadcast television's heyday—gender politics and communism.

The young girl, alive but complete with saintly aura, can be recruited for political purposes. For instance the 1997 New Labour manifesto for the British general election, which Labour won with a landslide, had winsome girls on virtually every page. New Britain looked like a marriage between Tony Blair and Miss Goody Two-Shoes. But the old democracies have little to say directly to young people. When girls appear in the hard news pages it's not for their own benefit or that of their peers; it's because of the "Totty Rule" or the "dead saint" rule. No wonder they avoid the political sphere—they don't want to play Dominique Swain to Tony Blair's Jeremy Irons.

It is left to entertainment culture and the retail trade—emblematized by the fashion world that reporters like Donal MacIntyre condemn—to take up the cause of civil society. This is a world in which young girls, both real and symbolic, have some agency. Lo-lo may not be old enough to vote, but she gets her citizenship from the box in her lounge room and the carrier bags in her bedroom. She's in the age of "democratainment" (Hartley, *Uses of Television* 154–65). National identity is a corporate sponsorship opportunity. Human rights are publicized by Benetton. The ethics of personal and civic conduct are taught daily in sitcoms and serials. *Home and Away* talks her through ethical dilemmas. The public sphere is down at the shopping mall.

To keep out of the news and retain agency in an age of binary anxiety, girls "need an edge" (as Chief Dan George famously recommended in *The Outlaw Josie Wales*). Like their fictional role models, they need a magical attribute to help them practice what they teach. Sabrina is a witch. Buffy is a slayer. Alex Mack is made of metal goo from *Terminator II*. In both *Sister Sister* and *Two of a Kind*, "the" young girl is two identical young girls. Moesha is played by pop star Brandy Norwood. *Clueless* girls are kind, generous, and clever, but they hide all that civility under drop-dead gorgeous bodies. Fluidity of identity and juvenile wish fulfillment are forged into weapons of mass instruction (as it were). The smartest person on television is Lisa Simpson. This little girl grows up. She kick-boxes in *Buffy*; she kicks head in *Xena*. She gets teenage kicks in Chemical Bros. videos. Her role models are girlie stars, and the frame of reference is worldly fashion, not saintly "innocence." American-dream girl is busy using democratainment to promote civil society with daughterly derring-do, whether at home (*Clarissa*), at school or college (*Sabrina*), or in the workplace (*Don't Shoot Me*)—the latter set in the offices of a fashion magazine.

The girl can look after herself, love her own, live it up, get a life, and make the boys look like "Doh" in her hands. Does television encourage equal self-esteem for boys? No chance. Their role models are lager-lout sportsmen. For them a lesson in civics is learning to watch kid's-television presenter and men's magazine favorite Gail Porter without their hands down their pants. The only time they do anything right is when a dream girl fixes it for them, like Lisa in *Weird Science*—a virtual beauty, half masturbatory fantasy, half older sister (no wonder the boys are confused). Things have gone so far down the road of promoting girls and neglecting boys, we're told, that boys are the new girls: Helpless, underachieving, locked into private life and personal obsession. And girls are the new boys: Running the country—or at least its public narrative.

But don't forget the Cold War. With visibility comes danger. Freedom breeds fear and desire loves death. America is still the sublunary equivalent of the Promised Land (Bewes 150). Un-American young girls are now fair game. Everywhere you look they have a death wish—Estella in *Great Expectations*, Morgan La Fay in *Merlin*, Matty in *House of Cards*, Joanne Whalley in *Edge of Darkness*. In entertainment culture, the young girl is placed in direct touch with promise. But in news her tragedy is promise unfulfilled. The young girl, dumbed down, endangered, and punished for her own unruly sexiness, and made public for her looks and not her acts, is a dramatization of a different (un-American) national destiny. If she's the hope for the millennium, then it's "no future," never mind bin Laden.

Among the lessons of Nine Eleven, therefore, appears to be this one: The need to recognize that the western imaginary is far from post-Christian, on both sides of the apparent opposition between news and fashion, sacred and profane, innocence and experience. Both news and fashion are apparently secular domains, but both remain redemptive discourses of perfectability in the here and now. The journalistic and archepiscopalian apologists of binarism have celebrated the "death" of postmodern relativism, seemingly with a sigh of relief. But the return of this new Middle Ages forces a choice between "absolutes"—truth or evil. When fashion is put on the "evil" side, while "truth" equates innocence with death, what should young girls choose?

WORKS CITED

Bewes, Timothy. "God Bless America: Just What Is It That Makes the Big Country So Different, So Appealing?" *Pop—Fashion*Art* 3 (2001): 148–50.

Califia, Pat. *Public Sex*. Pittsburgh: Cleis, 1994.

Casey, S. "Kittenwalk." *Who Weekly*, 12 May 1997: 42–50.

Corbett, B., and E. Symons. "Sex Symbol at 13 and *Dolly* Isn't Kidding." *Sydney Daily Telegraph*, 5 Mar. 1997, 13.

de Duve, Thierry. "Come On Humans, One More Stab at Becoming Post-Christians!" *Heaven*, ed. Doreet LeVitte Harten. Ostfildern, Ger.: Hatje Cantz, 1999, 74–90.

Giroux, Henry. *Channel Surfing: Race Talk and the Destruction of Today's Youth*. London: Macmillan, 1997.

Gorbachev, M. S. *Memoirs*. New York: Bantam, 1997.

Guilliatt, Richard. *Talk of the Devil*. Melbourne, Austral.: Text, 1996.

Harten, Doreet LeVitte, ed. *Heaven*. Ostfildern, Ger.: Hatje Cantz, 1999.

Hartley, John. *The Politics of Pictures: The Creation of the Public in the Era of Popular Media*. New York: Routledge, 1992.

———. "'When Your Child Grows Up Too Fast': Juvenation and the Boundaries of the Social in News Media." *Continuum* 12, 1 (1998): 9–30.

———. *Uses of Television*. New York: Routledge, 1999.

Jensen, Peter. "Presidential Address to the Sydney Synod, 26 October 2001." http://www.anglicanmediasydney.asn.au/synod2001/presidential_address.htm, 11 Nov. 2001.

Johnson, Rachel. "Skirting the Issues." *Australian,* 12–18 July 2001, "Media," 14.

Klein, Calvin, Inc. *New York Times,* 28 Aug. 1995, A5.

Lumby, Catharine. "Sex, Murder and Moral Panic: Coming to a Suburb near You." *Meanjin* 58, 4 (1999): 92–106.

Miller, Toby. "What It Is and What It Isn't. Introducing … Cultural Studies." *A Companion to Cultural Studies*, ed. Toby Miller. Oxford: Blackwell, 2001. 1–19.

Milliner, Karen. "Prints of Darkness." *Brisbane Courier Mail*, 17 Mar. 2001, 29.

Milton, John. *Paradise Lost*. Ed. John Leonard. London: Penguin, 2000.

———. *Areopagitica*. Ed. John W. Hales. Oxford: Clarendon, 1886.

O'Leary, Brendan. http://www.opendemocracy.net/forum/document_details.asp?CatID=98&DocID=658&DebateID=150. 15 Nov. 2001.

Paulino-Neto, Brigitte. "Contes et merveilles" [Fairy Tales and Wonders]. *Vogue Paris,* Nov. 2000, 69–70.

Pipher, Mary. *Reviving Ophelia: Saving the Selves of Adolescent Girls*. Sydney, Austral.: Doubleday, 1996.

Redfern, Lea. "The Paedophile As Folk Devil." *Media International Australia* 85 (1999): 50.

Slattery, Luke. "Wake Up and Smell the Cordite." *Australian,* 24 Oct. 2001, 30.

Walker, Jamie. "Full-frontal Furore Taints Affair of the Art." *Weekend Australian,* 17–18 Mar. 2001, 15.

Williamson, B., and W. Temple. "Model Agency in Sex Scandal." *Sydney Daily Telegraph,* 24 Nov. 1999, 5.

Wood, Gaby. "Idol Worship." *Observer* [*Life* magazine], 28 Nov. 1999, 30–33.

5

"As Wholesome As . . . ":
American Pie As a New Millennium Sex Manual

Sharyn Pearce

When *American Pie* opened in United States cinemas in the northern summer of 1999, it was generally described as yet another raunchy high school comedy geared for that lucrative 14–24 demographic of horny young males. Like the other hit comedies of that summer, *Austin Powers—The Spy Who Shagged Me, South Park—Bigger, Longer and Uncut,* and *Big Daddy,* it appeared to be a gross-out movie (in a season of apparently stunningly successful gross-out one-upmanship) which outraged propriety and good manners, and it was variously portrayed as risqué and reprehensible, featuring degrading, coarse material, out-of-control libidos, and reliant upon crass humor as a way of appealing to a dumbed-down market. Most critics assumed it to be a randy update of Reagan-era teen comedies, a recycling of that rather tired genre now quite literally preoccupied with bathroom humor. This view was furthered by a strong advertising campaign which was clearly marketed to a drooling teenage male audience and featured ad lines like "There's something about your first piece" (Gray 5), thus linking the film to the previous year's spectacularly gross hit, as well as making an overt connection between the "pie" of the film's title and its other usage as a vulgar term for female genitalia. And so one U.S. reviewer described the film as "degrading human sexuality to the level of a bowel movement," treating sex as "no more significant than a belch," and labeled the producers as "merchandisers of cultural rot" (Kavanaugh), while another, referring not so obliquely to the central masturbation incident in which the main character defiles the nation's ultimate symbol of purity, commented "I fear to think of the fate that now awaits various baked goods at fraternities around the country" (Lim).

But an alternative reading of *American Pie* sees it as a manual for self-formation, as a means whereby young men can progress relatively smoothly toward adulthood with particular reference to the management of sexual conduct. I would also add that it encourages critical self-reflection, moral commitment, and responsibility to others. Instead of simply dismissing the film as a crude 1990s remake of *Porky's*, for example, I would argue that it has more in common with other 1980s films such as *The Breakfast Club* or *Risky Business* because, like those texts, it provides a sympathetic portrait of white, middle-class youth as essentially confused but also innocent and doing their best to come of age. Centered as it is so securely within the visual and pedagogical machinery of Hollywood culture, *American Pie* is by no means a sensitive coming-of-age film, yet it manages—and quite endearingly, I think—to be both sweet and gross at the same time. Furthermore, this very low budget comedy (it cost merely US$11 million) has proved to be enormously successful, a huge hit both in the United States and elsewhere, even when pitted against shagadelic superstars, cult television cartoons, and film vehicles for Adam Sandler, currently America's biggest-earning actor. What I will attempt to do in this chapter is to explain *how* the film works as an up-to-the-minute sex education manual which is attuned to today's young people (especially young men), and which appeals *because* it is so contemporary in its frank treatment of sexuality.

Well-known sociologist of youth cultures Henry Giroux argues that

Teens and other youth learn how to define themselves outside of the traditional sites of instruction, such as the home and the school.... [L]earning in the post-modern age is located elsewhere—in popular spheres that shape their identities, through forms of knowledge and desire that appear absent from what is taught in schools. The literacies of the post-modern age are electronic, aural, and image based; and it is precisely within the diverse terrain of popular culture that pedagogical practices must be established as part of a broader politics of public life—practices that will aggressively subject dominant power to criticism, analysis and transformation as part of a progressive reconstruction of democratic society. (49)

Of course youth is at the center of a multitude of regulatory practices and techniques associated with pedagogy, especially if it is viewed as a problem or as a threat to the public order. This is particularly so where youth occupies a subversive space in which to explore sexual desire and if sexuality is viewed, as it so often is, as unmanageable and in need of control, surveillance, legal constraint, and other forms of disciplinary power. Young people today are subjected to an extraordinary range of processes directed at training and repressing the body through extended schooling, and sex manuals are usually considered as belonging to these regulatory processes because of their specific interests in and discourses about the disciplining of the body. Most usually researchers in this area have discussed sex education manuals in Foucauldian terms as working in the interests of the patriarchy/governmentality. This Foucauldian perspective is especially pronounced when critics examine nineteenth-century and early twentieth-century Anglophone sex education manuals, which, according to Jeffrey Weeks and others, are the means through which institutions produce strategic methods of control to induce docility in the social body and provide a discourse wherein power can be circulated in the social order so as to enforce control and repression. In this particular instance, however, I would argue that *American Pie* is actually a quite enlightened modern sex manual, precisely because it deals with such important topics as nonhegemonic masculinity and female desire. Few U.S. critics have actually noticed the subversiveness or the seriousness at the heart of this apparently tasteless film, although possibly Richard Corliss comes closest in his remark that "the film hints that a teenager's most poignant groping is for his elusive identity."

According to Judith Butler's concept of performativity, the body provides a surface upon which various acts and gestures accrue gendered meanings (36), and being masculine entails a performance which requires the production of specific bodily signs. For Butler, gender is not constructed as a stable identity, but one tenuously constituted in time, instituted in an exterior space through a stylized repetition of acts, by means of which the culture preserves gender and power differences. Butler stresses that gender is chameleonlike, that it is only as solid as the social and cultural practices that constitute it over time, and that these performances are open to unexpected variation and transformation (157). This view is reinforced by Steven Cohan and Ina Rae Hark in *Screening the Male*: "Masculinity is an effect of culture and construction, a performance, a masquerade rather than a universal and unchanging essence" (7).

Given, then, that gender is primarily an act of representation, that field of signification which strives to regulate the production of sex, gender, and desire can be contested through insubordinate performances of gender, where the body of youth, seen through an appropriation of popular culture, is presented as a site of resistance and expressed through a transgressive sexuality. Like so many other characters in 1990s films such as *The Full Monty*, the four lead actors in *American Pie* (Jim, Oz, Kevin, and Paul) constantly subvert traditional gender discourse and signs of conventional masculinity. While many (usually art-house) movies are concerned with a teenage girl's deflowering, this movie presents us instead with sexually inexperienced *boys* who, like their female counterparts, spend all their available time wondering what sex must be like, and in this particular instance trying to overcome the stigma of virginity by "depositing vital body fluids onto or into any imaginable object" (Kavanaugh). In keeping with the gender reversals which permeate this text, the central character, Jim, is portrayed as unconfident and hypersensitive, being overly concerned about his clothes (he practically lives in one favorite shirt) as well as his looks and self-image (he asks, in all seriousness, for instance, whether in trying to impress a girl he should adopt the persona of "cool hip Jim, or laid-back Jim").

The best instance of contesting hegemonic masculinity occurs midway through the movie, when Jim is called upon to perform a bizarre strip routine in his bedroom for the lovely Nadia, while his captivated friends watch the performance over the Internet. According to Laura Mulvey and others (including Kuhn, Kaplan) films deliberately create masculine structures of "looking," and the gaze is the main mechanism of filmic control. Because the male spectator shares the gaze of the male character, women become objectified erotic subjects, existing in films simply as recipients of the male gaze. Nadia has come for a history study session, but first of all she has to change out of her ballet clothes. But what starts out in this instance as the boys using the Net to "perve" on Nadia while she undresses in Jim's room and looks to be exploitative becomes something rather different when Jim, having raced back from his friend's house where he has been watching her on the screen, reenters the picture. "Now you have seen me," she pouts, "I want to see *you*," and she orders him to strip and perform for her. And so what initially appears to signal the apparent realization of a young man's ultimate fantasy of a beautiful and willing girl in his bedroom has in fact metamorphosed into something quite significantly different.

The usual sexual division of the gaze is reversed, and the customary inscribing of heterosexual masculinity has been altered to place female spectators in privileged positions. The gaze has been deconstructed, with the new female gaze being substituted for the concentrated stare, the conventional patriarchal gaze connoting power and dominance. The text resists the objectification of the woman characteristic of the male-centered narrative, replacing it with female subjectivity, desire, and agency. Like the "perve pages" in girls' magazines like *Dolly*, for instance, the audience is invited to take pleasure in male spectacle. The male body is now docile to female command while the female gaze, not at all repressed, looks actively and erotically, but in a nonthreatening and nonaggressive manner, controlling but also celebrating rather than criticizing what it is viewing.

In this particular instance Jim actively uses his body to ensure Nadia's spectatorial desire. Yet his is not a narcissistic, arrogant, aloof, or powerful sexual performance, and his vulnerable body is not well-toned. Jim's displaced performance is comic, tongue-in-cheek—burlesque even—and parodies the notion that, as both Steve Neale and Yvonne Tasker have argued, when male bodies are seen, the focus is on action. Indeed, if men are customarily supposed to be in active control of their bodies, then this aberrant behavior contrasts sharply, once more, with cultural expectations of gender. Moreover, this is certainly not a homoerotic spectacle: Jim's hyperactive routine, clad in unbecoming boxer shorts, appears, in fact, to be deliberately unsexy, and the horrified yet fascinated Net-watching males, heterosexuals one and all, find Jim's performance cringe-inducing rather than in any way arousing. Indeed, the resolute heterosexuality of this scene, with its firm exclusion of any overtones of gay sexuality, is absolutely in keeping with the film as a whole. The implied audience is definitely a heterosexual one, and there is no coded gay male discourse here (it is, after all, mainstream Hollywood cinema), and so "unsexy" male bodies would appear to be a necessary, even welcome ingredient. Yet, awkward as it is, there is no doubt that Nadia enjoys Jim's goofball routine, sees it as an amusing and entertaining form of sexual foreplay, and laughingly gestures to him to join her on the bed. It must also be admitted, however, that she has just been reading Jim's pornographic magazines, she is clearly interested in Jim anyway, and unlike Jim, who awkwardly manages premature ejaculation (twice) thus creating immense amusement for his friends watching on the Net, she is a sexually aware and confident young person who may indeed have intended to use the study session as an excuse to seduce him. However one chooses to "read" this scene, it is evident that if, as Mulvey ("Visual Pleasure") suggests, the film text constructs its spectators through processes that can be mapped onto the unconscious structures through which our gendered identities are produced, then in this instance, as in others, *American Pie* constructs a space for opposition and change and for an alternative audience positioning. In setting up the audience to share the spectators' look, the orthodox gendered alignment of looking, masculinity, and power is clearly being undermined.

Indeed, *American Pie* is a product of the 1990s in that it features the processes of reconceptualizing and exploring sexual bodies. The phallic imago of masculinity is blurred, and the male body is no longer characterized by a hard and ready phallus or understood as impenetrable, as a "war-body simultaneously armed and armored, equipped for victory" (Waldby 268). This text is not about thrusting, phallocentric power, but about fixations with bodily fluids (in the manner of *There's Something About Mary*), and other tokens of transgressive masculinity (the entire text is permeated with masturbation, premature ejaculation, and diarrhea). Moreover, in presenting masculinity as errant, abject, as a site of vulnerability, and in contradicting phallic control, I hope to demonstrate that this is very much a text of its time.

Now if *American Pie* is to be treated as a contemporary sex education manual, it is important to note that such manuals almost always inscribe and endorse the approved sexual conduct of the day—and in this case, the film reveals those values implicit in a new millennium manual. Nowhere is this contemporary evaluation more appropriate than with the topic of masturbation, which has traditionally posed a problem in sex education manuals, having been linked to nineteenth-century ideas that it caused moral as well as physiological damage (Nelson 532), and that sexual self-mastery, or the containment of desire, was important in achieving the development from boyhood to manhood as well as the perpetuation of the existing social order. As Walker's work on seminal loss has ably demonstrated, male sexuality was brought into the social dimension through theories of sexual fastidiousness and national energy, and the emphasis upon the importance of hoarding sexual capital ("spermatic economy," as it was sometimes called) arose from a wider social fear of the degeneracy of the body at both a personal and a national level. It was a commonly felt belief that youthful habits set a pattern for adult sexual attitudes, that a man's sexual character was both the model and source for the rest of his character, and that the habits of restraint developed in that area eventually led to the acquisition of virtues such as hard work, piety, and noble ideals. The years between fifteen and twenty-five, in particular, were associated with such an explosion of sexual energy and desire that if an adolescent could not control his sexuality, it was felt that he would be incapable of the power of restraint that was the signifier of manhood. Consequently, sex education manuals from the nineteenth century onward reinforced these notions that masturbation not only caused fatigue and debilitation but was especially endangering to the spirit. Moreover, if practiced to excess, it could lead to enfeeblement.

Sex manuals traditionally devoted many pages to strategies for masturbation avoidance, and a sampling of American methods might include crowding out lustful thoughts by thinking of a mother's pure love, reading the Sermon on the Mount, singing a soul-stirring hymn, seeking the company of sensible women, shadow boxing, walking very fast, cultivating a hobby, or changing position frequently when seated (quoted in Campbell 2). Perhaps the best known, and one of the earliest, American manuals, *What Every Young Man Should Know* (1897), counsels against this "secret vice," noting that self-abuse causes suffering for a boy's parents and family, his children may be born in poverty, and his offspring will be inferior because he has "injured his reproductive powers." Furthermore, the practice leads to "idiocy, and even death," the boy's mind fails, his health declines, and early death ensues: "Boys have to be put in a strait-jacket or their hands tied to the bedposts or to rings in the wall" (quoted in Campbell 3). And such creatures are instantly recognizable, as the boy who secretly indulges in this vice develops a shifty glance and pulls his cap down so as to hide his eyes when passing people in the street. Other ways of detecting possible debauchery include unnatural lassitude, especially in the mornings; strange appetites for clay, chalk, and slate pencils; round shoulders; twitching; pimples (especially on the forehead); pain in the back; headache; and full veins and palpitations (quoted in Campbell 3).

Warnings about masturbation are by no means confined to American cultural texts. In Australia in the 1920s, for instance, Marion Piddington's *Tell Them! The Second Stage of Mothercraft* lectures parents that it is their duty to cultivate eternal vigilance against "dysgenic" habits. Piddington advises that children must never touch their sexual organs, and so mothers must provide pants for small boys without pockets, or with the pockets firmly sewn up. She even informs a mother whose quiet son "doesn't like girls" and prefers to stay home and go to bed early rather than party with friends, that she is harboring a "likely self-abuser" (112). In the 1940s, a family counselor could still warn that the practice of self-abusing cannot be discovered "simply by looking at a person, although it often accompanies a general slackness of character and behavior" (Griffith 190), while the best-selling Australian sex education manual of the following decade resorts to slick semantics as a way of dealing with the problem:

Some young men find themselves in a good deal of distress in resorting to prayer and yet still finding that they are not able to overcome it. We would perhaps suggest that it is unwise for a lad to pray specifically asking God to help him overcome this habit of masturbation, for this tends to really impress the habit on his mind and entrench it deeper into his life. Rather we would suggest that he asks God to help him in the development of his life generally, and that God's purpose be fulfilled in every area of his life. This is positive and not negative praying. (Kenny 24)

Now, at the *fin de siècle* and into the "noughties," sex therapists and educators in America, Australia, and elsewhere no longer view masturbation as a mortal sin, nor do they see it, in its next historical progression, as a kind of necessary evil (to "blow off" excess sexual steam, for instance). Instead they encourage masturbation as an important part of maintaining a healthy sexuality and see it as an exercise in sexual independence and practicing sensuousness, arguing that a playful and happy approach to self-pleasuring serves as a kind of sexual apprenticeship. According to this perspective, men and their lovers benefit enormously via sexual self-experimentation. If this is leisurely, relaxed, unhurried, and tuned-in, men then develop into skilful and sensuous lovers. Australia's best-known family therapist, Steve Biddulph, claims that if masturbation is experienced without guilt and in a relaxed and trusting atmosphere, a boy learns to be receptive and surrendering, and it can be a spiritual experience. In case his remarks could be seen as too cloying, Biddulph also quotes Billy Connolly's (and Woody Allen's) quip, "the one advantage masturbation has over sex is that you don't have to look your best" (120). The attitudes in *American Pie* reinforce this relaxed attitude toward masturbation, which in fact permeates the film right from the opening scene, when Jim is watching a scrambled cable sleaze channel when his parents barge in unannounced, and this even includes Nadia masturbating in Jim's bed prior to the Internet strip scene. It's a film which *comes out* about masturbation in a very big way, and those characters who are most at ease with their bodies (like Nadia, for example) treat it as a pleasurable experience rather than a furtive and guilty "dirty secret." Additionally, it might also be noted that while in some instances solitary masturbation could still be viewed as a problematic practice (and Jim's surreptitious behavior is certainly questionable), mutual masturbation, in an age of AIDS/HIV and concerns about teenage pregnancy, might be viewed more positively and practically. (Kevin and his girlfriend Vicki have more or less been doing this prior to "taking the plunge" on prom night.)

In keeping with sex education manuals, which it could be argued have traditionally been concerned at least as much with moral as with sexual education, given their overriding preoccupation with the molding of future decent and responsible male and female citizens, what we see here overall is a privileging of a certain kind of masculinity through the camera's focalizing gaze—that is, the presentation of ideal sensitive "new age" guys or, to put it bluntly, terrific dating and later breeding material. In this text macho boys are held up to ridicule—boys such as Stiffler and the other sports jocks, who manically chant "You don't score until you score" in the final of the lacrosse match, or the odious Sherman, the self-styled "Sherminator," who boasts of his prowess with women and with "one lucky lady" in particular, only to be so severely embarrassed at the prom that he urinates in front of his peers (yet another sign of transgressive masculinity, of malperforming penises). *Their* posturing and masculine masquerades are shown to be a complete sham as hegemonic masculinity fails and is found spectacularly wanting—not least by the always-empowered girls as well as the newly empowered group of four, who come to realize that their pact to lose their virginity by prom night was infantile and that sexual performance for its own sake is unimportant. Moreover, in terms of the messages being sent out to the audience, it is hugely important that the four heroes get the girls, whereas the others do not. The film ultimately proves, as Fred Pfeil has remarked elsewhere, that sensitizing the reformed white male self is actually a very efficient way of re-empowering (64).

And so Oz, the shy, failed Casanova, joins the school singing group to seduce girls, but instead meets true love and gives up the sport that he has hitherto lived for. Kevin sleeps with his long-term girlfriend Vicki, who subsequently decides that it is time to move on. Then, in an amusing spoof of *The Graduate*, Paul is seduced by the older woman who likes her whiskey and her men aged eighteen, while Jim is deflowered by a secretly lascivious band geek, who, in keeping with the gender reversions and subversions which abound in the text, shouts "Say my name, Bitch!" as a prelude to their sexual foreplay. When he wakes up to find her gone, he chuckles delightedly, "I've been used—COOL!"

If exemplary role modeling is "the proper generic function of the Western movie hero" (Cohan 207), then this text fulfils a similar function, but with a new millennium spin. Young men are guided toward manhood, not through old-fashioned masculine valor, but in terms of their interaction with women. For masculinity in this film is broadly defined in terms of its encounters with the feminine, and in a further unusual touch, *American Pie* is not ultimately about bonding with other males, or about buddies—it is much more about the defining of a male in terms of how he relates to and empathizes with women. In the eternal rites of passage from boy to man, and from innocence to experience, this text is principally about the construction of "feminized" men who are more responsive to interpersonal relationships than the hegemonic norm. What is actually constructed in this film/sex education manual is a different type of masculinity, a new masculinity—much like the type identified by Steven Cohan in *Masked Men*, his study of Hollywood in the 1950s, where the more feminized, younger men like James Dean and Montgomery Clift, who are associated with feelings and emotions, are contrasted with John Wayne's now dated but traditional male hero (201–63).

In his germinal work, *Masculinities*, Bob Connell has identified a "new age" man created after contact with feminism as one who is supportive to women, critical of other men's attitudes, has the capacity to have feelings worth expressing, is sensitive, and has emotional depth (120–42). Given a textual narrative which focuses upon feelings, emotions, and the boys' handling of relationships (defined by Connell as *cathexis* 24), the mostly sweet and lovable main male characters in *American Pie* clearly develop into "new age" prototypes who are significantly molded by the women about them. Given that sex and sexual relationships form a large part of their development into Connell's ideal sensitive, heterosexual, new age men, it is highly significant these relations are consensual rather than coercive.

Crucially, in keeping with modern sex manuals, although not necessarily Hollywood mainstream movies, the girls in *American Pie* are not *just* the vehicle of male fantasies. They are fleshed out, not just flesh. This is something the film producers appear to have been aware of—they have commented, "the key to a sex comedy is not to have anything sexist or malicious" (quoted in Higgins). Seventeen-year-old girls have traditionally seemed more mature than their male counterparts, and, since 1970s feminism, they appear to be even more so. Certainly the girls in this film are more mature and far more in control of their sexuality than the boys. Naturally assertive, they all take the sexual initiative, and none is coerced into doing what she does not want to. This reading is confirmed by comments from one of the actors: "It doesn't feel like a guy-fest to me because the women in the movie have control," says Alyson Hannigan (aka *Buffy the Vampire Slayer*'s Willow), "so it's pretty much a chick flick in my opinion. [Women] may be more hesitant to see it, and guys will definitely turn out for the first weekend. But girls like to see it ... because it helps us to understand what dweebs they are" (Nashawaty 27). In her 1979 essay on melodrama, Laura Mulvey commented that "women have been largely without a voice, gagged and deprived of outlets, including that of popular culture" ("Notes" 39). In this film they *do* have a voice, albeit in an oblique way. *American Pie* is undoubtedly centered on the exploits of the four boys, but the self-reliant, assured girls are important in their own right—they are by no means treated perfunctorily as cardboard cutouts or sexual objects. Indeed, although the film appears to have been targeted toward males, and although the audience breakdown for gender, race, age, and class is unknown to me, it would scarcely be surprising if Hannigan was correct and that young females composed a quite significant proportion of its box-office takings.

American Pie is, in part, a tongue-in-cheek parody of man-to-man sex talks, of "secret men's business" generally. For instance, Kevin's older brother tells him of the whereabouts of a book, an instructional bible of sex techniques handed down from one generation of high school boys to the next. But Kevin is worthy of this only when he proves to his brother that he is concerned to make the sexual experience happy for his girlfriend as well, that he wants to "return the favor," as he puts it. His credentials having been verified, his visit to the secret place to find the book is cued in with the portentous music associated with the pursuit of a noble quest, and this music continues later as Kevin reads the dusty tome and notes in particular the pages dealing with the "tongue tornado." This in turn leads to the cunnilingus scene where Kevin pauses from the act to furtively glance at the "bible" for further inspiration, an episode described in *Rolling Stone* as "not disgusting, not sick and really very funny ... and we were also quite thrilled, as a matter of sexual politics, to see that it wasn't only guys getting off in the movie but girls as well" (Hedegaard 96). At regular intervals too, Jim's well-meaning father also offers wisdom to his excruciatingly embarrassed son, proffering magazines such as *Hustler* and *Shave*—("this one I'm not so familiar with—it focuses on pubic regions in detail—this looks just like some tropical plant—underwater" and so on). This lampooning of father–son sex talks is a clever feature in a film which can be read as one gigantic modern sex manual designed to subvert patriarchal domination via gross-out comedy, and which offers contemporary ideas and advice about masturbation, about being nice to girls, by treating them equally, and not using them, and by letting them take the initiative to accept or reject sexual advances.

Young producers Chris and Paul Weitz appear to have been keenly aware of contemporary changes in the cultural prescriptions of gender, of the fragile, provisional, and unstable makeup of masculinity and its many transient, unfinished, and incomplete guises (according to Judith Butler's theatrical metaphor which was invoked earlier). In *The Remasculinization of America*, Susan Jeffords presents successive popular restagings of the Vietnam conflict as a recuperation of the militaristic ideal of masculinity from the battering it received from both the feminist and antiwar movements, an argument which is articulated further in *Hard Bodies*, where she examines the 1980s as a reclaiming of the masculine body by promoting traditional narratives of spectacular white male action heroes standing for individualism, liberty, militarism, and a mythic heroism. Now, in the late 1990s, a further redefinition of the masculine has evolved, another phrase in the "extended narrative of national identity" (Jeffords 23), a movement away from the hardened bodies of those kings and warriors (to use Robert Bly's terminology) that emblematized Reaganism. There has been a noticeable change of direction away from the increasingly extravagant spectacles of violence and power (the recently disastrous *Pearl Harbor* notwithstanding) to inward, increasingly emotional displays of masculine sensitivity, vulnerability, traumas, and burdens (this exploration of their "feminine" sides is seen at its most mawkish, sanctimonious, and pathos-chasing in Robin Williams's movies such as *Good Will Hunting* and *Patch Adams*). And so the hardened, muscle-bound, domineering man of the 1980s becomes the considerate, loving, and self-sacrificing man of the 1990s—icons of the "new" masculinity seen most clearly in the progression from *Terminator* to *Terminator 2*: "Once he was programmed to destroy the future. Now his mission is to save it" (Jeffords 157).

According to *Rolling Stone*, the love message in *American Pie* exists simply as a cynical exercise, as a sop to get all the really important stuff, "the oral sex, the pie-screwing ... filmed" (Hedegaard 96). I argue precisely the other way around, that the titillating gross-out comedy is the lure to attract the audience's attention, to deliver the message which, in the end, is incredibly wholesome.

Not all the reviewers liked the discrepancy which lies at the heart of this teen film: Corliss, for example, complained of the discordant "mix of ... sex gags and woozy sentimentality." But ultimately *American Pie* is a sex manual of its time, decked out as a male initiation rites movie with a surefire appeal to a modern cine-literate youth market. In the end, as Giroux argues, it is a much more effective vehicle than a book. Finally, this reading is borne out in the interview in *Rolling Stone*, where three of the main male actors describe themselves as Christians, one describing himself as "a very sensitive guy, a very Nineties man," and a "born again virgin," justifying the movie, and his role within it, because "the underlying message is that sex is not the important thing—love is!" (Hedegaard 97). If popular culture is truly a region of cultural practice where masculinities are modeled, renegotiated, and reinforced, then *American Pie* is a very canny example of this kind.

NOTE

An earlier version of this chapter appears in *Manning the Next Millennium*, eds. Sharyn Pearce and Vivienne Muller (Fremantle, Western Australia: Black Swan, 2001).

WORKS CITED

American Pie. Dir. Paul Weitz. Screenplay by Adam Herz. Universal, 1999.

Austin Powers—The Spy Who Shagged Me. Dir. Jay Roach. New Line Cinema, 1999.

Biddulph, Steve. *Raising Boys*. Sydney, Austral.: Finch, 1997.

Big Daddy. Dir. Dennis Dugan. Columbia, 1999.

Butler, Judith. *Gender Trouble: Feminism and the Subversion of Identity*. London: Routledge, 1990.

Campbell, Patricia J. *Sex Education Books for Young Adults 1892–1979*. New York: R.R. Bowker, 1979.

Cohan, Steven. *Masked Men: Masculinity and the Movies in the 1950s*. Bloomington: Indiana University Press, 1997.

Cohan, Steven, and Ina Rae Hark. *Screening the Male: Exploring Masculinities in Hollywood Cinema*. New York: Routledge, 1993.

Connell, R.W. *Masculinities*. Sydney, Austral.: Allen and Unwin, 1996.

Corliss, Richard. Review of *American Pie*, dir. Paul Weitz. *Time*, 12 July 1999, 77.

Giroux, Henry A. *Channel Surfing: Racism, the Media and the Destruction of Today's Youth*. London: Macmillan, 1997.

Gray, Timothy M. "*Pie* Is Summer's Teen Sneak Feature." *Variety*, 12 July 1999, 5.

Griffith, Edward F. "Emotional Development." *The Road to Maturity*, ed. Edward F. Griffith. London: Victor Gollancz, 1944. 170–99.

Hedegaard, Erik. "There's Something About Virgins." *Rolling Stone*, 19 Aug. 1999, 94–100.

Higgins, Bill. "*Pie*; Not like Mama Made." *Variety*, 12 July 1999, 59.

Jeffords, Susan. *The Remasculinization of America: Gender and the Vietnam War*. Bloomington: Indiana University Press, 1989.

Kaplan, E. Ann. *Women and Film: Both Sides of the Camera*. New York: Methuen, 1983.

Kavanaugh, John F. "Movie Mores." *America*, 14 Aug. 1999, 24.

Kenny, P. L. *Guide to Virile Manhood: A Reliable Sex Education Book for Young Men*. Melbourne, Austral.: Father and Son Movement, 1957.

Kuhn, Annette. *The Power of the Image: Essays on Representation and Sexuality*. London: Routledge, 1985.

Lim, Dennis. "Losing It." *Village Voice*, 13 July 1999, 66.

Mulvey, Laura. "Visual Pleasure and Narrative Cinema." *Visual and Other Pleasures*. Bloomington: Indiana University Press, 1989. 14–26.

———. "Notes on Sirk and Melodrama." *Visual and Other Pleasures*. Bloomington: Indiana University Press, 1989. 39–44.

Nashawaty, Chris. "Pie in Your Face." *Entertainment Weekly*, 16 July 1999, 26–28.

Neale, Steven. "Masculinity As Spectacle: Reflections on Men and Mainstream Cinema." *Screen*, Nov.–Dec. 1983, 2–17.

Nelson, Claudia. "Sex and the Single Boy: Ideals of Manliness and Sexuality in Victorian Literature for Boys." *Victorian Studies* (Summer 1989): 525–50.

Pearl Harbor. Dir. Michael Bay. Touchstone, 2001.

Pfeil, Fred. *White Guys: Studies in Postmodern Domination and Difference*. London: Verso, 1995.

Piddington, Marion. *Tell Them! The Second Stage of Mothercraft*. Sydney, Austral.: Moore's Bookshop, 1925.

South Park—Bigger, Longer and Uncut. Dir. Trey Parker. Paramount, 1998.

Tasker, Yvonne. *Spectacular Bodies: Gender, Genre and the Action Cinema*. London: Routledge, 1993.

There's Something About Mary. Dir. Bobby Farrelly and Peter Farrelly. Twentieth Century Fox, 1998.

Waldby, Catherine. "Destruction, Boundary Erotics and Reconfigurations of the Heterosexual Male Body." *Sexy Bodies*, ed. Elizabeth Grosz and Elspeth Probyn. London: Routledge, 1995. 266–77.

Walker, David. "Continence for a Nation: Seminal Loss and National Vigour." *Labour History* 48 (May 1985): 1–14.

Weeks, Jeffrey. *Sex, Politics and Society: The Regulation of Sexuality Since 1800*. New York: Longman, 1987.

6

"The Seven Things All Men Love in Bed": Young Women's Magazines and the Governance of Femininity

Gordon Tait

From the mid-1970s to the mid-1980s, there was a decisive growth in the area of specialist women's magazines. Leaving aside such general titles as *Woman's Day* and *New Idea*, whose circulation remained fairly static, the readership of titles specifically aimed at young women increased by 2500 percent (Windshuttle 47). Furthermore, this upward trend not only resulted in an increase in the readership, but also the number of published magazines. According to Joseph Dominick (139), by the mid-1990s, women's magazines had become the largest single category of magazine published (ninety-two in the United States alone). The choice is now enormous, particularly for the young. Magazines such as *Cosmopolitan, Cleo, Dolly, Seventeen, Honey,* and *Elle* constitute but a tiny part of an extensive selection, covering a range of ages.[1] For example, *Dolly* and *Seventeen* are primarily aimed at teenagers, *Honey* and *Elle* are directed toward teenagers and women in their early twenties, and *Cosmopolitan* and *Cleo* are marketed at a range from the late teens to the thirties. As a consequence of the vast size and range of this market, Windshuttle states that anyone wishing to understand the condition of young women, or the relations between the sexes "needs to come to terms with the contents of women's magazines. Young women buy them in very large numbers.... [J]ust about every female beyond early childhood ... sees one of these magazines regularly. Hence, whatever attitude one takes to them, it must be acknowledged that their influence is pervasive" (247).

While more recent analyses have also pointed to the potency and importance of contemporary phenomena like music videos, all these commentaries still stress the centrality of women's magazines for investigating and interpreting twenty-first century gender relations and identities among the young (Jones &

Jones; McLoughlin). After all, the "pervasive influence" of women's magazines referred to by Windshuttle has long been regarded as a significant subject of discussion. In *The Feminine Mystique*, Betty Friedan was one of the first to argue that such an influence was almost entirely negative. She claims that these magazines have a significant part to play in reinforcing the subordinate status of women.

Friedan is not alone in this analysis. There is now a considerable literature, spanning more than three decades, which supports this viewpoint (Demarest Garner Kaiser; Peirce; Sullivan O'Connor Wilson). According to McRobbie (268), young women's magazines constitute a highly effective ideological site for the transmission of patriarchal values. Its success lies in the fact that it appears to be a site wherein young women are "free" from the elements of coercion so obviously in evidence within other terrains, such as the school and the family, and thus it is the illusion of freedom that is pursued within the covers of magazines. McRobbie looks forward to the production of a magazine for young women which does not simply, but subtly, reflect "styles created by men to transform them into junior sex-objects" (282). The production of such a magazine will form one part of a counterhegemonic process whereby young women learn to deconstruct the dominant, oppressive models of femininity, and, in the words of Ann Snitow, learn to "project a unique self" (quoted in Gilbert & Taylor 103).

IDENTITY MANAGEMENT AND YOUNG WOMEN'S MAGAZINES

This chapter will propose an alternative understanding of young women's magazines. Rather than locating such texts within an overall model of repression and patriarchal domination, it will be argued here that they can be regarded as practical manuals which enlist young women to do specific kinds of work on themselves. In doing so, they form an effective link between the governmental imperatives aimed at constructing particular personae (such as, for example, "the sexually responsible young woman"), and the actual practices whereby these imperatives are operationalized. These manuals do not prevent young women from learning to "project a unique self," they constitute a significant source of practices and techniques through which particular types of self are shaped.

In spite of some slight variations, the content of young women's magazines appears to be fairly consistent: Men and sex, fashion and beauty, celebrity gossip, and advice. Kathryn McMahon expands on this appraisal when she argues that, in effect, such apparently separate areas are simply variations on one central subject: Sex. In her article "The *Cosmopolitan* Ideology and the Management of Desire," she analyses the content of *Cosmopolitan* magazine over a twelve-year period, from 1976 to 1988. She found that the articles fell into six categories: (1) relationships with men, 77 articles; (2) the lives of celebrities, 51 articles; (3) advice about sex, 49 articles; (4) beauty, diet, and health, 34 articles; (5) psychological advice, 30 articles; and (6) work and money, 23 articles. She then goes on to say that these categories are actually misleading, since most were actually about sex anyway:

For instance, articles in the category of relationships with men and articles about the lives of celebrities contained sexually explicit material and dealt with sexual relationships.... Those articles in the category of beauty, diet and health were most often prescriptives on how to recreate oneself as a desired object. Those articles in the category of psychological problems and advice ... contained advice on depression after a relationship breakup, starting over after an affair, and sexual behaviours. Those articles about work and money eroticised relations of power on the job. (385)

Magazines aimed at the younger end of the market, such as *Jackie* and *Dolly*, have a similar, if more muted, preoccupation with sex and sexuality. Although there is no explicit sex in these articles, the pivotal moment in almost all cases concerns "the kiss"—preparing for it, selecting the right partner for it, and making sure that no other girl gets in first (Gilbert & Taylor 88). In direct correlation with the perceived degree of sexual maturity, magazines such as *Jackie*, *Seventeen*, and *Dolly* suggest practices and techniques aimed at how to talk to boys ("Ten Guy Goof-Ups You Gotta Avoid"—*Teen*, Mar. 1993), various ways of acquiring a first boyfriend ("Are You a Flirt?"—*Dolly*, Mar. 1994 "True Crush or True Love"—*Seventeen*, Oct. 1998), getting him to ask you out ("Making the First Move?"—*Seventeen*, Oct. 1993), managing the first date ("The First Date: Don't Blow It"—*Dolly*, Oct. 1994), and assessing your new boyfriend ("Love Test: Is It for Now or Forever?"—*Seventeen*, Aug. 1998), and so on.

Magazines like *Cosmopolitan* and *Cleo* are aimed at a more mature market and consequently address topics such as how to assess the suitability of a prospective lover ("Weenie or Whopper: Can You Assess His Size Without Taking His Clothes Off?"—*Cleo*, Feb. 1994; "Suss Out His Sexual Potential: Can He Go from So-so to Oh, Oh, Oh?"—*Cosmopolitan*, Sept. 1998), strategies for picking up men ("Pick Him Up Pointers"—*Cosmopolitan*, Nov. 2000), specific sexual techniques ("The Seven Things All Men Love in Bed"—*Cleo*, July 1994), and for keeping sex interesting in a relationship ("The Five Secrets of Sexual Touch"—*Cosmopolitan*, Oct. 2001).

However, having once identified and targeted a population, whether at the younger or more mature end of the market, the question then arises: How are personae created within these categories persuaded to carry out their respective moral obligations and induced to adhere to the relevant moral codes in matters of sex? To put it another way, how do you convince, for example, a *Cosmo* girl to act like one? Those young women who decide to adopt some (or all) of the practices constitutive of *Cosmo* girl, including sexual practices, do not make these choices at random. Simply painting a portrait of a particular persona, along with its associated lifestyle, is insufficient to convince young women to adopt that persona. As Foucault points out, targeted populations have to be enjoined to carry out such "work on the self" ("Technologies of the Self" 27). That is, they are persuaded to adhere to the *Cosmo* sexual code in a variety of ways. For example, they are persuaded by the promise of being sexually "self-fulfilled," by the desire not to be considered abnormal by their peers, by concerns over venereal disease, by worries about being overlooked by men, and so on. Each of these incitements plays a part in convincing young women, within the context of the magazines they read, to shape themselves in particular ways.

MODES OF PERSUASION

In 1980 *Cosmopolitan* magazine conducted an extensive survey of sexual practices among its readership. There were over 100,000 replies (as compared to only 6,000 in the Kinsey Report in 1953 and only 3,000 in the Hite Report in 1981). It was published in the September issue of the magazine as "The Sexual Profile of that *Cosmopolitan* Girl," then later as *The Cosmo Report* (1981). It is significant that the report began its introduction with the following *raison d'être* for the research: "What about you and me? Are our sexual practices and feelings typical? (Typical of whom?) Are we in tune with the times, or woefully behind or eccentrically ahead of them? (Where do we fit in? Is there some way we can measure ourselves?)" (Wolfe 17).

With chapters entitled "The Whens, Wheres and How-Oftens of Sex," "Sexual Practices," "Orgasm with a Partner," and "Lovers," the report sets out in precise detail just what constitutes sexual normality for young women. Furthermore, with a chapter on sexual fantasies and dreams, even the subjectivity of the *Cosmo* girl can be assessed and normalized. McMahon sums up this process when she states that *The Cosmo Report* represents "the construction of the norm as ideal: The *Cosmopolitan Girl*. The reader is expected to compare, which implies judgement, her own sexual experience in relation to this construct" (390).

Significantly, this form of normalizing within *Cosmopolitan* is not only common to most young women's magazines, but also to most other manuals on youth and sex, most of which have sections on what it means to be "normal" and how specific sets of differences can be assessed and addressed (Wooton).

Of all the normative knowledges specifying young people as their object, two are particularly influential: Psychology and medicine. In particular, psychology has a preeminent status in the management of subjectivity. The success of psychology (along with its associated disciplines) is symptomatic, not only of the growth in the knowledges claiming professional expertise within this domain, but also of their value in the government of populations (Rose, *The Psychological Complex*). However, these disciplines should not be understood solely in terms of their immediate regulative utility. They have also become axiomatic to constructing the practices by which a "self" is formed and directed: This includes mechanisms of self-understanding and evaluation, ways of thinking and talking about personal feelings, procedures for managing emotions, and so on (Rose, *Governing the Soul* 3). A concern for normal sexual and mental development of their readers is particularly evident within young women's magazines. Indeed, in "Are Those Sex Articles Really Necessary?" *Cosmopolitan* argues that magazines such as itself have a crucial role to play in producing an emotionally healthy population (91). After all, such publications invariably offer psychological advice to help readers overcome their social and sexual problems, and this advice is one of the few sources of information consistently available to young women.

The second mode of persuasion that warrants commentary involves the scientization, and in particular, the medicalization of sex. Magazines such as *Seventeen*, *Dolly*, *Cosmopolitan*, and *Cleo* all contain sections which provide medical advice for readers. This advice is most frequently regarding sexual problems. For example, the "problem clinic" in *Cosmopolitan* deals with issues such as concerns over frequency of masturbation, difficulties in having successful sexual intercourse, anatomical questions about genitals, worries about contraception and sexually transmitted diseases, and so on. Even those parts of young women's magazines which are not specifically addressing medical problems still adopt a scientific tone when dispensing advice. Furthermore, the sexual self-government of young women is most frequently driven by a scientific emphasis on the consequences of bad management—in particular, unwanted pregnancy and sexually transmitted diseases. Certainly, these problems do occupy a pivotal position within many manuals on sex education, in that they locate young women as a category which is inherently "at-risk" for these misfortunes yet able to be saved through appropriate instruction (Evans Jackson Phelps). However, the consequences of being allocated "at risk" status do not end simply with the provision of adequate knowledge about the mechanics of sex. Rather, young women have become an object of concern for a network of knowledges, professional groups, strategies, and manuals which advocate and inculcate the practices of self-management necessary to avoid "trouble"—be that becoming pregnant or catching a sexually transmitted disease.

Importantly, the processes of self-government necessary to avoid venereal disease do not simply revolve around instilling the reflex of using a condom, although it is not irrelevant. The central issue is really the moral problematization of promiscuity, in that the programs of self-management aimed at young women are more ethical than prophylactic. While *Cosmopolitan* and *Cleo*, which champion the right of single young women to have a sex life, continually stress the importance of taking measures to prevent sexually transmitted diseases ("I Lost My Virginity ... and Got 3 STDs!"—*Cleo*, July 2001), they also emphasize the importance of restraint and responsibility when having sex. That is, successful promiscuity (however limited) has to be carefully managed—i.e., "sleep with different men, [just] make sure it's safe sex" ("It's OK to Be a Bitch," *Cosmopolitan*, Sept. 1995).

More frequently, magazines aimed at a younger market either encourage abstinence ("I'm 27, Famous, and a Virgin"—*Girlfriend*, Aug. 1999) or warn against the social and medical consequences of becoming a "slag"—"flirts or sexually permissive women who flaunt their desire" (Gilbert & Taylor 82). This is generally accomplished indirectly through articles such as "We Had Sex and Then He Dumped Me" (*Girlfriend*, Oct. 1994), "I Had Sex with Him and Now I'm Sorry" (*Teen*, Nov. 1993), "I Got Drunk and Lost My Virginity" (*Dolly*, Oct. 1994), or even "Drugged and Raped She Thought She Could Trust Him, but She Was Wrong" (*Teen*, June 2001).

Governmental imperatives aimed at modifying the sexual conduct of the population do not operate simply by the power of decree. Rather, according to Foucauldian analysis, specific categories of person are recruited into programs of self-reformation. For example, the programs which develop out of governmental concerns over an issue such as youth pregnancies do not simply translate, at some later date, into an improvement in the relevant statistics. Instead, they operate by enlisting young women into doing specific kinds of work on the self—to shape the self, in this case, into the image of the "sexually responsible young woman." This work takes the form of the adoption of various "practices of the self." The case of young women's magazines provides an important example of this process, in that they provide a useful link between specific governmental aspirations and the adoption, by a targeted population, of practices that go some way toward realizing those aspirations. Such magazines provide a medium through which broad governmental programs actually get taken up as practices of self-government by young women.

PRACTICES OF THE SELF

These practices take many forms. For example, self-interrogation is now one of the central practices by which self-knowledge is gained. However, this practice is not a fundamental and inevitable part of what it means to be human, any more than is having a moral conscience. Rather, it is a particular historical and cultural attribute. There now seems nothing unusual about the extensive and repetitive self-interrogation that young women's magazines require from their readers. Young women are continually enjoined to scrutinize all aspects of themselves: Their sense of fashion, their body shape, their sexual preferences, their libido, their fantasies, their readiness for marriage, their fidelity, and so on. The "test yourself" questionnaire is now a standard device within most young women's magazines, where readers can assess themselves "objectively" and adjust their conduct/thoughts/aspirations accordingly. In this manner, self-interrogation gains the status of an exercise in scientific inquiry. Although some parts of the magazine appear to be simply informative (sex, celebrities, fashion, advice), even these provide a set of measures—an ideal—against which young women are expected to measure themselves. Ultimately, ideals such as "the *Cosmo* girl" affect the sexual conduct of young women, not simply because they provide a high-visibility role model, but because they encourage young women to evaluate themselves in relation to this model, to scrutinize their shortcomings, and then to embark upon various projects of self-modification.

Importantly, these practices of self-interrogation have largely operated in tandem with a second practice—the confession (Foucault, *History I* 58). Like the practice of self-interrogation, the confession also has a significant role within young women's magazines. First, it is common for such magazines to provide a regular forum for readers to write in and share their experiences. Essay-length letters are published detailing everything from birth to bereavement, from sexual experimentation to sexual abuse, and from happy beginnings to unhappy endings. This process is deemed to be therapeutic for the writer, as well as entertaining, informative, and cautionary for the reader. Second, advice within these magazines is most frequently dispensed through direct replies to readers' letters. Features such as the "problem page" and the "doctor's clinic" (*Cosmopolitan, Cleo, Seventeen, Elle*) combine the confessional with the process of government through expertise. Whether the problems are medical, psychological, or ethical, readers confess to experts, who offer advice and guidance, which is then translated into self-government. It can be argued that the phenomenal response to the questionnaire on sexual conduct published in *Cosmopolitan* (which gave rise to *The Cosmo Report*), is an example of the widespread elaboration of confessional practices. Young women were asked to detail the most intimate aspects of their sexuality for the magazine's survey, with which over 100,000 complied. Furthermore, within magazines like *Cosmopolitan,* it is often not simply the women who are urged to confess the most intimate details of their sexual practices and fantasies. Readers are also enjoined to persuade their boyfriends, lovers, and husbands to confess their sexual secrets—secrets which have permitted, in turn, the construction of a parallel persona to the "*Cosmo* girl": The "*Cosmo* man." ("A Survey for Him"—*Cosmopolitan,* Sept. 1995). Significantly, this willingness to confess not only provides, in this instance, the raw material for the construction of the "*Cosmo* girl" (and man), it also provides, in a broader sense, the raw material by which government can operate effectively. That is, the confession is not only a "practice of the self," it is also an important technique of government.

In spite of the centrality of self-interrogation and incitations to speak as practices of ethical self-management, not all practices of the self constitutive of a young woman's "habitus" (Bourdieu 83) are directed at mental or spiritual development. Some are directed at the body itself. Instructing readers on how to acquire specific bodily practices constitutes an important component of

young women's magazines. McRobbie, in her analysis of *Jackie*, contends that
the magazine makes it clear that the successful acquisition of femininity (in the
style championed by the magazine) is not a *fait accompli* for all teenagers.
Rather, becoming the kind of young woman that *Jackie* considers appropriate
requires hard work. This work involves, in part, learning to use the body in certain ways:

> Another useful expression though, is the pathetic appealing look, which brings out a
> boy's protective instinct and has him desperate to get you another drink/help you on
> with your coat/give you a lift home. It's best done by opening your eyes wide and drop-
> ping the mouth open a little looking (hanging your head slightly) directly into the eyes
> of the boy you're talking to. Practice this. (*Jackie*, 15 Feb. 1975, quoted in McRobbie 263)

Such techniques of the body, albeit for a more mature readership, are also detailed in magazines like *Cosmopolitan* and *Cleo*. Aside from the wealth of articles on diet and exercise regimen, these magazines often suggest appropriate
bodily techniques for observing social protocols and encouraging sexual attraction. Indeed, the techniques of the body associated with sexual conduct are
often quite explicit, such as those detailing bodily techniques for getting more
satisfaction out of sex ("How to Please a Man with Your Hands"—Cosmopolitan, Nov. 2000; "The Orgasm Workout: Clench Your Way to Ecstasy"—*Cleo*,
Jan. 1994). Detailed instructions are also given in a variety of sexual techniques,
techniques which then constitute an important part of every "*Cosmo* girl's"
erotic repertoire ("The Bad Things Nice Girls Do in Bed"—*Cosmopolitan*, Mar.
2001; "Drive Him Wild"—*Cleo*, Feb. 1994; "The Secret Sex Moves That Will
Rock His World"—*Cleo*, Oct. 2000).

To summarize: Techniques of ethical self-formation are central to the management of sexual conduct, since they constitute an integral part of the habitus by which young people are shaped. Such practices are not restricted to
adoption of certain stylistic codes. They also include a multiplicity of mental,
spiritual, and physical practices, such as self-interrogation, incitements to
confession, specific ways of sitting and walking, the regulation of the body
through exercise and diet. More often than not, these techniques of self-
formation are graded according to age, the outcome being the production of
very different personae from within the pages of *Cosmopolitan* to the pages
of *Seventeen*.

At this point, it is important to make two qualifying points. The first is that
young women's magazines are by no means the only manuals which detail ways
of constructing an appropriate "self." Such manuals are widespread, encompassing all aspects of identity formation. For example, books such as Kaye Wellings's
First Love, First Sex, Robert Francoeur's *Becoming a Sexual Person*, and Jenny
Davis's *If Only I'd Known* cover much of the same ground as the magazines
aimed at the younger end of the market, although in a more academic and therapeutic register. Indeed, Wellings's book also includes advice/directions on danc-

ing, dating, kissing, petting, masturbation, first intercourse, and so on. It even includes a chapter entitled "Am I Normal?" a description of introspective techniques for getting through "to the real person underneath" (16) and directions on appropriate bodily gestures and posture.

The second point is that neither the array of possible sexual/social identities nor the various practices of self-formation detailed by young women's magazines is adopted unproblematically by the readers. Young women take a multitude of positions with regard to these texts: They can be read for information, for guidance, for amusement, for boredom relief, or simply for the horoscopes; the identities on offer can be taken up, disregarded, overlooked, built upon, mutated, adopted partially, or adopted sporadically; likewise, the techniques of the self proposed by these magazines can be utilized, experimented with, adapted, laughed at, or just plain ignored. This is not to suggest that such manuals of self-formation are therefore unsuccessful. Rather, the relationship between the content of young women's magazines and specific practical outcomes is a complex and context-bound one.

CONCLUSION

The arguments in this chapter concern the manner in which young women learn to construct specific types of relationships with themselves. The intention has been to provide an alternative approach to the issue of young women's magazines. This approach avoids some of the problems associated with a particular kind of feminist theory—that is, a paradigm which has generally explained such magazines almost exclusively in terms of social control. Such a critical feminist approach neatly delineates the good from the bad, the dominant from the counterhegemonic, and the oppressors from the victims. Such domain assumptions lead to a predictable conclusion: Femininity is shaped by domination and repression. In contrast to this approach, it has been my contention that the Foucauldian reinterpretation of power as productive and organizational opens up research to a variety of conclusions, conclusions which can be assessed from case to case. This is not to say that the exercise of power cannot still be coercive; however, I have argued that, for the most part, contemporary forms of rule operate by targeting populations, organizing their conduct and capacities, and channeling their aspirations. The examples outlined in this chapter illustrate the manner in which specific populations—in this case, early teenage girls in *Dolly* and *Jackie* and more mature young women in *Cosmopolitan* and *Cleo*—can be differentially and precisely targeted and their conduct shaped and governed. While young women's magazines are just one of many sites within which this process occurs, they still constitute an effective mechanism for the formation of particular kinds of gendered identities.

NOTE

1. All magazines cited in this chapter refer to the Australian edition.

WORKS CITED

"Are Those Sex Articles Really Necessary?" *Cosmopolitan*, Oct. 1993, 90–96.
"Are You a Flirt?" *Dolly*, Mar. 1994, 46.
"The Bad Things Nice Girls Do in Bed." *Cosmopolitan*, Mar. 2001, 170–71.
Bourdieu, Pierre. *Outline of a Theory of Practice*. Cambridge, Eng.: Cambridge University Press, 1997.
Davis, Jenny. *If Only I'd Known*. London: Orchard, 1995.
Demarest, Jack, and Jeanette Garner. "The Representation of Women's Roles in Women's Magazines over the Past 30 Years." *Journal of Psychology* 126, 4 (1992): 357–69.
Dominick, Joseph. *The Dynamics of Mass Communication*. New York: McGraw-Hill, 1996.
"Drive Him Wild: Foreplay Is Something to Be Savoured, Not Rushed." *Cleo*, Feb. 1994, 104.
"Drugged and Raped: She Thought She Could Trust Him, but She Was Wrong." *Teen*, June 2001, 62.
Evans, Lynette, and Helen Jackson. *Questions You Ask About Sex*. Ringwood, Austral: Penguin, 1989.
Faust, Beatrice. *Women, Sex and Pornography*. Harmondsworth, Eng.: Penguin, 1980.
"The First Date: Don't Blow It." *Dolly*, Oct. (1994), 76–80.
"The Five Secrets of Sexual Touch." *Cosmopolitan*, Oct. 2001, 198–99.
Foucault, Michel. *The History of Sexuality, Volume I: An Introduction*. Harmondsworth, Eng.: Penguin, 1976.
———. *The History of Sexuality, Volume II: The Uses of Pleasure*. Harmondsworth, Eng.: Penguin, 1987.
———. "Technologies of the Self." *Technologies of the Self*, ed. Luther Martin, Huck Gutman, and Patrick Hutton. Amherst: University of Massachusetts Press, 1988. 16–48.
Francoeur, Robert. *Becoming a Sexual Person*. New York: Macmillan, 1991.
Friedan, Betty. *The Feminine Mystique*. New York: Dell, 1963.
Gilbert, Pam, and Sandra Taylor. *Fashioning the Feminine: Girls, Popular Culture and Schooling*. Sydney, Austral.: Allen and Unwin, 1991.
"How Men Want to Be Seduced." *Cosmopolitan*, Dec. 1994, 76–82.
"How to Please a Man with Your Hands." *Cosmopolitan*, Nov. 2000, 234–38.
"I Got Drunk and Lost My Virginity." *Dolly*, Oct. (1994), 108.
"I Had Sex with Him and Now I'm Sorry." *Teen*, Nov. 1993, 42–43.
"I Lost My Virginity ... and Got 3 STDs." *Cleo*, July 2001, 104.
"I'm 27, Famous, and a Virgin." *Girlfriend*, Aug. 1999, 22.
"It's OK to Be a Bitch!" *Cosmopolitan*, Sept. 1995, 52.
Jones, Marsha, and Emma Jones. *Mass Media*. Hampshire, Eng.: Palgrave, 1999.
Kaiser, Karen. "The New Women's Magazines: It's the Same Old Story." *Frontiers* 4 (1979): 14–17.
"Love Test: Is It for Now or Forever?" *Seventeen*, Aug. 1998, 23.

"Making the First Move?" *Seventeen*, Oct. 1993, 130–34.

McLoughlin, Linda. *The Language of Magazines*. New York: Routledge, 2000.

McMahon, Kathryn. "The *Cosmopolitan* Ideology and the Management of Desire." *Journal of Sex Research* 27, 3 (1990): 381–96.

McRobbie, Angela. "*Jackie:* An Ideology of Adolescent Femininity." *Popular Culture: Past and Present*, ed. Bernard Waites, Tony Bennett, and Graham Martin. London: Croom Helm and Open University Press, 1982. 263–83.

"The Orgasm Workout: Clench Your Way to Ecstasy." *Cleo*, Jan. 1994, 64–68.

Peirce, Kate. "A Feminist Theoretical Perspective on the Socialisation of Teenage Girls Through *Seventeen* Magazine." *Sex Roles* 23, 9–10 (1991): 491–500.

Phelps, Kerryn. *Sex: Confronting Sexuality*. Sydney, Austral.: HarperCollins, 1993.

"Pick Him Up Pointers." *Cosmopolitan*, Nov. 2000, 302.

"Pucker Up: How to Get You and Your Lips Ready for Action." *Seventeen*, Feb. 1992, 20.

Rose, Nicolas. *Governing the Soul: The Shaping of the Private Self*. London: Routledge, 1990.

———. *The Psychological Complex: Psychology, Politics and Society in England 1869–1939*. London: Routledge, 1985.

"The Secret Sex Moves That Will Rock his World." *Cleo*, Oct. 2000, 74–79.

"The Seven Things All Men Love in Bed." *Cleo*, July 1994, 86–88.

Sullivan, Gary, and P. J. O'Connor. "Women's Role Portrayals in Magazine Advertising: 1958–1983." *Sex Roles* 18 (1998): 181–88.

"A Survey for Him." *Cosmopolitan*, Sept. 1995, 184–86.

"Suss Out His Sexual Potential: Can He Go from So-so to Oh, Oh, Oh?" *Cosmopolitan*, Sept. 1998, 184–87.

"Ten Guy Goof-Ups You Gotta Avoid: Find Out What Really Turns Them Off." *Teen*, Mar. 1993, 12–14.

"True Crush or True Love?" *Seventeen*, Oct. 1998, 11–12.

"Warm, Wet and Wild." *Cosmopolitan*, Feb. 1994, 10–11.

"Weenie or Whopper: Can You Assess His Size Without Taking His Clothes Off?" *Cleo*, Feb. 1994, 56–60.

"We Had Sex and Then He Dumped Me." *Girlfriend*, Oct. 1994, 74–77.

Wellings, Kaye. *First Love, First Sex: A Practical Guide to Relationships*. London: Greenhouse, 1986.

"What Women Do Wrong in Bed." *Cosmopolitan*, June 1993, 50–51.

Wilson, Sally. "The Image of Women in Canadian Magazines." *Mass Media and Social Change*, ed. Elihu Katz and Tamas Szecsko. London: Sage Publications, 1984. 231–45.

Windshuttle, Keith. *The Media*. Harmondsworth, Eng.: Penguin, 1984.

Wolfe, Linda. *The Cosmo Report*. New York: Arbor House. 1981.

Wooton, Vicki. *Be Yourself: Love, Sex and You*. Ringwood, Austral.: Penguin, 1989.

7

Living in a Young Country?
Youthful Creativity and Cultural Policy
in the United Kingdom

David Buckingham

This is a new age, to be led by a new generation. Let me talk to you about my generation. We grew up after the Second World War. We read about Fascism, we saw the Soviet Union, and we learned to fear extremes of Left and Right. We were born into the welfare state and the NHS [National Health Service], and into the market economy of bank accounts, supermarkets, jeans and cars.... We built a new popular culture, transformed by colour TV, *Coronation Street* and the Beatles. We enjoy a thousand material advantages over any previous generation; and yet we suffer a depth of insecurity and spiritual doubt they never knew.
        Tony Blair, Speech to the Labour Party Conference, 3 October 1995

In 1996 in the run-up to a general election which his party was to win with a historic landslide victory, Britain's Labour leader Tony Blair published a volume of speeches symptomatically entitled *New Britain: My Vision of a Young Country.* The rhetoric that characterizes these speeches has since come to define the discursive parameters of British political debate: Social inclusion, rights and responsibilities, decency and morality, community, citizenship, and stakeholding—these and other characteristic "New Labour" terms have emerged as the key political tokens in contemporary policymaking. As is well known, Blair's "vision" is one of "democratic socialism," rather than "statist socialism"—let alone the "student Marxism" he repeatedly sweeps aside. Far from being incompatible with the efficient management of the capitalist economy, civic virtues of the kind listed above are seen to be indispensable if Britain is to compete in the new global economic order: Indeed, the reinvention of civil society positively requires "partnerships" between the public and the private.

"Youth" is central to Blair's conception. Words like *new, modern, change,* and *renewal* recur with mantralike insistence (Fairclough). Far from being an "old," declining postimperial power, living on its past (Wright), Blair calls on Britain to become "a country convinced that its best times can lie ahead" (x):

I want us to be a young country again. With a common purpose. With ideals we cherish and live up to. Not resting on past glories. Not fighting old battles. Not sitting back, hand on mouth, concealing a yawn of cynicism, but ready for the day's challenge. (65)

Blair's "vision" is certainly wide-ranging. The "young country," he asserts, will be united, not divided by an antiquated class system. Its economy will be based on "partnership" between bosses and workers; it will be well educated and technologically literate; it will have modernized public services; and it will be a "decent" society, based on strong families and a keen sense of the individual's moral responsibility to the community.

Perhaps surprisingly, *New Britain* contains little mention of cultural policy. Nevertheless, in the quotation at the head of this chapter, Blair talks about "his" generation both in terms of material wealth and in terms of culture. While not exactly "young," Blair self-consciously represents what the Americans call the "baby boomer" generation; and he is at pains to differentiate himself from what he calls the "old and dead political culture of Tory Britain" (70). In the first year of the New Labour government, there was much talk of the "rebranding of Britain" and the emergence of "Cool Britannia." Just as Harold Wilson had awarded honors to the Beatles in the 1960s, so Blair entertained high-profile "youth" stars such as Oasis "bad boy" Liam Gallagher and television presenter Chris Evans at 10 Downing Street. The work of young British artists such as Damian Hirst—while distinctly more challenging—was also briefly claimed for this project of glamour by association. Like Bill Clinton with his saxophone, Blair was repeatedly pictured with his Fender Stratocaster guitar, in jeans and open-necked shirt; and old photographs of him with his student band "Ugly Rumours," complete with appropriately early-70s hairstyles, were released to the press.

In the event, "culture" has become a key part of New Labour's economic and ideological project—albeit one that does not always sit easily with other elements of it. One of the incoming government's first actions was to replace the Conservatives' Department of National Heritage with the Department of Culture, Media and Sport (DCMS)—a symptomatically modernizing and "democratic" move. Through a range of subsequent policy and funding initiatives, the government has sought to equalize access to cultural goods, to stimulate the growth of the cultural industries, and to maximize the social benefits of creative participation in the arts, particularly for disadvantaged or "socially excluded" young people. There has been a massive increase in funding for cultural activities, both from new sources such as the National Lottery, the Millennium Commission, and the National Endowment for Science, Technology and the Arts and by means of general increases in funding for established bodies such as the national and regional arts councils. Given the relative underfunding of the arts and cultural activities over the preceding two decades, this has seemed to some like the coming of a new golden age.

In this chapter, I intend to focus on this invocation of "youth" and its role in the recent development of cultural policy in Britain. In particular, I want to consider the issue of "creativity," which has become another of New Labour's key slogans. As I shall indicate, *youth, creativity,* and *culture* are all shifting signifiers: Their meanings are at once inclusive and exclusive, vague and yet highly precise. And, of course, it is this quality that enables them to perform their political work. While I certainly intend to avoid an automatic "yawn of cynicism," I do wish to suggest the need for some sharper critical thinking here.

A CREATIVE DREAM

Stephen Daldry's Oscar-nominated film *Billy Elliot* (2000) represents both the aspirations that are at stake in this emphasis on youthful creativity and some of its most telling limitations. It is, in many respects, a paradigmatic New Labour movie. Set against the backdrop of the miners' strike in the north of England in the mid-1980s, the film tells the story of its eponymous hero's efforts to overcome the constraints of his working-class upbringing and train as a ballet dancer. Dance is clearly seen here as a means of escape; and some of the most remarkable dance sequences in the film show Billy chafing against the frustrations imposed by the small mining town. He has to overcome the homophobic prejudices of his father and his older brother and their prejudice against the middle-class teacher who recognizes Billy's potential; and while both eventually come to support Billy, the working-class family (with the significant absence of the mother, who has died) is mainly depicted as violent, narrow-minded, and authoritarian. Billy finally escapes to the Royal Ballet School in London, and the closing scene shows him performing on the London stage in *Swan Lake* as his family looks on from the audience.

Throughout the film, Billy's father and brother are frequently seen on the picket line and in pitched battles with the police, although the motivations for the strike remain unexplained and the film's sympathies here are far from clear. However, the miners' strike is more than simply a backdrop to the story of Billy's discovery of his creative talents. In fact, there are striking parallels—reinforced by the script and the editing—between the two narratives. Billy's father goes back to work as a strikebreaker explicitly in order to "give the boy a chance" and earn some money for his education; as he announces to his fellow workers that Billy has been accepted by the Royal Ballet School, they inform him that the strike has collapsed; and the shots of Billy leaving for London are intercut with shots of the miners being shut in the cage and descending into the pit as they return to work. As Billy's individual escape attempt succeeds, so the struggles of organized labor are defeated: It is as if they are inversely related to each other. The individualistic story of salvation through art seems positively to require the negation of collective social movements. The working-class child can only succeed if he escapes from his origins; and in the process, those origins must be defined as merely damaging and worthless.

A CREATIVE STORY

Britain's culture minister, Chris Smith, is fond of telling a real-life story that has much in common with the fictional tale of Billy Elliot. The story is set on a so-called "socially excluded" estate in Bristol known as Hartcliffe, which (according to Smith) was transformed through the efforts of one teacher. Vic Ecclestone, a teacher in a local comprehensive, began working with a group of "difficult" boys on a dance project. The boys were initially resistant but eventually became very engaged with what they were doing. The project evolved into a performing group, which toured around the country and abroad; and the group's success in turn led to the regeneration of the whole community. Hartcliffe changed from being a place people were embarrassed to say where they came from to a place whose name was spoken with pride.

This story, or versions of it, has been told at numerous conferences; and it appears both in Chris Smith's book *Creative Britain* (136–37) and in a Policy Action Team report published by the Department of Culture, Media and Sport (DCMS) for the government's Social Exclusion Unit (27–28). The story exemplifies a belief in the transformative role of the arts—and particularly of creative *participation* in the arts—as a means of overcoming what the government now encourages us to call "social exclusion." To be sure, Smith's story is not as virulently individualistic as *Billy Elliot*. In this account, the arts function as a catalyst for other changes, not just in the individual but also in the wider society. Participation in the arts, it is argued, builds confidence and self-esteem, encourages personal growth, fosters social cohesion, improves educational achievement, and gives young people the skills they need for employment. In these ways, the arts can bring about the social and economic transformation of disadvantaged communities. As Smith would have it, "creativity will increasingly be the key to a country's cultural identity, to its economic success, and to individuals' well-being and sense of fulfillment" (quoted in DCMS 5).

I cannot vouch for the accuracy of the Hartcliffe story, although there is probably more to be told. My concern here is more with its political function and its consequences. Why is New Labour telling us this story about youthful creativity, and what political purposes does it serve? Why has creativity become such a prominent theme in current debates, not just about cultural policy but also in the wider educational and political arena? And how should those who work with young people—particularly in the field of arts education—respond?

As I have implied, this new emphasis on youthful creativity reflects a broader move toward democratization than is apparent in many other areas of Labour's cultural policy. It is an emphasis that is now being pursued in a whole range of funding policies and initiatives aimed at encouraging community-based grassroots arts projects, particularly in disadvantaged areas. Of course, gross inequalities in arts funding persist—as is most clearly represented by the controversies surrounding the funding of London's Royal Opera House. Yet at least on the level of rhetoric, New Labour has much less invested than the Conservatives in maintaining distinctions between high culture and popular culture. On the contrary, its key terms are those of access, inclusion, and diversity: Art, it argues, is for everyone, not just for the elite.

As the Hartcliffe story implies, culture and the arts appear to have been conscripted into a far-reaching—and broadly egalitarian—social and economic project. While I support these aims, I also fear that the appeal to "creativity" may come to function as a magical solution for a whole range of problems, particularly those that cluster around the real or imagined dangers of youth. These are problems which, in many other respects, the government seems either unable or unwilling to address, except by much more directly disciplinary means. There are significant tensions in this respect between the government's policy on culture and its policies on education, on criminal justice, and on welfare benefits. In this context, creativity becomes a kind of fairy dust: Sprinkle enough of it about and it will seem as though the world has been magically transformed. By contrast, I want to suggest that, if these new democratic emphases in cultural policy are to be sustained and implemented, they will need to find their counterparts in educational and social policy more broadly: There will need to be a more sustained and comprehensive effort to equalize opportunities, to reduce inequalities, and to support young people's attempts at self-expression—even if they result in dissidence and dissent.

DEFINING CREATIVITY

Smith's *Creative Britain* is one obvious point of reference here, but there are many others. In this chapter, I will also be referring to *The Creative Age* (Seltzer Bentley), published by the New Labour think tank Demos; the report *All Our Futures: Creativity, Culture and Education* (National Advisory Committee), (the so-called "Robinson Report") commissioned by the Department for Education and Employment (DfEE) in conjunction with the DCMS; and the most recent and far-reaching manifestation of this emphasis, the DCMS Green Paper *Culture and Creativity: The Next Ten Years*. This prominence of *creativ-*

ity in the speeches of a government minister, in the work of a leading think tank, and in a series of government-sponsored reports reflects a much wider emphasis in contemporary cultural and educational policy. Creativity is also part of the rationale for some of the government's more radical experiments in educational policy, such as Education Action Zones (Buckingham Jones), specialist schools and community-based learning centers. It is a key theme in documents on education produced by bodies like the Arts Council of England and the Royal Society of Arts (Bayliss) and in the educational rhetoric of key players in the cultural industries examples of the range are the filmmaker Lord (David) Puttnam (the first head of the General Teaching Council) to Greg Dyke, the director general of the BBC, and Gerry Robinson, chairman of the Arts Council of England and author of *The Creativity Imperative: Investing in the Arts in the 21st Century.*

Perhaps predictably, creativity is defined here in very diverse—and in some instances, very inclusive—ways. There is a general agreement that creativity is a good thing, and that we need lots more of it; but very few of these documents address in any detailed way how we might recognize creativity when we see it, how we might evaluate it, and how it might relate to the other qualities that might be involved in the arts or in learning. In some instances, creativity appears to be synonymous with the arts, but in others it is seen as a much wider phenomenon. For Smith, creativity is aligned with the "creative industries"— although this is itself a relatively inclusive notion, encompassing advertising and "designer fashion" alongside more traditional art forms. For Demos, however, creativity is defined much more broadly: It is "the application of knowledge and skills in new ways to achieve a valued goal" (Seltzer & Bentley 10). From this perspective, creativity is a matter of problem-solving, applying new knowledge to unfamiliar situations and a willingness to make mistakes in pursuit of a goal—qualities that are not at all confined to artistic activity, narrowly defined.

In the Robinson Report, there is a significant and unresolved tension between the narrower identification of creativity with the arts and the broader argument for creativity as a quality that should be developed right across the curriculum. Part of the report's aim is to reverse the marginalization of the arts in education that has been taking place in Britain over the past twenty years; but in doing so in the current political context, the report cannot be seen to be falling back on dangerously liberal or progressive ideas or simply arguing its position. The report is therefore torn between its defense of the arts and its argument that creativity is just as much an aspect of science subjects as it is of the arts. In its recognition of the need to bridge "the two cultures" and its acknowledgment of "multiple intelligences," this is a powerful argument (Gardner); but on another level, it could be seen to marginalize the arts still further. For if all curriculum subjects involve creativity, why do we need the creative arts at all? Significantly, some policymakers have argued that Robinson failed to go far enough in this direction and remained too arts-focused. While the Department for Education appears to be quite happy with generalized notions of creativity, it is still distinctly uneasy about the arts.

ACCESS AND INCLUSION

How are these ideas of youthful creativity currently being used in cultural and educational policy in the United Kingdom? In the following section of this chapter, I want to focus on key aspects of this new agenda and to indicate some of the problems with each of them.

The idea that creativity provides a means of overcoming "social exclusion" and providing "access" for disadvantaged groups. As my quotation marks imply, there is much to be said about the political work such terms perform. As Norman Fairclough argues in *New Labour, New Language* (2000), to talk about "social exclusion" rather than inequality is to engage in a kind of euphemism—albeit one which slips back into a deficit model of the poor. The "socially excluded" are somehow seen to be lacking in social networks and in meaningful social interaction: They simply don't go to the right parties. By extension, they are also often seen to be morally and psychologically inadequate. They lack "self-esteem" and the resources for "personal growth." In the words of the architect of New Labour, Peter Mandelson, they are "cut off from what the rest of us regard as normal life" (quoted in Fairclough 52).

One consequence of this shift in terminology, according to Fairclough, is that social policy comes to be seen as a *choice* between longer-term measures to alleviate poverty—such as redistributing wealth—and short-term measures that appear to "tackle social exclusion." This is a particular danger for community arts projects aimed at young people: As Sara Selwood has argued, such projects can serve merely as "a form of temporary social service for young people who are disadvantaged or 'excluded'" (337). Even more cynically, creativity could be seen here as a way of coping with the threat of the underclass—a way of deflecting potential opposition or unrest into activities that are believed to be less challenging to the social order.

The majority of policy documents in this field do not overtly subscribe to this time-honored view of cultural activity as a kind of psychological safety valve. Nevertheless, there is a recurrent view of participation in the arts as an essentially neutral good. Like Ambrosia, the arts will spread harmony and enlightenment. Creativity, it would seem, somehow automatically makes you a better person. From this perspective, it seems almost perverse to insist that the arts and culture are inevitably tied to social interests or to the operation of social power—or indeed to point out that they often possess a conflictual or critical edge.

More specifically, one might wish to question whether involvement in the arts is actually capable of delivering these broader social goals. In practice, the Labour government has achieved very little in addressing fundamental inequalities; the gap between rich and poor in Britain is widening, and poverty is rising, particularly among children and young people. At the very least, involvement in the arts is unlikely to make much difference to these things unless it is combined with rather more fundamental policies that reduce inequalities of income and extend social welfare rather than seeking to undermine it. In this respect, we also need to consider the different meanings and consequences of "access." Different social groups clearly stand to benefit in very different ways from their involvement in the arts—in what they do with the opportunity, in how they are able to capitalize and build upon it, and in potential outcomes. The meaning of *access* will vary significantly with people's existing social, educational, and cultural capital. It is not enough simply to provide equality of opportunity, without also addressing the inequalities that people bring to their involvement in the arts in the first place.

CREATIVITY AND COMMERCE

Cutting across this broadly democratic emphasis on access and inclusion is another key emphasis—on the economic value of culture and creativity. Chris Smith, for example, is eager to emphasize the growing economic value of the cultural industries—they apparently generate £50 billion of economic activity every year, amounting to 4 percent of Gross Domestic Product—and their role in securing Britain's economic competitiveness in world markets. Britain, it is proclaimed, leads the world in areas such as fashion and computer games design (Smith 31–33). These arguments reflect a series of slippages that are characteristic of New Labour's economic rhetoric (Fairclough). The "national" interest seems to be indivisible from the interests of businesses—indeed, of the *multi-national* companies who are, after all, the organizations that largely own and control the cultural industries. Here, as in much New Labour policy, the neoliberal economic order seems to be taken as given: The only question that remains is how well "we" can compete within it.

In some ways, Smith is right to reject a puritanical distinction between culture and commerce. Historically, it is impossible to identify a time when artistic or cultural production was *not* tied up with the operations of the market or with the economic power of particular social classes, for example via systems of artistic patronage. Yet while culture and commerce are inextricably entwined, they have also been in some fundamental respects opposed. At least since the Romantics, the arts have been a vantage point from which people have criticized the imperatives of business. In practice, the market may have a certain economic interest in cultural diversity; but in promoting the arts as simply another business, it may prove unwilling to permit more fundamental forms of opposition.

In fact, there has been a significant escalation in the scale of commercial involvement in the arts over recent years. In *No Logo* Naomi Klein, for example, points to the ways in which commercial interests have increasingly penetrated so many areas of social and cultural life—not least education and youth culture itself. Klein argues that contemporary capitalism is no longer about advertising, or even sponsorship, but about branding, a much more invasive form of promotional culture that has become almost impossible to avoid. To say the least, there is a striking contrast between this view of the new economic order and New Labour's emphasis on public–private partnerships, in which commercial involvement is increasingly seen as the solution in every area of social policy, from education to transport to cultural activity.

What appears to be emerging here is a new educational-cultural complex, which (like the military-industrial one) is largely dominated by global economic forces. For arts education practitioners, this frequently results in some awkward questions about where we draw the line. One of the problems with public-private partnerships is that the public has for so long been deprived of adequate funding that it tends to roll over obediently when the possibility of commercial sponsorship comes along. It is clear what commercial corporations gain from sponsoring the arts, particularly if they are connected with the disadvantaged: In addition to the feel-good factor of being seen to be socially responsible, they are simultaneously managing to implant their brand in the consciousness of consumers (particularly young people, who are one of the most difficult markets to reach). The more awkward issue here has to do with what public institutions—educational or community arts organizations, for example—get in return. While it would be unduly purist to reject such partnerships outright, one could certainly urge public organizations to drive a much harder bargain than they often do.

CREATIVITY AND EMPLOYMENT

These last two themes come together in a third key emphasis, which is the notion of creativity as a central skill or requirement for the world of work. This is most strongly articulated in Demos's *Creative Age* (Seltzer & Bentley), but it is also a key emphasis for Chris Smith and the DCMS Green Paper. It is argued that involvement in the creative arts will equip young people with the skills they need for jobs, not only in the expanding cultural industries but also in the economy more broadly. Paid employment is seen to be the most significant and lasting way to tackle social exclusion. The assumption here, of course, is that unemployment (or underemployment) is a consequence of a skills shortage, or at least a failure to match the available labor with the available jobs. The argument assumes that there can and will be meaningful jobs for all, and it fails to take account of those among the "socially excluded" who, for various reasons, may never be able to enter paid employment.

At the same time, there is an argument here about the *kinds* of work people will be doing. In the new global economy—the so-called "knowledge economy"—creativity is seen as a necessity for the workforce. The economy, it is argued, no longer needs wage slaves or hired hands. On the contrary, according to Charles Leadbeater in *Living on Thin Air: The New Economy*, it needs free-thinking, problem-solving entrepreneurs—flexible, creative thinkers who can respond quickly to an ever-changing economic and cultural environment. This is a vision of a largely casualized workforce, of outsourcing and "portfolio careers." Workers must be responsible for developing and updating their own skills; they must be prepared to be mobile and to "make their own careers." In this new ideological definition of work in advanced capitalist economies, conflicts between those who own the means of production and those who work for them have all but disappeared.

But *whose* work does this vision actually describe? Ultimately, the notion of "creative entrepreneurship" is only ever likely to apply to a small proportion of the workforce and to certain categories of workers. What for some may prove to be a productive environment of creative flexibility for others is simply a recipe for insecure and poorly paid employment on the margins of the service economy. More specifically, there is little evidence that involvement in the creative arts actually results in "socially excluded" young people becoming more employable or gaining skills that they can trade in on the job market. In the area of media, for example, new digital technologies are frequently seen to offer great new opportunities for disadvantaged young people: The creative skills they develop through their own leisure uses of these media (for example, in playing and creating computer games) are, it is argued, precisely the skills that are needed at the cutting edge of the industry. This is largely wishful thinking. There are certainly some instances of digital "rags to riches" stories, but they are by definition unrepresentative (Schon et al.). Evidence from surveys suggests that the majority of young people who enter employment in the media industries do so by virtue of social contacts and are effectively working for nothing or relying on a private income (British Film Institute).

This relates back to the question of access. Under certain circumstances, the "informal" cultural competencies that are developed in youth cultures can become a valuable commodity in some areas of the employment market. But it is much harder to trade in this form of cultural capital if you do not also have social capital (that is, contacts and particular kinds of "social skills") and a certain degree of formal educational capital (such as a degree of literacy) as well. Again, these resources are much more available to some social groups than to others.

CREATIVITY AND EDUCATION

Education is, of course, a key theme in this debate. For Smith, education in the arts is a crucial guarantee of access and participation in the cultural democracy he seeks. "Nurturing the spark of creativity" through education is, he argues, important both for individual fulfillment and for "our economic success as a country" as well (33). For Demos, the primary emphasis here is on "learning beyond the classroom," outside formal education (Bentley); while the Robinson Report and the DCMS Green Paper attempt to carry this through in terms of the curriculum in schools and in calling for "creative partnerships" between schools and cultural institutions of various kinds.

Nevertheless, an emphasis on creativity would seem to be strikingly at odds with the general direction of British education policy, which appears ever more insistent on the maintenance of narrowly defined academic "standards." The apparent neglect or marginalization of the Robinson Report is quite revealing in this respect. Copies of the summary report were not sent out to schools, and there are as yet few signs of implementation, particularly when compared with one of the government's parallel initiatives on citizenship education. There may in fact be several reasons for this: The report itself is perhaps overlong, and it has far too many recommendations. Government representatives have typically dismissed it as "politically clumsy." Yet the key problem with the report is that many of its arguments are quite at odds with New Labour's education policy. Among other things, the report calls for a slimming down of the national curriculum, a reduction in national testing, and significant limitations on the powers of school inspectors. It argues for much greater trust to be placed in teachers and for them to be given greater freedom to experiment, rather than simply to "deliver" a given curriculum. Implicitly, however, the report is rather pessimistic about the likelihood of these things coming to pass: The notion that the arts might be a guaranteed educational entitlement for all children in schools is something it implicitly seems to regard as somewhat utopian. (For a fuller discussion of the report, see Buckingham & Jones.)

"Creativity," then, seems quite at odds with the government's growing obsession with the measurement of performance and its ever-narrowing conception of what counts as valid learning in schools. Yet these emphases in educational policy are merely part of a more general disciplinary emphasis in social policy relating to children and young people. The authoritarian crackdown on youth crime, the implementation of curfews, the lowering of the age of criminal responsibility, the withdrawal of social security benefits for sixteen- and seventeen-year-olds, the end of free higher education—these and other developments are quite contrary to the culturalist rhetoric of access and empowerment, and indeed to the celebration of the "young country." Meanwhile, there is a growing "curricularization" of children's leisure through homework clubs and summer universities. It is as though education has come to be seen as the *work* of childhood, and it cannot be allowed to stop once children walk out the classroom door. Idle hands must be kept busy, lest they cause trouble for the rest of us.

If creativity is genuinely an imperative, cultural policy clearly needs to be aligned with these other areas of social policy. Without policies that provide resources and support for young people, that permit a culture of dissent and debate—and even tolerate some apparently "antisocial" behaviors—creativity will be little more than the icing on the cake.

CONCEPTUALIZING "YOUTH"

If *creativity* and *culture* are somewhat loosely defined throughout these debates, so too is notion of youth. This is partly a question of where youth begins
and ends. In the United Kingdom, a growing number of young people are now
choosing (or being forced) to stay living with their parents, not least as a result
of the demise of student grants. Within some areas of European social policy,
"youth" appears to last until the age of twenty-five, or even thirty. Meanwhile,
market pressures have been seen to push the "end of childhood" ever earlier:
children's television programs, magazines, and pop music have increasingly
taken on the characteristics of "youth"—or at least "teenage"—media. Youth
has become a symbolic commodity that can be used to market a whole range of
goods to those who fall well outside its generally accepted biological boundaries: "Youth" sells to fifty-something rock fans, just as it does to prepubescent
followers of the boy bands.

More significant, perhaps, is the issue of how particular values come to be associated with youth. In this instance, the positive valence of youth in New
Labour's cultural policy could be seen to reflect a necessary repression of its opposite—the figure of the troublesome, antisocial (working-class, male) youth.
The kids are all right, it would seem, only as long as their energies are channeled in responsibly "creative" directions.

In fact, there is a notable parallel here between the ambivalent reinvention of
youth in cultural policy and the reconceptualization that has taken place within
academic research. Broadly speaking, mainstream research on youth culture
has tended to reinforce the dominant definition of youth as a "problem," and
whether that problem has been seen to be social or psychological in origin, the
implicit solution has generally been to call for increases in state regulation
(Griffin). By contrast, cultural studies research has increasingly emphasized the
opposite side of the coin, depicting young people as an inherently progressive
social force and emphasizing the implicit and explicit ideological "resistances"
of the more "spectacular" forms of youth culture. This shift toward a more celebratory stance is particularly marked in the work of Paul Willis. To compare,
for example, Willis's *Learning to Labour* with his *Common Culture* provides a
clear indication of some very fundamental changes. In place of the broadly Al-
thusserian account of ideological reproduction that characterized the earlier
book, the emphasis in *Common Culture* is on young people's autonomy and
freedom. Young people are no longer seen here as passive "dupes" of ideology
who simply accept the social roles that are imposed upon them. On the contrary, the emphasis is on what Willis terms the "symbolic creativity" of young
people's appropriations of popular cultural forms.

Willis's work is particularly notable in this context because of its influence
on cultural policy. The work represented in *Common Culture* was undertaken
as part of a "Commission of Enquiry" into youth culture under the auspices of
a leading United Kingdom arts funder, the Calouste Gulbenkian Foundation

(Willis *Moving Culture*). It is this that accounts for the book's somewhat combative stance toward "elite" art forms and its enthusiastic celebration of the creativity of "everyday" cultural practices such as watching television, listening to music, and even hanging out in pubs. In a direct affront to what he calls "old-fashioned Marxist rectitudes," Willis argues that it is through "the commercial provision of cultural commodities" rather than through the official institutions of "high art" that "the main seeds for everyday cultural development" are to be found. While Willis's arguments can hardly be said to have unsettled the traditional elitism of arts funding, they have certainly influenced the development of policies on youth arts and on access to the arts more generally (for instance, in the case of schemes such as the Arts Council's "Arts for Everyone" and "New Audiences").

Yet, as I have argued elsewhere ("Re-reading" 203–8), *Common Culture* is characterized by a kind of "morale-boosting" rhetoric about youth that seems strangely at odds with the political context in which it was written—in effect, at the peak of Thatcherism. With the Left in retreat, and class politics implicitly abandoned, "youth" becomes the vehicle for a whole range of frustrated aspirations. In the process, youth comes to be conceived as a homogeneous category, and youth culture as automatically politically "progressive."

More recent work on youth culture has sought to move beyond this approach and the vestiges of the "Birmingham tradition" from which it derives. Work on popular music has begun to undermine what might be termed the "myth of authenticity" that informs much youth culture research. The notion of "repressive tolerance"—that the expression of authentic needs (whether by producers or consumers) has been systematically distorted and exploited by the profit motive—has become ever harder to sustain in the wake of empirical study, for example on the origins of genres such as acid house or punk (Redhead). Researchers have acknowledged that "needs" and "authentic expressions" are themselves defined and constructed in discourse—not only in media discourse, but also in the discourse of individual "consumers" (Widdicombe Woofitt). Youth culture is not a force outside the market but is inextricably connected with it and it operates its own (class and gender-based) hierarchies that significantly undermine generalized definitions of "youth" as a homogeneous category (Thornton). The beginnings of this new paradigm in youth culture research begin to point beyond the easy celebration that characterizes the work of Willis and others—and indeed, some of the arguments of would-be policymakers.

FROM POLICY TO PRACTICE

For all its problems, the new emphasis on youthful creativity I have discussed in this chapter represents an important opportunity. There is an emerging rhetoric here that can be used to good effect. Nevertheless, it is important to be realistic about what can possibly be achieved. This will require a certain amount of self-examination among arts education practitioners—a degree of clarity and rigor about the aims of the work and about its effectiveness.

Of course, there is a long history of practice in this field. Despite the claims of novelty in some of the policy discourse, attempts to engage young people in the creative arts (and particularly disadvantaged young people) did not begin last week or last year. Nevertheless, as the sector expands, many new people will be getting in on the act, and not all of them will know what they are doing or why they are doing it. Quite correctly, evaluation has become a key issue in arts funding policies; and there are genuine questions about the quality of what is provided and the quality of the learning young people are experiencing that urgently need to be addressed (Woolf). This will necessarily involve a rather more rigorous idea of what might count as evidence and of how we might establish and prove some of the assertions we might wish to make about the effects of participation in the arts.

In terms of practice, the main danger here is that all sorts of promises are made which simply cannot be delivered—and that creative participation in the arts will be seen to have a power that is much greater than it can ever possess. If we are genuinely interested in tackling social exclusion or inequality, the arts can be only one part of a much broader strategy; and without that broader strategy, cultural activity may well remain quite superficial and tokenistic. Meanwhile, it is vital that those involved in arts education—particularly in the informal or community sector—begin to articulate what they need if these claims are to be fulfilled, such as long-term funding, adequate salaries and employment conditions, training and opportunities for in-depth evaluation—and indeed greater accountability in arts funding itself.

WORKS CITED

Arts Council of England. *Leading Through Learning*. London: Arts Council, 1998.

Bayliss, Valerie. *Opening Minds: Education for the 21st Century*. London: Royal Society of Arts, 1999.

Bentley, Tom. *Learning Beyond the Classroom*. London: Routledge, 1998.

Billy Elliot. Dir. Stephen Daldry. Universal, 2000.

Blair, Tony. *New Britain: My Vision of a Young Country*. London: Fourth Estate, 1996.

British Film Institute. *Media Industries Tracking Study Report*. London: British Film Institute, 1998.

Buckingham, David. "Re-reading audiences." *Reading Audiences: Young People and the Media*, ed. David Buckingham. Manchester, Eng.: Manchester University Press, 1993, 202–18.

Buckingham, David, and Ken Jones. "New Labour's Cultural Turn: Some Tensions in Contemporary Educational and Cultural Policy." *Journal of Education Policy* 16, 1 (2001): 1–14.

Department of Culture, Media and Sport. *Culture and Creativity: The Next Ten Years*. London: Department of Culture, Media and Sport, 2001.

Fairclough, Norman. *New Labour, New Language.* London, Routledge 2000.

Gardner, Howard. *Multiple Intelligences: The Theory in Practice.* New York: Basic Books, 1993.

Griffin, Christine. *Representations of Youth.* Cambridge, Eng.: Polity, 1993.

Klein, Naomi *No Logo.* London: Flamingo, 2000.

Leadbeater, Charles. *Living on Thin Air: The New Economy.* London: Penguin, 1999.

National Advisory Committee on Creative and Cultural Education (NACCCE). *All Our Futures: Creativity, Culture and Education.* London: Department for Education and Employment/Department of Culture, Media and Sport, 1999.

Policy Action Team 10. *The Arts and Sport: A Report to the Social Exclusion Unit.* London: Department of Culture, Media and Sport, 1999.

Redhead, Steve. *The End-of-the-Century Party.* Manchester, Eng.: Manchester University Press, 1990.

Robinson, Gerry. *The Creativity Imperative: Investing in the Arts in the 21st Century.* London: Arts Council of England, 2000.

Schon, Donald, et al., eds. *High Technology and Low Income Communities.* Cambridge, MA: MIT Press, 1999.

Seltzer, Kimberley, and Tom Bentley. *The Creative Age.* London: Demos, 1999.

Selwood, Sara. "Cultural Policy and Young People's Participation in the Visual Arts." *Journal of Art and Design Education* 16, 3 (1997): 333–40.

Smith, Chris. *Creative Britain.* London: Faber, 1998.

Thornton, Sarah. *Club Cultures.* Cambridge, Eng.: Polity, 1995.

Widdicombe, Sue, and Robin Woofitt. *The Language of Youth Subcultures.* Brighton, Eng.: Harvester, 1995.

Willis, Paul. *Common Culture.* Milton Keynes, Eng.: Open University Press, 1990.

———. *Learning to Labour.* Farnborough, Eng.: Saxon House, 1977.

———. *Moving Culture.* London: Calouste Gulbenkian Foundation, 1990.

Woolf, Felicity. *Partnerships for Learning: A Guide to Evaluating Arts Education Projects.* London: Regional Arts Boards and the Arts Council of England, 1999.

Wright, Patrick. *On Living in an Old Country: The National Past in Contemporary Britain.* London: Verso, 1985.

8

The Unheimlich Maneuver:
Uncanny Domesticity in the Urban Waif Tale

Claudia Nelson

In 1866 Hesba Stretton published *Jessica's First Prayer*, the tale of a London street child who befriends an unsympathetic coffee seller known to her as Mr. Daniel. Simultaneously a representative of bourgeois respectability and a man characterized by his "mysterious and fugitive air ... as if he dreaded observation" (403), Daniel eventually raises Jessica to the bourgeoisie while she strips him of his secrecy and brings him, unwittingly, to God. Among the most popular fictions of its century, *Jessica's First Prayer* "sold over two million copies and was translated into fifteen European and Asiatic languages," reports Lance Salway (35); Czar Alexander III, Leslie Howsam adds, made it required reading in Russian schools (289). It also inaugurated a new genre. Waif tales by Stretton herself and by imitators such as Mrs. O. F. Walton (*A Peep Behind the Scenes* [1877], *Christie's Old Organ* [1882]) and "Brenda" (*Froggy's Little Brother* [1875]) proliferated in the late nineteenth century, manipulating the conventions of sentimentality in an effort to enact emotional and social change.

Peter Hunt contends that within children's literature, "There are 'live' books and 'dead' books, books which no longer concern their primary audience (and [which] concern no-one else except historians)" (200); by Hunt's standards, *Jessica's First Prayer* and its Victorian successors belong to the latter category. But those interested in contemporary adolescent fiction should nonetheless care about Stretton's narrative, if only as influential forerunner: The genre of the waif tale is by no means moribund. Representative titles from the 1990s include, for instance, Paula Fox's *Monkey Island* (1991), in which an eleven-year-old, once comfortably off, is abandoned in a Manhattan welfare hotel by his pregnant mother; Theresa Nelson's *Beggar's Ride* (1992), in which a girl sexually abused by her mother's boyfriend flees to the comradeship of a gang of homeless youths in Atlantic City; Terence Blacker's *Homebird* (1993), in which a middle-class British teenager devastated by his parents' incipient divorce runs away to live in a squat; Russell Banks's *Rule of the Bone* (1995), in which the drugged-out but abused narrator's mother and stepfather throw him out of their trailer in upstate New York; and Beverley Naidoo's *No Turning Back* (1995), in which a twelve-year-old Johannesburg black with a violent stepfather bounces from the streets to the home of a white shopkeeper to a shelter. All these novels—and many others that resemble them generically—share with their Victorian forebears the assumption that the social problem of the homeless teenager is really the domestic problem of the failed parent. Like Stretton's Jessica, daughter of an alcoholic actress who has rejected her maternal responsibilities (and who seeks to torpedo Jessica and Daniel's domestic idyll in the 1904 sequel), the teenagers in these texts have parents who see them not as children to be nurtured but as prey.

In their characteristic insistence that their protagonists are not merely lacking homes but escaping them, traumatized and angry even as they seek to construct homes of their own, novels about homeless children often manipulate what Freud identifies as the tension between the *Heimlich* and the *Unheimlich*—the domestic versus the antidomestic, the knowable versus what must be repressed.[1] This preoccupation, I argue, is one that contemporary fiction for young adults, particularly fiction emanating from Britain and the Commonwealth, has inherited from the Victorian waif tale.[2] The uses to which the tension is typically put have changed over time, perhaps; the evangelicalism of *Jessica's First Prayer* has given way to a more secular brand of social criticism. Yet today as in the past, narratives that ostensibly indict the social conditions that permit homeless children employ the uncanny to suggest that the ultimate culprit is a parental (or quasi-parental) inability to nurture, or indeed to tolerate, the young. On one level, *Jessica's First Prayer* may be seen as a psychological mystery story revolving around shame, horror, and identity and full of anxieties that can be resolved only by Mr. Daniel's unlikely transformation into benevolent father. This fascination with simulacra and substitutes, particularly those blurring the boundaries between reality and artifice, emotional life and emotional deadness, is crucial to the uncanny; as Elizabeth Elam Roth puts it, Freud's admiration for E. T. A. Hoffmann's mastery of the uncanny grows out of Hoffmann's ability to cast "into doubt the humanity of lifesize, animated beings" (39). But it is also crucial to the urban waif tale from its inception onward, since a preoccupation of the genre is to cause readers to question the humanity of the "lifesize, animated beings" called mothers and fathers.

To illustrate this argument and thus to delineate a generic convention that may not be immediately apparent, the present chapter juxtaposes Stretton's tract with three urban waif tales from another historical moment: Robert Swindells's Carnegie Medal thriller *Stone Cold* (1993), Melvin Burgess's dystopian fantasy *The Baby and Fly Pie* (also shortlisted for the Carnegie in 1993), and an Australian example, Libby Hathorn's *Feral Kid* (1994). All four emphasize such aspects of the uncanny as horror and its repression, doubling, and what Freud calls "intrauterine" (womblike) space (244). But more specifically, these texts also use the uncanny to deconstruct the domestic myth and to identify displaced youths as refugees from monstrous homes. *Jessica's First Prayer* and *Stone Cold* employ contrasting yet complementary conceptions of fatherhood—in one case a fatherhood flawed by its difference from childhood, in the other a fatherhood whose danger lies in its perverse kinship with the adolescence it menaces. *The Baby and Fly Pie* hinges upon its protagonists' inability to recognize the unmotherliness of mothers. And the title character of *Feral Kid* experiences a series of inadequate parents of both genders before he leaves the city, apparently to make common cause with a foster grandmother. In each case, the horror at the heart of the fiction is ultimately a family horror.

In Freud's 1919 essay "The 'Uncanny,'" he defines the *Unheimlich*, or uncanny, as "that class of the frightening which leads back to what is known of old and long familiar" (220). This definition draws on the complex of meanings assigned to the German word *Heimlich*, which can signify both "familiar, homely, pleasantly domestic" and "concealed, kept from sight, withheld from others" (222–23). Thus *Heimlich* and *Unheimlich*, the domestic and the uncanny, overlap: "*Heimlich* is a word the meaning of which develops in the direction of ambivalence, until it finally coincides with its opposite, *unheimlich*" (226). What is ultimately most frightening and *Unheimlich* is what is most intimate and personal; we repress some private fear or desire and are subsequently horrified to encounter it as something exterior to ourselves, "a doubling, dividing and interchanging of the self" (234). But while Freud emphasizes the *Unheimlich*'s connection to the maternal, Carol Clover has noted of slasher films that the *Unheimlich* is often "decidedly androgynous: Female/feminine in aspects of character and place (the 'intra-uterine' locale) but male in anatomy" (215). And indeed, in both Victorian and contemporary fictions, secrets manage to be at once male and female, paternal and daughterly, inside and outside the social order. Such ambiguities, it seems, are central to repression.

Repression, in turn, drives the narratives discussed here. In *Jessica's First Prayer*, it is the repression of self that Stretton criticizes. Here Mr. Daniel—whose real surname is Standring but who, like many denizens of waif tales, hesitates to divulge his true identity—is concealing his proprietorship of a coffee stall, a business he considers incompatible with his more respectable work as chapel-keeper. Jessica is associated with the stall, since it is there that she has bonded with Mr. Daniel, who sometimes grudgingly gives her coffee and stale buns. In her filthy rags, Jessica embodies for Daniel his own "unrespectable" behavior in secretly managing the stall: The proper middle-class adult male can be doubled by the improper and destitute girl child. Thus, when he sees her at the chapel, a blatant contrast to the fashionable people with whom he would like to associate, the experience is horrifying to him: "His grave face grew ghastly pale, and he laid his hand upon the door to support himself until he could recover his speech and senses.... [He] hovered about a good deal, with an air of uneasiness and displeasure" (414). Hitherto *Heimlich* in the sense that she has been concealed, Jessica now confronts her double in an uncanny way as a living reminder of his secret shame.

Nor does Jessica embody the repressed for Daniel alone. Although it is impossible to make her respectable by giving her new clothing or sending her to school, as her mother would pawn the one and forbid the latter, Jessica is lent, for churchgoing purposes only, "a little cloak and bonnet, which had once belonged to the minister's elder daughter" so that she will have "a somewhat more respectable appearance in the eyes of the congregation" (420). In her natural state, that is, she is a figure too horrifying to view, a reminder of social realities that "nice" people prefer to forget. J. S. Bratton suggests that Stretton identifies with Jessica, since while living in Manchester the author "had felt herself on the brink of social extinction, living in squalid lodgings, with no settled income, and cut off from the protection of her home community" and "had regularly attended a chapel for over a year before anyone there condescended to speak to" her (86). Whether or not Jessica is a downmarket double of her creator, the child's outcast state is insisted upon; she disturbs even the minister's small daughter, who is "anxious about her behavior, and ... [makes] energetic signs to her when to stand up and when to kneel" (414).

But one sign of Jessica's virtue is that as an outcast, she has nonetheless internalized the values of her society—even though Stretton identifies these values as false. She assents to her own repression because, like the middle-class pharisees who surround her, she equates respectability and virtue. As she remarks to Daniel early in their acquaintance, "I've been watching you hundreds of times afore you saw me, and the police leaves you alone, and never tells you to move on. Oh, yes! you must be a very good man" (406). Just as the main function of both coffee stall and chapel-keeping for Daniel is to provide him with money (the sign of respectability, if not necessarily of godliness), Jessica's lack of funds and status makes her socially threatening to representatives of the middle class. Understanding and even sharing their anxiety, she is willing to efface herself, forbearing to beg and coming to the stall only at negotiated intervals.

Still, Stretton's ultimate point, of course, is that the universal disapproval of Jessica is ill founded; the Victorian emphasis on respectability threatens to repress Christianity itself. The faith that Jessica develops as soon as she encounters religion illuminates the hypocrisy and concern for appearances that characterizes everyone else in the story except the minister's younger daughter (who has not yet learned propriety) and the minister himself. And at that, as Daniel remarks, the minister is less gifted than Jessica at saving souls: "You're ... a great preacher, and many people flock to hear you ... but all the while, hearkening to you every blessed Sabbath, I was losing my soul, and you never once said to me, though you saw me scores and scores of times, 'Standring, are you a saved man?'" (423). It is Jessica, not the worthy minister, who brings Daniel to Christ; in other words, it is the repressed, the secret, the apparent enemy of what is cozy and domestic (*Heimlich*) in Victorian society that is ultimately most valuable, outshining even the good father. In a reversal of the usual Victorian gendering of public and private spheres, Jessica is associated with the streets and with the more overtly commercial of Daniel's businesses. Normally, Victorian texts code the home as virtuous and the marketplace as fallen; yet when we discover her lying "upon a scanty litter of straw" in a stable (421), we realize that this dwelling has sacred meaning precisely because it is a stable and not a home. Finally Jessica is "public" in a positive sense: She represents values of which all can, and should, partake. Daniel learns to function rightly (as opposed to respectably) only when he learns to accept, rather than repress, Jessica's *Unheimlich* virtues, welcoming them into his home by adopting her as his daughter. To become worthy, the home must embrace the street, since excessive privacy (*Heimlichkeit*) is cold and sterile.

If *Jessica's First Prayer* critiques Daniel's repression of self, in *Stone Cold* it is most obviously the repression of others that is at issue. Like Stretton's tale, *Stone Cold* focuses on the bond between a homeless child in London (here, a boy who calls himself Link) and a mysterious representative of "respectability" (a man who calls himself Shelter). But the connection between Link and Shelter is more sinister than that between Jessica and Daniel, since Shelter's interest in teenage waifs is in making them "respectable" by killing them, giving them army haircuts and military-surplus boots and stowing them where they will be off the streets forever. As he puts it, his "mission" is to "clean up the garbage," to remove the "dossers and junkies and drunks" who are dragging down the country (12). What is to be repressed, in other words, is weakness, slackness, and human frailty, traits to which Shelter considers himself immune even though the army has discharged him "on medical grounds"—presumably because of his mental instability.

Shelter's repressiveness is the central crime of the novel, but Swindells also presents it as an exaggeration of traits already "normally" present in both an uncaring society and an untenable foster father–son relationship: Vince, Link's mother's boyfriend, has forced him from the house by accusing him of parasitism and delinquency, precisely the charges that Shelter levels against his "recruits" before he murders them (5–6). Just as Shelter may hate and fear his victims because they embody a vulnerability he cannot bear to recognize in himself, Vince seems threatened by the oedipal attachment between Link and his mother and seeks to destroy it by replacing it with new sexual content. As Link explains, "the one thing that really bugs me is the way he leers at Mum and comes out with this very suggestive stuff about going to bed and rounding off a decent night. In all the years Dad was with us, I never once knew him to mention sex in my hearing, or even hint at it. This slob leers and winks and nudges with one eye on me to see how I'm taking it.... It makes me puke" (4).

Vince's crime, in short, is less that he has replaced dad (who eloped with a receptionist when Link was fourteen) than that he has replaced Link and his sister, distracting their mother's attention and using sexuality to oust them from their home. In a sense, then, he is Link's double, functioning, as Roth comments of the double within the Freudian uncanny, "to retard and impoverish the ego's development" (42). The same might be said of Shelter and his seven "recruits," for if Shelter's animosity toward street waifs partly arises from their difference from himself (they are undisciplined, untidy, *unheimisch* [threatening, uncanny, sinister]), it also arises from his repressed awareness of their kinship to him. When he recalls his career as a master sergeant who "turn[ed] dirty, scruffy, pimply youths into soldiers. Into men" (11), we understand that he spent his professional life transforming living recruits into simulacra of himself and now spends his retirement doing the same to the bodies in his collection. As Link realizes during the final horrific confrontation, in which Shelter introduces him to his decaying victims before trying to garrote him, "He'd done something to their heads—they were all like his" (127).

Indeed, Shelter and his victims share more than a haircut. He too is resentfully jobless, expelled from his "home" in the army and forced into idleness; he too jettisons his real name for his operations on the street; he too is an element that society would like to repress. What Link remarks of himself is equally true of Shelter: Passers-by "don't want to think about me. They don't like reminding I exist. Me, and those like me. We're living proof that everything's not all right and we make the place untidy" (1). Link sardonically calls himself a "serial killer" because he fantasizes about murdering men who have offended him (40). Moreover, like Stretton's Jessica, he internalizes the views of himself that impel Shelter's hatred: "*I* wouldn't have hired me" (78). If, as Freud remarks, madness is uncanny because it forces the observer to recognize the madness "in remote corners of his own being" (243), Shelter's psychopathology and Link's status as "some sort of freak" (94) draw them together—and their first-person narration forces the reader into the equation as well.[3]

The uncanny normality of madness becomes the more apparent because the crime site here is not the street but the home. Shelter disposes of most of his victims in a manner that is *unheimisch* because it is *heimisch*: Masquerading as a do-gooder, he invites them in for a bath, a change of clothes, a meal, lets them stroke his cat—"A cat speaks of warmth, comfort, placid domesticity," he notes (16)—and fractures their skulls as they drink soup on the sofa. He then disposes of the bodies in a cozy space under the floor, the kind of *Heimlich/Unheimlich* place that represents for Freud the "intrauterine," commenting paternally that he is granting them "an end to hunger and a roof over their heads.... I sometimes think I spoil 'em" (101). On the one hand, Shelter is a professional father whose insanity restates in exaggerated form the ukases that "normal" fathers traditionally issue their adolescent offspring: Cut your hair, take a bath, wear appropriate clothing, don't make noise, stay home at night. On the other, as his womblike crypt and obsessive housekeeping signal, his success as mass murderer depends upon his ability to masquerade as male mother. To lull his victims into trusting him, he poses as fond cat owner; Link (who is himself feminized by his long hair and nails as well as by his vulnerability) looks on contemptuously as Shelter "cradle[s the cat] in his arms, crooning. Rock[s] it like a baby ... the great soft noodle" (123). Unaware of his danger, the prospective "recruit" dismisses his stalker as "what my granddad used to call a Mary Ellen—the sort of man who wears frilly aprons around the house and may be seen in the garden, pegging out clothes" (125). What Clover identifies as the androgyny of the *Unheimlich* is here characterized as lethal.

Shelter makes a conscious effort not to follow a pattern in his murders, since consistency makes detection easier; thus he targets girls and Afro-Caribbeans as well as white males. Nevertheless, his victims are not merely all homeless, they are also all young, in their late teens or early twenties. The age difference between the forty-seven-year-old killer and his monstrous progeny, the corpses he (re)produces, reaffirms a theme prominent throughout the narrative, namely that parents cannot be trusted. Indeed, all Link's relationships with members of the older generation end in their betrayal of him: His father's desertion sabotages his academic performance and leaves the family vulnerable to Vince; his mother, once "wrapped up in her family" and "always there when you needed her" (4) doesn't stick up for him against Vince's aggression (6); his "girlfriend," Gail, turns out not to be the runaway she has posed as but an adult reporter working undercover on a story about homeless youth. Link's near-fatal encounter with Shelter is merely the most dramatic moment in a series in which he is always cast as the deceived, the patsy, the expendable one. As he points out, in the end he is still homeless. Unlike Stretton, Swindells suggests that the family cannot be recuperated.

The question of whether a viable family may be constructed also underlies *The Baby and Fly Pie*. Burgess's alternative-reality novel postulates a world in which the welfare state has vanished, leaving behind an underclass that supports itself in various shady ways. That the poor will abandon their children is taken for granted. Waifs must either scratch a living on the streets, where police may summarily execute them, or be enslaved by women known as Mothers, who provide food and shelter (after a fashion) in return for the children's labor. Young children, known as "rubbish kids," work as scavengers in dumps; older ones may be sold into still less salubrious lives. Domestic comfort and secure families are luxuries of the rich.

Burgess's protagonist, a "rubbish kid" nicknamed Fly Pie, is unusual in having a sister. Jane has looked after the younger Fly since they arrived on the streets (when Jane was four) and has found comparative security for them by getting them under the sway of the grotesque Mother Shelly, whose "family" numbers some one hundred children. In this environment, they have drifted apart to some extent; Fly is initially unaware, for instance, that Jane, now fourteen, has been sold as a prostitute. Their reunion occurs when Fly and his friend Sham, amusing themselves by jumping off a building into a mountain of discarded boxes, find a wounded kidnapper who has snatched a baby from her fabulously wealthy parents and is demanding a ransom of £17 million. Bleeding and feverish, the kidnapper needs help. Fly acts as messenger; Sham looks after the baby; and Jane is imported to nurse the man. Soon, however, the kidnapper dies, and the three inherit the baby. Longing to do things "right," Jane refuses to ask a ransom, so a "reward" of £3 million is negotiated. But the handoff goes awry because little Sylvie's parents, Mr. and Mrs. Tallus, have no intention of rewarding individuals whom they see as criminals. Sham sees his danger and abandons his comrades, Fly escapes, and Jane is killed.

The novel is organized around the construction of a series of unstable homes. The first of these fragile domestic spaces is the pile of cardboard boxes, an unmistakably "intrauterine locale": Not only does the boys' play mimic an inverted birth ("'It's hot,' he shouted in a muffled voice. 'It's hot in here!' ... I started fighting my way down—swimming and crawling and climbing at the same time, smashing up as many boxes as I could to get there [the pile's center]" [15]), but once they reach their objective, they find, appropriately, a baby. This nest gives way to others—a plastic tent, a shack shared with an old man named Scousie, a rented room, a middle-class house belonging to an elderly woman—but in each case we must follow the pattern laid down at the outset by looking for the unexpected element at the heart of the home. And consistently, what we find is a paradox, a conflation of opposites on the order of the union of *Heimlich* and *Unheimlich*. Homes built at the intersection of such warring tendencies, Burgess suggests, cannot last.

Baby Sylvie is a case in point. She is at once a "rubbish kid" herself, found in the trash, and an aristocrat; she is an unimaginable treasure and, it turns out, an unimaginable danger. As Fly knows all along, for boys like him treasure *is* trash: "Treasure isn't for rubbish kids, you see. It's too much. Really it just wastes a kid's time. If you were sensible you'd chuck it away if you found some treasure because it just spells trouble" (10). But while Sylvie brings disaster, at least she does so innocently. In contrast, the "homes" that follow the boxes are sites of malevolence and betrayal. Scousie's beloved son, a gangster who tries to appropriate Sylvie, beats him up. The gray-haired woman who succors the children when they arrive at her house in a downpour hopes to delay them so that they may be apprehended and executed. And, most shattering of all, Mrs. Tallus, who has become the center of Jane's fantasies, turns out to be ruthless, a tigress deprived of her young and looking for prey. It is not maternal nurturing but destructiveness that underlies homes in this fiction, and Jane is the ultimate victim.

Jane's death is foreseeable from the beginning. From the streetwise point of view represented by Sham and often also by Fly, she is too innocent to live. "She hasn't got what it takes," says Sham (72); Fly remarks, "I didn't like her around. She didn't know the right things" (31). Her desire to live by the ideals that she associates with the "respectable" world disastrously recalls Jessica's perception that respectability equals virtue. That Jane's insistence on retaining her innocence strikes Sham and Fly as not merely misguided but also obsessive, however, signals the presence of repression. What Jane is repressing, and why she is doing so, becomes clear when Fly mentions that from early childhood onward she used to comfort him (and herself) with a fantasy about how they came to the streets. In this fairy tale, the brother and sister were neither abandoned nor, as Fly hypothesizes, the children of someone executed by the police. Rather, "Our mum and dad had lost us years ago by accident. They were very unhappy about it and they were always out looking for us. One day, they'd find us." As Jane tells it, mum and dad "were rich! Dad worked in a big business and Mum stayed home all day just so she could look after us" (44).

This scenario reassures the children precisely because it leaves no room for anger or blame. The mislaying of the children, which happens during a "special surprise trip" organized for their pleasure, occurs in the subway after the influx of a horde of passengers and may be construed as the children's own fault or the result of a natural phenomenon: In the crowd, "we found we were following the wrong people. We got lost. It's easy to get lost in London" (45). Mum and dad, after all, were devoting themselves to their offspring, dad more than succeeding as breadwinner, mum relinquishing her other interests to serve as caregiver. The traditionalism of the family here imagined, which smacks of the 1950s or even the 1850s, apparently mandates faith in domesticity-as-religion as well. In a world in which no one has a concerned parent and mothers exploit rather than nurture, Jane and Fly's mum and dad cared. The children's natural anger at the position in which they find themselves is repressed, displaced by the fantasy that this position is temporary and accidental.

Fly remarks that while he's too old to credit such tales, nevertheless he likes to "pretend every now and then that maybe it [is] true after all" (45). Jane's greater commitment to the fantasy that she created is evident in her efforts to appear well groomed, to teach herself to read and write, to "say 'thank you' nicely" (31), to conceal her prostitution from her younger brother. Clearly she is trying to grow up into someone who might belong to the family she has imagined for herself. The power of the fantasy is also at work in her readiness to trust the Talluses, whose description matches that of Jane's imagined parents: Mr. Tallus is a wealthy businessman, Mrs. Tallus is a stay-at-home mother, and both are desperate to recover the child lost through no fault of theirs. Fly notes that Jane "spoke about Mrs Tallus as if she was our aunt or something" (154), but in fact the relationship that Jane appears to have in mind is closer still. In seeking to please Sylvie's mother, Jane is seeking to please the mother she has internalized: "'She loves her baby so much,' said Jane wistfully. 'She was crying on the phone. She kept asking me to give Sy to the police, but I told her we wanted to prove to her that we could do things right. It's important, you see?'" (148).

As Freud suggests, what is repressed becomes uncanny when our repressed emotion takes shape outside us. In this novel, the moments of horror are moments of violence or cruelty occurring between parents (or parent substitutes) and children. Such transactions go both ways; we are to be equally repelled by Scousie's son's beating of his father and Mrs. Tallus's rejection, "ugly and full of rage," of a baby whom she has momentarily thought to be her own and whom she then literally throws away (161–62). Arguably, however, the ultimate representative of the uncanny here is Sylvie, whose paradoxical role as "rubbish kid"/treasure, object of love/commodity, symbol of hope/bringer of death mirrors the tensions inherent in Jane and Fly's own self-perceptions. The children's reaction to Sylvie fluctuates between affection and irritation, behavior that one might see as characteristic of someone unaccustomed to infants who is dragooned into babysitting. But in psychological terms, one might also argue that it is because Sylvie functions as the uncanny double of the children's past selves that their response to her is ambivalent.

In Burgess's novel, awareness of the uncanny is situated primarily in the reader. In contrast, *Feral Kid* shows its characters—especially the protagonist, thirteen-year-old Robbie—repeatedly experiencing moments of horror brought on by confrontations that evoke buried memories. The plot is simple: Abandoned by his murderous father, Robbie winds up in Sydney, where he encounters Mandy, a drug-using young prostitute, and the sinister Pale, another escapee from the social-welfare net, who cajoles and intimidates him into participating in a series of thefts. One of these acts is the attempted mugging of an elderly widow, Iris Walker, who has recently moved in with her daughter but who longs for her old home in Queensland; during the mugging, Iris and Robbie unaccountably become friends, and the end of the novel sees them making their separate ways to Queensland and (presumably) a happy ending. Given the unembellished nature of this narrative line, we are the more likely to notice the patterns with which Hathorn is playing, the most important of which employ the uncanny in one way or another.

Like Burgess's novel, *Feral Kid* is structured around Robbie's progression from one terrifying home to another. The first of these, the rooms he shared with his adored grandmother, his mentally handicapped sister, and his father, disintegrates when his father catches his grandmother preparing to abscond with the children and, apparently, beats her to death before disappearing himself. Robbie is then quartered with a hostile foster mother who ships him off to reform school; escaping from the school, he finds that the concept of "home" loses all stability, as he is rarely in the same place from night to night. He sleeps two nights in a park in a nest constructed by Pale, one night in Mandy's squat, one night in a viaduct (again with Pale), one night in a garage while he eludes the police, and several nights in Pale's favorite hideout, an underground reservoir temporarily emptied for repairs.

This pattern works, on the one hand, to deconstruct the image of "home" by associating it with instability, hostility, and danger rather than with security and love; these homes are far from *Heimlich*. On the other hand, it also lends itself to an emphasis on "intrauterine" spaces, here associated, as is typical of waif tales, with fear. Pale opines that houses are not to be trusted because "They catch you and hold you down to things" (22); Robbie evidently agrees, fearing in his park nest that "the grass tussocks would reach down and cover him, suffocate him" (25), terrified that he will be trapped and drowned when the reservoir is refilled. The viaduct, a "great, yawning, dark hole stopped up with a few straggly strands of barbed wire" (93), turns out to contain a sight presented as intensely horrific, the corpse of Pale's kitten, who has been strangled by one of Pale's associates; the reservoir, another black hole that feels "like death," feels haunted by another murdered child, Pale's friend Ritch (140). Womb imagery proliferates in Hathorn's novel, which repeatedly shows Robbie squeezing through narrow apertures into cavernous dark spaces, but these returns to primal maternity are never comforting. When Pale tells of breaking into a car, demolishing a violin he finds there, and returning the destroyed instrument to its case as a horrible surprise for the owner, Robbie experiences an uncanny moment, feeling "like the violin himself," for he remembers "waking up in the night, long ago, to the sound of something being smashed in the room next door" (77). Wombs, like houses and the violin case, cannot protect their occupants. Indeed, we become used to encountering parent figures who menace the young: Robbie's foster mother; a pursuer who reminds him of his father and who chases him into yet another abyss; Mandy, who approaches him sexually while high, under lights that turn her face into "a blotch of dark holes," panicking him (80). Even Pale's cat has failed to safeguard her offspring.

Only Iris, whose womb is too old to function, is not linked to terror. Throughout, she has reminded Robbie of his grandmother; his flight to her old home makes the conflation complete, in that we discover that her Queensland associates include people of Robbie's surname, evidently his great-uncle and great-aunt. This coincidence reverses the uncanny: The projected reunion is a future event rather than a memory, *Heimlich* rather than *Unheimlich*, and Iris's doubling of the grandmother causes a thrill not of horror but of delight. Having found an acceptable substitute for his lost protector at last, Robbie will have no need for repression; once the tale is no longer a waif tale, the uncanny can dissipate.

Contemporary commentary on horror, especially within film theory, relies heavily on Freud's insight that the uncanny is the return of the repressed. Robin Wood, for one, takes up Freud's idea of the double to note that "the relationship between normality and the Monster ... constitutes the essential subject of the horror film," and that this "relationship has one privileged form: The figure of the doppelgänger, alter ego, or double" (79). Similarly, Barbara Creed draws on both Freud and Julia Kristeva to describe the monstrous as "an encounter between the symbolic order and that which threatens its stability" (49)—though, as I have suggested, all these novels, inheritors of a Victorian anxiety about whether domesticity and respectability can live up to the demands we make of them, surround the concept of "order" with ambiguity. And Noel Carroll, observing that "psychoanalysis is more or less the *lingua franca* of the horror film" (17), anatomizes the double in terms of what he calls "fission," in which "a character or set of characters is multiplied into one or more new facets each standing for another aspect of the self, generally one that is either hidden, ignored, repressed, or denied by the character who has been cloned" (21).

Carroll's taxonomy of horror plots likewise depends upon repression; what he calls the "Discovery Plot," for instance, in which—as in these waif tales of the 1990s—man meets monster, employs a "delay between discovery and confirmation ... involv[ing] the audience not only in the drama of proof but also in the play between knowing and not knowing, between acknowledgment versus nonacknowledgment," that recalls the conflict between the adolescent and "parental authority figures" (23). This approach is fruitful for prose texts as well. In *Stone Cold*, Link horrifies Shelter because there is indeed a "link" between them, while Shelter horrifies us because of the parody of parenthood he represents; in *The Baby and Fly Pie*, readers may identify with Jane's understanding of the goodness of bourgeois life even while we see, with Sham and Fly, that this understanding is false. Conversely, *Feral Kid* reveals the inadequacy of the "respectable" point of view represented by Iris's daughter and by a well-to-do man who criticizes his teenage daughter for briefly shielding Robbie, so that the discovery upon which the happy ending depends is our realization that despite her class membership, Iris is not really "respectable" at all.[4] In the 1990s as in the 1860s, the meeting of the street and the domestic, the strange and the familiar can only unsettle our ideas about respectability, the family, and the self. The powerful responses elicited by all these works suggest that their appeal is more emotional than intellectual. While these authors seek to convey the need for social change in our approach to homelessness, the real function of their stories is more visceral: Whether tearjerkers or thrillers, each encourages adolescent readers to doubt the competence, the benevolence, even the sanity of parents. Representing what it is not "respectable" to represent but keeping it safely within the boundaries of fiction, urban waif tales at once discuss the uncanny and embody it—situating our emotional thrill, as always, at the place where *Heimlich* and *Unheimlich* meet.

NOTES

I thank Anne Morey for her contributions to the talk on which this chapter is based.

1. There are exceptions to the pattern; Jonathan Lewis Nasaw's *Shakedown Street* (1993), for instance, features a protagonist who lacks a home but is not alienated from her family, since her companion on the streets is her mother. Such a story line, however, is anomalous.

2. The American waif tale, typically more upbeat than its British counterpart, tends to follow a different set of rules; space precludes their discussion here.

3. Waif tales frequently use first-person narration, a technique that facilitates horrific effects. As Carolyn Steedman notes, "as soon as a writer allows a distance between the character and the reader—allows objectivity or irony to enter the text—then the uncanny cannot take place" (149).

4. For instance, her daughter sees Iris as irritatingly eccentric, overly trusting, and perhaps senile and worries about the possibility that she will somehow destroy the daughter's home.

WORKS CITED

Bratton, J. S. *The Impact of Victorian Children's Fiction.* London: Croom Helm, 1981.

Burgess, Melvin. *The Baby and Fly Pie.* London: Puffin, 1995. First published in 1993.

Carroll, Noel. "Nightmare and the Horror Film: The Symbolic Biology of Fantastic Beings." *Film Quarterly* 34 (Spring 1981): 16–25.

Clover, Carol J. "Her Body, Himself: Gender in the Slasher Film." *Representations* 20 (Fall 1987): 187–228.

Creed, Barbara. "Horror and the Monstrous-Feminine: An Imaginary Abjection." *Screen* 27 (Jan./Feb. 1986): 44–70.

Freud, Sigmund. "The 'Uncanny.'" Trans. Alix Strachey. *Works*, Standard ed., vol. 17. London: Hogarth Press, 1955. 217–52.

Hathorn, Libby. *Feral Kid.* London: Hodder, 1996. First published in 1994.

Howsam, Leslie. "Hesba Stretton (Sarah Smith)." *Dictionary of Literary Biography*, vol. 163. Detroit: Gale, 1996. 287–91.

Hunt, Peter. "Passing on the Past: The Problem of Books That Are for Children and That Were for Children." *Children's Literature Association Quarterly* 21, 4 (Winter 1996–97): 200–202.

Roth, Elizabeth Elam. "Aesthetics of the Balletic Uncanny in Hoffmann's 'Nutcracker and Mouse King' and 'The Sandman.'" *Children's Literature Association Quarterly* 22, 1 (Spring 1997): 39–42.

Salway, Lance. "Pathetic Simplicity: Hesba Stretton and Her Books for Children." *The Signal Approach to Children's Books*, ed. Nancy Chambers. Metuchen, NJ: Scarecrow, 1980. 34–45.

Steedman, Carolyn. *Strange Dislocations: Childhood and the Idea of Human Interiority, 1780–1930.* Cambridge, MA: Harvard University Press, 1995.

Stretton, Hesba [Sarah Smith]. *Jessica's First Prayer.* 1866. Rpt. *Masterworks of Children's Literature*, vol. 5, part 2, ed. Robert Lee Wolff. New York: Chelsea, 1985. 403–25.

Swindells, Robert. *Stone Cold.* London: Hamilton, 1993.

Wood, Robin. *Hollywood: From Vietnam to Reagan.* New York: Columbia University Press, 1986.

9

"I'll Never Be the Same After That Summer":
From Abjection to Subjective Agency in Teen Films

John Stephens

"Teen film" consists broadly of three attributes: A bundle of genres recognizable through their familiar, though constantly evolving, formulas; the structures or frameworks which give shape to particular films; and an implied audience and its viewing position. More recently, teen films are increasingly apt to be self-reflexive about their genres, even flaunting genre characteristics, as occurs, for example, during the opening minutes of *Scream 2*. The self-reflexive characteristics of many modern examples, such as the *Scream* trilogy, are also apt to include a thematizing of the narrative dichotomy between subjectivity which becomes abjected and the abjected character who struggles back to subjective agency. The dichotomy underlies modern thrillers, such as *I Know What You Did Last Summer*, and "chick flicks," characterized in the opening of *Scream 2* as "Sandra Bullock movies" (that is, films such as *While You Were Sleeping* or *Hope Floats*). Because teen genres are fluid, and hence a particular film is apt to incorporate features from numerous (other) recognized genres (thriller, horror, sci-fi, comedy, romance, romantic comedy, road movie), the dichotomy of subjective growth and abjection is widely deployed. This chapter will explore how this deployment across a range of films exerts a culturally normative pressure, whether ironically in *The Opposite of Sex*, perhaps the wittiest interrogation of teen genres, or euphorically in *Can't Hardly Wait*, with its comic distribution of rewards and punishments, or as negative exemplum in the dark morality story *I Know What You Did Last Summer*.

Viewers' recognition of the imbrication of narrative forms with the filmic resources and generic conventions which produce them is requisite for making sense of teen films. They render their images more readable by deriving them, to varying degrees, from popular culture, to the extent that the metonymic use of popular culture is a defining aspect of film in the 1990s and constitutes a chronotope (that is, a conjuncture of period, setting, and cultural situation). In theme and ideology, teen films are primarily concerned with subjectivity and intersubjectivity and with the social contexts in which these are produced, lost, or denied. A grounding presupposition is commonly the loss or failure of family, resulting in chronic states of abjection.

Teen films are generally conceived around certain experiences envisaged as key transition points along the border which separates childhood from adulthood: Graduating from one educational institution and entering a higher; first sexual experiences; leaving home; and sometimes childbirth. The action of the film may involve completing a significant journey, quest, or a comparable challenge; it may involve the death of a friend or a loved one; and it tends to be imbricated with the romance genre, commonly as shaping a desirable outcome, as in *Can't Hardly Wait*, but may also be a thwarted possibility, as in *I Know What You Did Last Summer*, or even a focus for parody in *The Opposite of Sex*. What is largely at stake in crossing the border is a development of subjective agency from the lesser potentiality of childhood to the greater potentiality of adulthood—a point self-consciously made early in *I Know What You Did Last Summer* as the principal characters anticipate "a last summer of immature adolescent behavior" before beginning college. It is at this point that an adolescent is especially vulnerable to abjection. Agency in teen films is often posited upon resistance to the acceptable behaviors established by and within the adult community—a perspective affirmed by the teen horror film *Disturbing Behavior*, in which model young adults are produced by microchip implants inserted to control behavior, although, significantly, the process is also likely to result in insanity. Subjective agency is thus here only possible for the minority of characters who choose nonconformity and alienation. They are abjected by the community and have chosen self-abjection as the only means by which they may possess some element of agency. But theirs is a path fraught with risk, since it can entail exclusion from all intersubjective relationships, and *Disturbing Behavior* shares with other teen films an interest in abjection as itself a boundary state from which the abjected will either spiral down to social dysfunction, insanity or death or else turn existence around to wrest some form of agency from it. Not surprisingly, films will often include characters who demonstrate both kinds of outcome (*The Lost Boys*; *Can't Hardly Wait*). However, the normative assumption is that abjection can (and should?) be overcome (*Reality Bites*; *Excess Baggage*).

The analysis of fictive characters in relation to the theory of abjection is, principally, extrapolated from Julia Kristeva's *Powers of Horror*, although often implicitly modified by the more general senses of *abject* as "what is contemptible" and "what has been cast aside." The concept has been applied in film analysis since the mid-1980s (see, for example, Barbara Creed's *Horror and the Monstrous-Feminine*), especially with reference to the representation of female characters. Significant for teen film is Kristeva's description of the causes of abjection as "what disturbs identity, system, order. What does not respect borders, positions, rules. The in-between, the ambiguous, the composite.... Any crime, because it draws attention to the fragility of the law, but premeditated crime, cunning murder, hypocritical revenge are even more so because they heighten the display of such fragility" (4). Whereas the abject in itself is not necessarily merely a negative, its status as "the place where meaning collapses" (2) and the "I" disappears renders it threatening both to the subject who embodies it and to social order and cohesion more generally. Hence the abject becomes abjected, cast out, in a move which reaffirms and upholds consensual forms of identity and social organization.

In her study of abjection in horror films, Creed lists the following "abominations" which the modern horror text has derived from what historical religion descried as abject: Sexual immorality and perversion; corporeal alteration, decay, and death; human sacrifice; murder; the corpse; bodily wastes; the feminine body; and incest (252). These elements readily spill over into related teen genres and are notably present in hybridized texts like *The Lost Boys* and *I Know What You Did Last Summer*. These films might be aptly described as "coming-of-age arrested" narratives, insofar as principal characters at the point at which they should be moving toward maturity and adult agency are instead cast into abjection. This state of being trapped at the boundary is metonymically figured in *The Lost Boys* by the vampire boys' underground hideout—which is both womb and a culture arrested at a moment in the recent past—and by the boundary condition between human and vampire which Michael (a restless new arrival in the community) enters and will leave only either by committing a murder (and becoming fully vampire, fully abject) or by destroying the vampire king (and returning to the path of the fully human). Creed identifies various ways that horror films illustrate the operation of abjection on the sociocultural arena, two of which are of particular relevance to teen genres. First, images of abjection, especially the corpse, whole and mutilated, and bodily wastes such as blood, sweat, and tears are heavily deployed in "coming-of-age arrested" films—notably in the "slasher" narrative of *I Know What You Did Last Summer*. For the audience of a horror film, Creed suggests, viewing "signifies a desire not only for perverse pleasure (confronting sickening, horrific images, being filled with terror/desire for the undifferentiated) but also a desire, having taken pleasure in perversity, to throw up, throw out, eject the abject (from the safety of the spectator's seat)" (253). These desires are compounded in *I Know What You Did Last Summer* by the abject nature of both the stalker/slasher and his victims. That is, even when the audience has worked out that the slasher is Ben Wilson and that his actions emphatically qualify as "premeditated crime, cunning murder, hypocritical revenge," moral alignment with the victims is precluded because the victims refuse to face up to the consequences of their own, unpremeditated, act of murder, the act which condemned them to abjection in the film's opening minutes.

The second operation of abjection on the sociocultural arena that Creed points to is that in horror film the function of the monstrous is "to bring about an encounter between the symbolic order and that which threatens its stability"—that is, that which crosses or threatens to cross the "border" is abject (253). In teen films which thematize abjection, across a spectrum from horror to carnivalesque realism, the monstrous (or an equivalent deviancy) occupies the border between normal and supernatural or between the performance of proper and improper gender roles. There is, however, considerable variation in the realization of the latter. In *Can't Hardly Wait*, for example, what is identified as "jock" masculinity is equated with abjection through the implicit assumption that the borders and rules are situated differently for teens and adults, so that in failing to make the transition the aggressively masculine Mike becomes abjected, while in contrast the intelligent and sensitive male (Preston) progresses from abject to agent. The monstrous is here thematized by an embedded, frame-breaking episode in which Mike's forerunner as school "sexual icon," Trip McNeally, makes an unexplained appearance to Mike during the party which marks the end of school days. Functionally, the scene derives from Dickens's *Christmas Carol*, in that Trip is the ghost of what Mike will become and signifies that now is the beginning place of his abjection. Trip is an overweight, beer-swilling, belching, farting slob, who perceives his own abjection as a consequence of the preference of college girls for mature, intellectual, socially aware males—that is, males who have successfully negotiated the teen/adult border. His "adult" advice to Mike—to hang onto his high school girlfriend and to wear flip-flops in the shower to avoid warts—is too late, on the one hand, and too trivial, on the other, to make a difference, but most of all it is an advocacy of abject stasis: The choice for the becoming adult must be between growth and abjection, not between stasis and abjection. Mike's immediate response is to seek out Amanda and offer to "take her back," but she has already moved on in quest of the more mature, more intersubjectively grounded relationship presaged in the "found" love letter from Preston. The film implicitly affirms that the new masculinity represented by Preston is still heterosexual, however, underscoring this by the jibe "fag!" flung at Mike from the crowd at his moment of deepest humiliation when he is publicly spurned by Amanda. Outside the ambience of Hollywood, on the other hand, the English realist narratives *Beautiful Thing* and *Get Real* depict young gay males progressing from abject to agent, and in doing so rewrite the script for "proper masculinity" in teen film.

The most fully realized depiction of abjection in contemporary teen films is perhaps to be found in *I Know What You Did Last Summer*, particularly in that the few principal characters who survive to the end of the film achieve only a temporary illusion that they have overcome abjection. This perspective coincides with representations of abjection in other popular media genres. Thus a pertinent comparison can be made with the final episode of the "Glory" series of *Buffy, the Vampire Slayer*, which offers perhaps one of the most exquisite representations in contemporary popular culture of the unresolvable struggle between abjection and agency. Although the Slayer's social role is to patrol and maintain the boundary between the normal and the supernatural, her subjectivity is marked as abject: The in-between, the ambiguous, what disturbs identity. While Buffy finally obtains the means to defeat the narcissistic goddess Glory, whose physical dominance over Buffy throughout the series has highlighted the abject in her role, the episode's frame insists on her abjection. It opens with a routine episode—saving an obviously abject male from a particularly large and predatory vampire—but now with a twist. First, this vampire doesn't recognize that Buffy is the Slayer, and hence her identity must be established by her action in slaying him; and second, to the rescued man's astonished query, "How'd you do that? ... You're just a girl," she replies, "That's what I keep saying." Interpellated as the Slayer by destiny and society's need (and, of course, by the text), Buffy's abjection inheres in the impossibility of ever being "just a girl" and following an everyday subjective development. The episode ends with a conjuncture of two incidents which restate Buffy's abjection. First, having finally defeated Glory with the aid of a troll-god's hammer, Buffy walks away from the broken body of Ben, who, in an inversion of Jungian psychology, functions as Glory's animus, unconscious, and would-be conscience, and to whom she transmogrifies in moments of seeming weakness (early in the episode Glory refers to him as "that little nagging pinch of humanity"). However, Giles, the Watcher (Buffy's adult guide and mentor), then squats beside him and explains that Buffy did not kill him because "She's a hero, you see. She's not like us;" then, because Ben's continuance will enable Glory's return at a later time, Giles smothers him. Buffy has already gone on to try to rescue her "sister," Dawn, but faced with the realization that either she or Dawn must die to avert catastrophe, chooses her own death. This is, of course, a grand heroic action, the great altruistic choice heroes must eventually make. What the conjuncture of these incidents within the frame suggests is that the choice is always already made ("This is the work that I have to do," says Buffy in her voiceover from the void), but the depiction of Buffy's intense love for Dawn just before she makes her leap into the energy field reminds us that the distinction between agency and abjection inheres not in the choice itself but in the self-orientation of the chooser. But does Buffy thereby elude abjection? The episode's closing frames zoom in on the headstone of Buffy's grave and its understating inscription:

Beloved sister

Devoted friend

She saved the world

A lot

The Gift

Then the screen fades to black. The effect is clearly designed to evoke the pathos of loss, but it also cannot but signify the crossing of the border between life and death, where development is no longer arrested, but terminated. Agency and abjection thus seem locked in an unresolved dialogue.

Buffy, we know, even at this moment of writing, will experience a rebirth. Within the predominantly realistic *I Know What You Did Last Summer*, what causes abjection seems likewise indestructible, and perhaps what this indicates is a perception, shared with *Buffy*, that abjection is a condition of culture. In its early scenes the film is very self-conscious about its narrative and psychological conventions. Its opening sequence, in which a young man sits drinking on the edge of a high cliff from which he suddenly falls (is, in fact, pushed), is initially uninterpretable except as an example of abjection, the in-between of earth, sea, and sky figuring that of life and death. The film then cuts to a beauty pageant, the emblem of abjected femininity within patriarchal culture, introducing its four main characters during a sequence which gives full scope to the voyeuristic-scopophilic gaze. Julie, Ray, and Barry look down from a balcony at the stage on which the young contestants, including their friend Helen, are posed. In a shot-reverse-shot sequence, Ray comments on Helen's "ample" breasts, Julie objects to the sexism of the display and the comment, and then the camera returns the gaze to the stage and a few seconds later tracks in onto Helen from a low angle, confirming Ray's observation. The moment of resistance is merely token, and the film will eventually play out the function of the gaze in the psycho-thriller teen flick: Male characters die when suddenly ambushed by the killer, but Helen and then Julie are subjected to protracted pursuit while the camera plays over their bodies, helpless and disheveled, generously proportioned and sexually attractive.

Masculine desire and voyeuristic pleasure are nevertheless given a more contemporary twist in *I Know What You Did Last Summer*, in accord with recent trends in the horror genre which position children in the place of abjection. Sobchack argues that by the 1980s the horror film had moved "from the representation of children as 'terrors' to children as terrorized" (12), and that "the ascription of responsibility for the breakdown of traditional family relations... has been transferred from child to parent" (13). Her reference was to preteen children, but the principle seems also to apply to *I Know What You Did Last Summer*, and, of course, is familiar in films from other genres—*Excess Baggage* and *Beautiful Thing*, for example—where fathers are the root of abjection. None of the principal four characters has a present and functional father (unlike those of Lois Duncan's novel on which the film is loosely based), and the stalker, Wilson, is the model of an obsessive/possessive father, unable to let go of the dead daughter whose name is tattooed on his arm. It is eventually disclosed that what the film's opening sequence showed was Wilson's revenge on the young man he held responsible for his daughter's death. While revenge for his own injury is the overt reason he hunts Julie and the others, it is clear that his obsession is also a form of abjection, a variant of the patriarchal impotence which Sobchack identifies in the modern horror film—a perversion of paternal love, or now displaced incestuous desire, into hatred for young men and for all young women not his daughter. The focus on abjection seems even more obvious if the film is compared with its pretext: It is, in Wagner's terms, an *analogy* (227) of Lois Duncan's 1973 young adult novel of the same name[1] but shifts away from the novel's complex moral dilemmas and instead develops its themes and its narrative and visual strategies by drawing on the horror genre and especially the "slasher" films (the scriptwriter, Kevin Williamson, also wrote the script for *Scream*). Music and sound effects are used to build tension, with numerous dark scenes, stalkings in enclosed spaces, and sustained sequences in which tracking shots create the expectation of surprise or attack. Like other teen films, the characters meet challenges in passing from the relative innocence of youth into the adult world. In this case, however, the entry into adulthood is a fall into irremediable abjection, a fall which, in conformity with horror film, is framed contiguously (but not causally) by entry into active sexuality. Thus, after the beauty contest the four principal characters drive to an isolated beach, where, as the film self-consciously gestures at its own knowingness, they retell versions of the urban myth about the escaped lunatic/slasher/man with a hook for a hand who murders the male partner of a couple making out in a car in a lonely place. Julie, the most questioning of the four characters, and the character whose point of view the film most generally aligns with, suggests that the story is a fable warning girls of the dangers of premarital sex, and that the hook is an obvious phallic symbol representing the fear of castration. These motifs of abjection are, however, only discussion points, and the two couples soon move to separate parts of the beach and themselves engage in premarital sex. Julie and Ray's relationship is at this point depicted as tender and caring and is the film's only moment of intersubjective agency. Soon after, the road accident in which Wilson is knocked down, and the subsequent disposal of his still-living body into the sea, mark the entry into abjection.

I Know What You Did Last Summer seems generically rather different from contemporary teen films—such as *Reality Bites*, for instance—mostly because of the "slasher" elements and a resolution which affirms abjection. It nevertheless converges with them in some obvious ways, as for example its configuration of characters in a pattern familiar in the teen chronotope: Serious, studious girl (Julie); beauty queen (Helen); overindulged, macho, and generally unpleasant rich boy (Barry); and an attractive, sensitive, but poor boy (Ray). Although Helen and Barry are less unlikable than in Duncan's novel, their lack of introspection seems to render them very prone to abjection. A fifth, more minor character, Max, functions early in the film as an emblem of the abject. He is the young male excluded from the popular group but too pushy in his attempts to belong. Humiliated at his first appearance in the film when he awkwardly but insistently attempts to ask Julie out, he comes under suspicion of following the other four when he drives up to them just after the encounter with Wilson and speaks to them both aggressively and knowingly. He is, somewhat inexplicably, Wilson's first victim—perhaps for no other reason than that the other characters falsely suspect him of being their stalker and that the act suggests Wilson's behavior is both insane and random, but thematically and, from an audience perspective emotionally, Max dies precisely because he is so abjected. The film's configuration of characters corresponds most closely with that of *Can't Hardly Wait*, though the latter is labeled comedy and achieves a comic resolution and, as pointed out above, certain characters abjected by the social dynamic of high school emerge as agential characters. In contrast, by the end of *I Know What You Did Last Summer* the stalker has killed off two of the four main characters, along with Max, Helen's sister Elsa, and a bumbling police officer. The close of the film evokes the possibility that Ray and Julie will, as Julie earlier expressed it, "salvage some small fraction of a life," but agency is distinctly lacking. Most of the principal characters are dead, no just outcome has been possible, since the slasher, Wilson, is hunting victims who are themselves morally compromised and repeatedly refuse to confront their condition. The status quo can never be restored because of the deaths and because, when the surviving characters shortly before the end think the persecution has finished, they explicitly decline a last opportunity to accept responsibility for their past actions. The ending contrasts strongly with the close of Duncan's novel, where the stalker has been captured, the four main characters are all alive (though two have been injured), and the more ethically inclined characters, Julie and Ray, finally confess their part in the fatal hit-and-run accident which was the catalyst for the novel's events.

The close of the film looks back to a common horror motif, wherein the monstrous irruption that is the cause of abjection has been pushed back but not eradicated. It thus also formally opposes the closure of "comic" teen films, which reinscribe "normality," characteristically encapsulated as heterosexual coupling, a pattern already established with *Rebel Without a Cause* (see Castiglia). *I Know What You Did Last Summer* gestures toward this reinscription, with Julie and Ray once more a couple, only to shatter it with the closing frames of the film (a fade to black as Julie is attacked by an unseen assailant) and hence to reassert the film's pervading dystopian vision. Unlike the comic teen films, then, the teleology of "normal" moral perspectives and family values which can function as a springboard for maturation is inscribed only as something lost.

A further marker of the persistence of abjection is evident in Julie's role, in that she contrasts with the slasher film character that Carol Clover calls "the Final Girl," the hero who at the close asserts her agency by overcoming the killer. Julie fits the role during the film's early stages as "the only character to be developed in any psychological detail" and "the only one to deduce from the accumulating evidence the patterns and extent of the threat; the only one, in other words, whose perspective approaches our own privileged understanding of the situation" (236). She shares with other Final Girls the horror at encountering the corpses of her friends, but unlike them she cannot take effective action on her own behalf. Rather, as she scrambles in the hold of the boat she is trapped on, looking in vain for somewhere to hide, the camera dwells on the metonyms of her abjection—her panicky movements; her sweaty body in its disheveled clothes; her breasts ever on the verge of slipping out of her low-cut blouse. There is a clear sense of relief when, in the struggle between Wilson and Ray, Wilson becomes tangled in the boat's rigging and is flung overboard, but there is no hint of the regendering that Clover (244) discerns in the modern slasher film. Rather, Julie is reinstated in feminine pulchritude, not for the purpose of closing with the normality of heterosexual coupling and growing up, but so that this illusory outcome can collapse again when she enters the shower in the closing frames. *Psycho*, of course, is not far away here. As many film theorists have argued since Laura Mulvey's *Visual Pleasure and Narrative Cinema*, techniques used to position the audience and to construct the gaze of the camera in "classic" cinema are gender-specific and have a determining role in the production of images of femininity and masculinity. Classic films rarely depict the viewpoint of female characters, representing them instead as visual and narrative objects, rather than as perceiving and acting subjects (see also Hedges; Jacobs; McCallum, "Present"). Although Julie is represented as a perceiving subject and, in her successful attempts to establish Wilson's identity, as an active subject, the end of the film returns her to the abjected female role. Mulvey designates woman as "image" and the male as "bearer of the look": "In a world ordered by sexual imbalance, pleasure in looking [scopophilia] has been split between active/male and passive/female" (11). Women are typically figured as the object of the camera's gaze and hence "the centre of the male gaze, its object and fetish, the cause and recipient of desire, pity and cruelty" (Kolker 132)—that is, abjected.

Exploring the imperative to take responsibility for one's actions produces a more positive representation of the abjection/agency dyad, in a different generic mix, in *Reality Bites*. In this film's radical form of metadiegesis (the assumption of the storytelling function by a character in the story), the main character, Lelaina, is making a documentary about her friends and herself. The structure of frame plus embedded film enables a complex depiction of the principal characters, here another configuration of five: Serious girl who wants "to somehow make a difference to people's lives" (Lelaina); self-depreciating emotional isolationist (Vickie); gay male abjected by fear of coming out (Sammy); attractive, sensitive, drop-out philosopher (Troy); and an outsider to this group, Lelaina's sometime boyfriend, the yuppy Michael. In the never-ending contest between solipsism and intersubjectivity, each in her or his own way is ensnared in solipsism. Opening the film with a university graduation ceremony thus functions only to foreground the "coming-of-age arrested" theme, as the characters face a world without evident desirable pathways. As in the later *Can't Hardly Wait*, the "monstrous" element in *Reality Bites* is a social formation, here commodity culture as represented principally by conspicuous consumption and popular television. This is just as surely a source of abjection as solipsistic masculinity, in that the addiction to surfaces and trivia blocks the quest for subjective agency. One telling way the film thematizes this situation is by means of the contrast and conflict between Michael, the quintessence of commodity culture, and Troy, the only character in these films to succumb to the lure of abjection as a self-conscious consequence of his existential despair about society. Michael, despite his best intentions, seems beyond redemption: He is a little older than the others and depicted as so thoroughly interpellated by his milieu that self-awareness seems impossible. Moreover, he does not realize his own state of abjection, so that he can neither resist nor embrace it. He is instrumental, however, at his last appearance in the film, in prompting Troy to see that his own dictum, "Everyone dies all by himself," is a disabling cliché. For Troy the beginning of subjective agency is the overturning of that cliché by a decision to dismiss old conflicts and go to his dying father. Troy's trajectory most clearly maps the shift from abjection to subjective agency experienced to various degrees by the four friends.

Reality Bites opens and is interspersed with excerpts from Lelaina's documentary and also includes a travesty of it after Michael appropriates it and arranges for it to be cut and edited. The documentary material itself effectively breaks the fictional frame in various ways. The jerky hand-held style implies that the spectator is witnessing "reality," as it does in so many contemporary police television dramas, but in combination with Lelaina's direct involvement with her subjects and the fact that she, the filmmaker, is frequently also included within the frame, the strategy also at the same time draws attention to the processes of production. The film in this way asserts both the reality of the ceaseless struggle between abjection and agency and the film's own authority in depicting it. As the documentary drops out of the discourse and gives way to illusionistic realism, Lelaina and Troy finally discover that a central source for subjective agency is intersubjectivity in the caring form that does, deeply, "make a difference to people's lives." The film carefully lays the ground for this through its dialogical relation between primary and secondary narratives; each parodies, undercuts, and comments on the other. Furthermore, both the primary narrative and the documentary overtly play with generic conventions. For example, in one scene Vicky and Lelaina overtly parody generic codes associated with television soaps, here *Melrose Place*, to discuss responses to the possibility that Vicky has AIDS, perhaps the late twentieth century's ultimate image of abjection, and the use of the confessional interview to document the family background and personal goals of the four friends. The effect is to break the fictional frame of both narratives, but it is also to elaborate central thematic concerns with the struggle to achieve subjective agency in a culture constructed out of surfaces and bricolage. Similarly, the commercially edited version of Lelaina's documentary signifies oppositionally to the other two narratives, especially in light of Lelaina's rejection of commodity culture in her graduation valedictory speech. The conflict between commodity culture and youthful idealism is encapsulated in the two responses to her closing rhetorical cry, "What are we going to do now? How can we repair all the damage we inherited? ... The answer is ... ," where her own open-ended response, "I don't know," is replaced by "pizza." The reshaped and edited version draws attention to processes of production, but it also elaborates theme through the contrast between the commercialized version and the interrogative, often idealistic, values espoused in the raw material. What it is that the answer "pizza" devastatingly does is foreclose the process of inquiry and growth presaged in the young graduate's "I don't know."

The filmic and narrative techniques of *Reality Bites* disrupt the illusion that the film represents a hermetically sealed world unfolding before the eyes of an audience of mere onlookers. This constitutes a departure from the typical pattern for teen films wherein a multistranded narrative situates its audience in a gap-filling role, but not a role which involves ideological choices. Instead, contemporary teen films seem to be increasingly employing metadiegetic strategies, so that an overt self-consciousness about the conventions used may nudge audiences toward a more analytical subject position. Thus a different take on the passage from abjection to agency in a commodity culture appears in *Excess Baggage*, a combination of romantic comedy and thriller. This is a straightforwardly linear narrative and, as a romantic comedy, pivots on the heterosexual romance outcome. Because it also has a strong element of the "road movie," it is unusually limited in its *dramatis personae*. It is more common for the narrative of a teen film to be structured as an unfolding of the interconnected or parallel stories of four or more varied characters, and this is a key contrast with older formulations of teen film genre, such as *Rebel Without a Cause*, which is rather framed as a male-male-female triangle (see Castiglia). Such constructions of thematically paralleled narratives are exposed as convention in *The Opposite of Sex* through the ironizing combination of voiceover and split-screen presentation.

Multistranding in itself does not necessarily disrupt the closed relation between spectator and screen as envisaged by Mulvey, partly because stories are subsumed within larger metanarratives and partly because unitary camera perspective tends to restrict point of view and have implications for the representation of intersubjectivity. The use of frame-breaking devices in film can foreground the cinematic process privileging the signifier. Metadiegesis breaks the fixation of the spectator's gaze by foregrounding fictionality, as in *The Opposite of Sex*, and, at least potentially, by disrupting diegetic levels of narration and, hence, conventional processes of audience alignment with representations. Direct address to the audience is a conventional form of metadiegesis in many film, television, and literary genres, but its effect is still to break the fictional frame of the narrative and overtly engage the audience in a collaborative role. *Clueless*, for example places voiceover and direct address in dialogic relationships and thereby draws attention to processes, generic conventions, and ideas. Similarly, voiceover is a conventional strategy for summarizing information, situating a narrative and aligning the audience with characters, as in the beginning of *Excess Baggage*.

Excess Baggage is nevertheless still self-conscious about its genres and themes. In an early monologue, when Emily is goading her reluctant captor,

Vince, she parodies a common view of what constitutes teen films: "You steal. Probably got a hard-on doing it. All part of life on the razor's edge, run till you drop, never say die." The irony here is that Emily can despise Vince's abjection because she has not yet identified her own condition as abject. A later dialogue, however, articulates the genre's less explicit significance, the necessity of subjective agency:

Emily: How am I supposed to explain eighteen years of being unwanted and unwelcome? I've always been a commodity to him [Alexander, her father]. I always thought that there was nothing and no one in the whole world that would make me feel who I was, except my father.
Vince: Listen. You find yourself. I mean, you show yourself who you are. You don't need your father to be telling you who you are.

At the same time, the positioning of spectator in relation to each of the characters by means of varying camera distance and the structuring of the scene through a series of shot–reverse shots underlines that "finding yourself" must also be an intersubjective process.

Thus *Excess Baggage* is driven by a motif which is both part of the genre's framework and a cue to the viewing position of the genre's implied audience: deep-seated intergenerational alienation. Other framing elements suggested by the film are mostly connected with its chronotope. Perspectival alignment is with Emily, a character from America's affluent white community, whereas her main interaction is with a character from a different socioeconomic group (on the one hand, Emily's father makes his dirty money from corporate crime; on the other, Vince steals cars). The adult world is corrupt or deficient and is contrasted with the world of young adults, which is capable of idealism and is still in a state of potentiality and becoming. Young people in teen films are therefore often literally (as in *Excess Baggage*) or figuratively (as in *Reality Bites*) on the run from the adult world. An important implication of this is that youth culture more readily crosses boundaries pertaining to class or race, is in touch with feelings, and operates more intersubjectively—that is, constructs subjectivity dialogically through interrelationships with others (see McCallum, *Ideologies* 7–8). Most adults, in contrast, have passed beyond the possibility of such behaviors and are locked into individualistic isolation. *Reality Bites* implies that if agency is not grasped within the relatively short transition period at or toward the end of the teen years, development may remain arrested, as it has for Michael.

The abjection–subjective agency dyad and the teen film conventions which, with few exceptions, plot the development from the former to the latter are very sharply delineated by their systematic inversion in *The Opposite of Sex*, a film offering a canny perspective on the genre through a merciless deconstruction of *Clueless* and the "producers' genre" derived from it.[2] Here Dedee, the narrator and main character (blond, of course, albeit played by Christina Ricci), supplies a self-reflexive voiceover affirming her own solipsism and opportunism and foregrounding the film's recurrent parodic and frame-breaking elements. She even draws attention to the factitiousness of closure in *Clueless*, and so on, by ending the film with a direct address which sends the audience away before the close predicated on the genre overwhelms her. The film frequently reminds its audience that they are not within the illusionistic cinematic suspense of a story unfolding as if the outcomes are as yet unknown, but viewing a story narrated retrospectively by its principal character. Hence she offers such warnings as "I don't have a heart of gold, and I don't grow one later," thereby mocking the convention of character development, and foregrounds the factitiousness of narrative structure and visual representation. Thus, as she is packing to run away, she remarks to the audience, "Oh, this bit where I take a gun is like, dah . . . , important. It comes back later, but I'm putting it in here for foreshadowing, which we covered when we did Dickens. If you're smart you won't forget I've got it."

As she walks from the house into the night a few frames later, she gestures vigorously at the off-screen film crew to turn off the lights so she can creep off in the dark. After she shoots her abject boyfriend Randy (marked as abject because he only has one testicle and embraces a satirized version of southern fundamentalism), she harangues the audience, "What, do you think I'd be the dead one? I'm the fucking narrator. Keep up!" And when she is giving birth, she introduces a split screen to give the audience the chance to watch something else if they are bored with cinematic representations of labor wards.

The most subtle narrative irony of *The Opposite of Sex*, however, comes at the close when Dedee finds that her narrative (and hence her life) are finally subject to her culture's metanarratives. To run away yet again and to go on refusing relationships is to embrace the existence of the isolate, the abject, and so she finally concedes that "Okay, so maybe I'm wrong. Maybe [relationships are] not all shit when you think about it. I thought the whole idea was I know what happens next." Her final rebellious gesture, as she tells the audience to leave and not watch (and presumably not gloat over) her as she turns toward responsibility, emphasizes the power exerted by the assumption that characters must progress from abjection to subjective agency. Dedee's final concession, "I'll give you this much, though. I never was the same again after that summer," simultaneously mocks and reinscribes that normative assumption.

Contemporary teen films, narratives originating in abjection and moving to closure in subjective agency through processes of causality, question the illusion that the films are simply mimetic and hence seem to promote a focus on story at the expense of spectatorship. In each example I have considered there are metadiegetic or frame-breaking strategies which give at least some prominence to the film's thematic elements, although this does not mean that they call the normative assumptions, the underlying metanarratives, into question. Quite the contrary. The pervasive effect is to affirm that the thoughtful viewer who does "keep up" will acknowledge the development from abjection to agency as pivotal for the human transition from teen to agential adult.

NOTES

1. An analogy, according to Wagner, describes a case in which a film draws on an existing novel but is a "considerable departure for the sake of making *another* work of art" (227).

2. The term is from Altman, who defines a producers' genre as an identifiable cluster of films deliberately commissioned to replicate elements such as particular actors or story motifs which have been linked to the box-office success of an earlier film (30–48). Thus Alicia Silverstone's role in *Excess Baggage* reprises elements of her role in *Clueless*, particularly a state of cluelessness associated with being the motherless, materially indulged daughter of a wealthy father, inhabiting a commodity culture. *Excess Baggage*'s Emily has a harder edge than Cher, however, in keeping with the overtly criminalized chronotope she inhabits and the deployment of elements from the road movie and Mafia film.

WORKS CITED

Altman, Rick. *Film/Genre*. London: British Film Institute, 1999.
Beautiful Thing. Dir. Hettie MacDonald. World, 1996.
Buffy, the Vampire Slayer, Series 5 ("The Gift"). Dir. Joss Whedon. Warner, 2001.
Can't Hardly Wait. Dir. Harry Elfont and Deborah Kaplan. Columbia, 1998.
Castiglia, Christopher. "Rebel Without a Closet." *Engendering Men: The Question of Male Feminist Criticism*, ed. Joseph A. Boone and Michael Cadden. New York: Routledge, 1990. 207–21; 315–16.
Clover, Carol J. "Her Body, Himself: Gender in the Slasher Film." *Feminist Film Theory*. Ed. Sue Thornham. Edinburgh, Scot.: Edinburgh University Press, 1999. 234–50.
Clueless. Dir. Amy Heckerling. Paramount, 1995.
Creed, Barbara. "Horror and the Monstrous-Feminine: An Imaginary Abjection." *Feminist Film Theory*, ed. Sue Thornham, Edinburgh, Scot.: Edinburgh University Press, 1999. 251–66.
Disturbing Behavior. Dir. David Nutter. Beacon, 1998.
Duncan, Lois. *I Know What You Did Last Summer*. London: Hamish Hamilton, 1982.
Excess Baggage. Dir. Marco Brambilla. Columbia, 1997.
Get Real. Dir. Simon Shore. Graphite, 1999.
Hedges, Inez. *Breaking the Frame: Film Language and the Experience of Limits*. Bloomington: Indiana University Press, 1991.
Hope Floats. Dir. Forest Whitaker. Twentieth Century–Fox, 1998.
I Know What You Did Last Summer. Dir. Jim Gillespie. Columbia, 1997.
Jacobs, Lea. "The Women's Picture and the Poetics of Melodrama." *camera obscura* 31, 1 (1993): 121–47.
Kolker, Robert. "Woman As Genre." *Women and Film*, ed. Janet Todd. New York: Holmes and Meier, 1988. 130–49.
Kristeva, Julia. *Powers of Horror: An Essay on Abjection*. Trans. Leon S. Roudiez. New York: Columbia University Press, 1982.
The Lost Boys. Dir. Joel Schumacher. Warner, 1987.
McCallum, Robyn. *Ideologies of Identity in Adolescent Fiction*. New York: Garland, 1999.

————. "The Present Reshaping the Past Reshaping the Present: Film Versions of *Little Women.*" *The Lion and the Unicorn* 24, 1 (2000): 81–96.

McMahan, Alison. "The Effect of Multiform Narrative on Subjectivity." *Screen* 40, 2 (1999): 146–57.

Mulvey, Laura. "Visual Pleasure and Narrative Cinema." *Screen* 16, 3 (1975): 6–18.

The Opposite of Sex. Dir. Don Roos. Rysher, 1998.

Psycho. Dir. Alfred Hitchcock. Shamley, 1960.

Reality Bites. Dir. Ben Stiller. Universal, 1993.

Rebel Without a Cause. Dir. Nicholas Ray. Warner, 1955.

Scream. Dir. Wes Craven. Dimension, 1996.

Scream 2. Dir. Wes Craven. Craven-Maddalena, 1997.

Sobchack, Vivian. "Child/Alien/Father: Patriarchal Crisis and Generic Exchange." *camera obscura* 15, 7 (1986): 7–36.

Thornham, Sue, ed. *Feminist Film Theory: A Reader.* Edinburgh, Scot.: Edinburgh University Press, 1999.

Wagner, Geoffrey. *The Novel and the Cinema.* Rutherford, NJ: Farleigh Dickinson University Press, 1975.

10

Hitting Below the Belt:
Action Femininity and Representations
of Female Subjectivity

Kerry Mallan

Buffy: "Do I appear shy, coy, and naïve or unrestrained, insatiable, and aggressive?"

"Never Kill a Boy on the First Date"

EMERGENCE OF THE FEMALE ACTION HERO

Filmic embodiments of female action heroes such as *Buffy, the Vampire Slayer*, Diana (*Girlfight*), *Xena: The Warrior Princess*, and *Lara Croft* are representative of a new era of action genre in which "women *have* taken central roles" (Tasker 68). Promotional advertising and general press commentaries on female heroes invariably rejoice in these women's ability to "kick butt" (presumably male butt) and promote the aggressive femininity which is implied in "girl power" discourse. Another feature of the publicity is the visual representation of these young women which clearly inscribes them as predominantly white, heterosexual, and beautiful. In this respect, female action heroes, who emerged in the late 1980s[1] and gained momentum from the mid 1990s onward, are as much characterized by their physical ability to karate-kick, overpower men, and use weapons with skill as they are by their physical appearance and wardrobe: Hence Buffy's dilemma in the opening quotation. What form of femininity should she embody on her first date with a boy? The humorous throwaway comment rings with a deeper resonance as it encapsulates the contradictions and complexities associated with the current wave of popular feminism promoted through the media and directly targeted at youth audiences.

The marketing and promotion of the dual idea(l) of "babe" and "action girl" cause an inevitable tension between a celebratory, postfeminist "girl power" rhetoric and a deeper feminist politics which seeks to deconstruct the image of femininity currently on offer in the media. For mass media producers, their involvement takes a form of negotiation which, on the one hand, reflects the cultural politics and mood of contemporary (western) societies and, on the other hand, ensures financial profit. For youth audiences, their reception of these film and television texts is less definite. Certainly, youth is a key consumer group for the genre, but what young people might derive from it is not so clear.

By examining the treatment of action femininity in *Buffy, the Vampire Slayer* and *Girlfight*, I want to wrestle with the tensions and contradictions that emerge in these texts in terms of the representations of femininity and female subjectivity. As an example of popular feminism, *Buffy, the Vampire Slayer* appears to complicate, through strategies of humor and ironic self-reflexivity, the dominant paradigm of woman-as-spectacle and object of the male gaze. By contrast, *Girlfight* works against popular representations of action femininity and endeavors to offer what I see as a more convincing account of female subjectivity together with a resistant form of femininity. Finally, the discussion considers youth audiences and the kinds of emotional and intellectual rewards they might derive from these texts in terms of their shifting and diverse identities.

BENEATH THE SURFACE OF POPULAR FEMINISM: WHAT'S AT STAKE FOR A VAMPIRE SLAYER?

A feature of postmodern society is its attraction to surfaces and its refusal, often through a form of ludic textuality, to acknowledge that a deeper reality exists behind phenomena. In terms of popular feminist texts, such as *Buffy, the Vampire Slayer* and others, the producers' attention to surface images results in an intentional superficiality—a strategy which elicits a certain appeal for the genre and acts as a form of self-protection against any charges of abrogating a social responsibility to address more serious, foundational concerns. *Buffy's* creator, Joss Whedon, has flippantly described the show as *"My So-called Life meets The X-Files"* (Reid-Walsh 502). This slick, wry comment eschews serious probing into any deeper meanings the series might suggest. By comparing his extra-ordinary life with another popular television series which is concerned with extraordinary phenomena, Whedon provides a good media headline while signaling to the reader that he is hip (like *Buffy's* cast and the youth who watch it). However, just as postmodernism distrusts metanarratives, it also cautions against relying on authorial intentions for understanding the meaning of a text. With these thoughts in mind an analysis of *Buffy,* as an example of action femininity which has attracted a devoted worldwide following of fans, entails an attention to surfaces, to linguistic playfulness, and to the imbrication of youth with the narrative and discursive constructions of gender, identity, and subjectivity.

Buffy, the Vampire Slayer represents American youth by focusing on selected and possibly the most relevant aspects for the implied youth audience—high school, dating, the prom, sexual relations, dances, fashion, music, and friendships. There is also the visual appeal of the "Goth" subcultural element—the vampires and other demons with their aesthetic fashion style (black clothing, Victorian era dress, sensuous fabrics), their "death-look" makeup, and flashback references to Victorian history. The script too is an acknowledgment of its audience, in that the language used by Buffy and her friends is a hybrid form of colloquial American English and a particular kind of teenspeak, termed "Slayerspeak" by *Entertainment Weekly* (quoted in Wilcox). Such linguistic inventiveness is a device for demarcating youth as a separate category from adulthood and highlights the gap between the generations, as Buffy states in one episode: "I think I speak for everyone here when I say, 'Huh?'" ("Invisible Girl"). Furthermore, the show aligns itself with its primary audience by emphasizing youthful friendships and loyalty as well as the superficiality of youthful narcissism with its celebration of commodity culture and desire to belong to the "in" group. This point is made explicit by Cordelia (the embodiment of youthful superficiality), who warns Buffy on her first day at Sunnydale High School: "You want to fit in here, the first rule is know your losers. Once you can identify them all by sight they're a lot easier to avoid" ("Welcome to the Hellmouth"). The use of real bands playing at the Bronze, the favorite local teen nightclub, is a further attempt at mimesis and a direct appeal to the show's target audience. The bands' music forms a pleasurable part of the nondiegetic soundtrack.

The series focuses on youth having to deal with problems on their own and without the assistance of adults, who are largely portrayed as clueless or cynical. Despite *Buffy's* superficiality, several episodes include issues and concerns that many young people experience in real life (for example, adolescent rites of passage, urban male gangs, violence toward females, Internet predators, and death of a mother). Yet the series manages to distance itself from any moralizing or therapeutic function through its use of humor, which derives from a playful pastiche of its Gothic origins (complete with premodern vampires) and contemporary concerns of youth living in postmodern American society. The upbeat linguistic humor, therefore, allows for ironic relief from the feeling of unease evoked by the visual images of vampires and Gothic-inspired mise en scène. However, despite its blatant youth-centered imagery and rhetoric, *Buffy* maintains a conservatism with respect to its reification of American commodity culture, predominantly heteronormative relationships, and Anglo superiority (Owen).

On the surface, Buffy appears more likely to be a popular cheerleader than a heroic vampire slayer. However, her attempts at cheerleading result in a bumbling display of ineptitude. It is obvious that her real talents lie in her ability to kickbox and deliver deadly stakes to the hearts of the evil vampires. As her Watcher and high school librarian, Giles, remarks: "You have a sacred birthright, Buffy. You were chosen to destroy vampires, not to wave pompoms at people" ("Witch"). However, Buffy soon learns that her "birthright" comes at a cost, and she often laments her destiny as a slayer and longs to live the life of a "normal" teenager. There is a double irony operating in this desire, as the series privileges normality despite its underlying storyline of a girl slaying vampires. Not only does normality structure the lack that Buffy's desire can never fill, it also serves as a "regulating feature to demarcate appropriate behaviors and privileges affecting all characters" (Ono 172). Despite Buffy's vigilance and successful efforts in her quest to save the world from vampires, her loner status (although she has a small band of loyal friends), combined with her extraordinary physical strength and karate and kickboxing ability, mark her as an outsider. The construction of Buffy's identity as based on difference supports Schick's observation that "identity is inseparable from that of alterity—indeed, identity itself only makes sense in juxtaposition with alterity" (21). The viewer, in coming to know who Buffy is, at the same time comes to know who she is not. While Buffy is easily distinguishable from the bland and the boring, she is also acutely aware of the ways in which she is the "other." This representation of the hero as a marginal Other is not an uncommon characteristic of traditional heroic narratives.

Notions of identity and alterity, of "us" and "them," operate not only between Buffy and her peers, but also between Buffy and the vampires. There is a perverse twist in that Buffy falls in love with a former vampire (Angel) and is the love object of another (Spike). While she is a vampire slayer, she must nevertheless identify with them and the places they inhabit—graveyards and the Gothic underworld of dungeons and sewers—a space aptly named the Hellmouth, which is (ironically) situated underneath Buffy's high school. This shifting relationship between place and identity disrupts the glossy, youthful, and seemingly static world of Sunnydale. Furthermore, Buffy's double identity as teenage girl/Slayer is discursively constructed through, and indeed relies upon, her participation in a network of places, of different "sites of discourse" (Schick 24)—the school library (which is the meeting place for Buffy, Giles, and her close circle of friends), the school, the graveyard, her home, and the caverns of Hellmouth. Each of these sites constructs a fluid identity with its own social topography and hierarchical positioning. For example, Buffy does not excel at schoolwork, but her kickboxing is outstanding. Buffy's movements across these different spaces disrupt the spatialized discourses of gender and heroism which traditionally imagine men and women as belonging to, and performing in, separate spaces. In terms of the female action genre, Buffy's performance in dark, dangerous, and public places resembles a form of phallic "masculinity" that is traditionally associated with the heroic narrative and the idealized body construct of the male action hero. Buffy's weapon (a wooden stake), actions, poses, sheer physicality, and strength interrupt the discursive configuration of her feminine body as the petite, sexualized object of the male gaze.

It is the slippage between Buffy's active heroic body and her eroticized body-as-spectacle that complicates the conventional objectification-identification paradigm of visual pleasure (Mulvey, "Visual") and is the source of tension relating to questions of representation and reception in a genre which traditionally has offered limited scope for active female subjectivity. The contradictions in Buffy's construction as both female action hero and sexual object of heterosexual male desire are not easily resolved. Undoubtedly, *Buffy* offers a space for both male and female viewing pleasure through its humor and excess, but whether *Buffy* offers an alternative to conventional modes of viewing or is just another form of masculine impersonation cannot be so confidently claimed. For this reason, the "action girl" persona cannot simply be utilized as a way of rectifying what was excluded or defined as inferior within patriarchal culture and conventional cinema. Furthermore, its deployment in shows like *Buffy* remains a deeply ambivalent process.

DIS/CLAIMING THE GOTH

In her analysis of slasher films, Clover cautions that the female hero, despite appearances to the contrary, may still function as "a congenial double for the adolescent male" (51). In this sense, the ambivalence of the powerful yet "girly" action hero permits a vicarious pleasure of the fantasy of the phallic woman for male viewers without causing any serious disruption to the heteronormative construct of male sexuality. Clover's observation opens up further ambivalences regarding Buffy as a feminist text. At a primary narrative level, Buffy struggles against vampires, but at a metanarrative level, she represents the struggle against the legacy of victimization which is part of the paradigmatic Gothic plot and women's subjugation in patriarchal societies generally. In many ways, *Buffy* conforms to the Gothic tradition especially in terms of its excessive imagery in coloring, lighting, and mise en scène. Most of the action takes place at night, which provides the perfect backdrop for encounters of the deadly kind in underground darkened caverns, mortuaries, and graveyards. Bubbling pools of green liquid, stalactites and stalagmites, and burning candles are additional visual effects used to convey an ambience of "otherworldness" that Buffy and her "slayerettes" encounter.

In other ways, *Buffy* works against its Gothic origins. Buffy is hardly the helpless, confused, and frightened heroine of the popular Gothic. On the contrary, she is strong, assertive, and brave. Her performance of energetic and combative physical movements embody a rhetoric of expressive and rigorous bodily aesthetics which eclipses the familiar female victim characterization of this genre. Her embodied rhetoric is a persuasive element for representing an agential, female subjectivity. However, as Clover's previous comment implies, her heroic female body cannot be rendered "mute" in terms of sexuality. In showing Buffy's body in action, there is an interplay between male and female bodies (and also between female bodies) which is sexually charged in its emphasis on rhythms and the interaction of flailing limbs and other body parts. The fast-paced soundtrack heightens the thrill by adding to the momentum and the excitement of the fight scenes while at the same time ensuring continuity of the combative sequences.

Yet, despite her apparent agency, Buffy is vulnerable when it comes to her first romantic relationship with Angel. Angel, like many male Gothic characters, is the embodiment of the "Shadow Male" (Modleski) who initially appears like Mister Right but harbors a murderous side. Angel is a two-hundred-year-old vampire who carries the curse of the gypsies for having killed one of their teenagers. Rather than stake him, the gypsies want Angel to live a life of tormented guilt over his past deed, and thus they restore his human soul so that he will feel the pain of his past. This is an inversion of vampire lore, wherein vampires have the memories of humans but their human soul has been replaced by a demon (Wilcox). Despite his lackluster personality and humor bypass, Angel's dark brooding good looks make him the ideal romantic male counterpart for Buffy as befits the romantic Gothic narrative of a love match made in hell. As Giles wryly comments, "A vampire in love with a Slayer. It's rather poetic, really—in a maudlin sort of way" ("Invisible Girl").

When Buffy loses her virginity on the night of her sixteenth birthday, the punishment for acting upon her sexual desires is that Angel experiences "a moment of true happiness," thereby breaking the spell and heralding the return of his vampire self—Angelus ("Surprise"). Angelus dismissively reduces their lovemaking to a one-night stand, telling Buffy, "You've got a lot to learn about men, kiddo—but I guess you proved that last night" ("Innocence"). Despite the subtext of the dangers of overt female sexuality and the love-them-and-leave-them attitude of males that the above scene supplies, Buffy is able to invert the dominance/submission binary which underpins the romance genre by realizing that her duty as a slayer must override her personal desires. By killing Angelus she saves the world from another vampire. As their act of sexual intercourse caused Angel to be reborn as the vampire Angelus, when Buffy eventually drives a sword through Angelus's heart it is a perverted act of infanticide, for she kills the demon she brought to life. The act also is a reverse copy of their original lovemaking in that Buffy is able to penetrate the body of the "other" with her sword as phallus substitute. Yet this scene's reliance on a phallus substitute poses the question of whether woman's own desires or subjectivity can ever be adequately represented within (and without relying on) a phallic system of representation.

While Buffy is cast as heroic in terms of her actions and unfailing devotion to Slayer duty, she is inevitably positioned as both victim and victor. In killing Angelus, Buffy denies her own desires. Furthermore, in true heroic spirit, she makes the ultimate sacrifice by plunging to her death in a vortex of electric energy so that she can save the world from an apocalypse. Buffy's death invokes the fantasy of a regained order and is the enactment of an ominous and ambiguous warning (and key motif of the series) that "death is her gift" ("The Gift"). While this scene can be read as a revision of the heroic narrative by having the woman as victor, she is also a dead one; this highlights the ambivalent nature of the act as the ultimate heroic gesture or another romantic device to ensure sympathy for the woman. Buffy's dead body is positioned seductively in the foreground of the frame, lying on her back with her right leg in a bent-knee position and head to one side. She is observed by her friends, who act as rhetorical battle-worn figures in the apocalyptic mise en scène. Buffy, as in life, is the central focus, and yet, despite her heroic/selfless gesture, her body does not evoke the image of a martyr. Rather, she is the object of sight, an object of aesthetic consumption for her friends and the viewer, all of whom are involved in a voyeuristic surveillance of the dead female body. There are no markings on her body to suggest a previously lived existence as both woman and action hero—no scars, no blood, no signs of damage, no dirty marks on her white top. To do so would disrupt the aesthetically fashioned sign of the idealized beautiful dead woman as a site of spectacle. While death is the negation of a life and subjectivity, this scene provides a contradiction between words and image. As we "see" death we "hear" a very much alive Buffy in voiceover reassuring her friends to: "Be brave. Live—for me." But there is no need for concern for Buffy fans, since the scene forms the end of season five, and as season six (at the time of writing) is already on air in some countries, viewers can be assured that, phoenix-like, Buffy will rise again and may even achieve a "higher" status than before.

While *Buffy* is able to combine realism with fantasy to produce a text which is a pastiche randomly cannibalizing styles drawn from Gothic literature, other popular cultural texts, and the quest narrative, it never reneges on its loyalty to contemporary consumer capitalism both on and off screen. The show's endorsement of "girl power commerce" (Ono 165) is visible in the way that Buffy/Sarah Michelle Gellar has become the quintessential youth commodity with her face/body promoting Maybelline cosmetics and other consumer goods from T-shirts to notepads. This doubling and cloning of her image in a *mise en abyme* of circular self-reference suggests that despite her action persona, her power ultimately resides in her face and body to sell an idealized femininity which is blond, beautiful, and white. To answer the question posed at the beginning of this section, "What's at stake for a vampire slayer?" it would appear that there is not much to lose, but a lot to gain in terms of market profitability and celebrity status.

GIRLFIGHT: RESISTANT FEMININITY IN ACTION

Whereas *Buffy* promotes a white, middle-class, individualistic, and pleasurable ideal of female identity (Ono 165), *Girlfight* is a female Bildungsroman on the desire of a young Latina woman to become a successful boxer. Set in the Bronx, a more racially mixed area than the fictional and predominantly Anglo (Californian) suburb "Sunnydale" which is Buffy's locale, this film offers a representation of female power and subjectivity which does not rely on superhuman strength or a vivacious, wisecracking personality common to the female action genre. A further difference between the two texts is that *Girlfight* was written, directed, and produced by women.[2] While a feminist film need not necessarily be produced by women, a feminist writer and director will undoubtedly reside both inside and outside the text. This is not to suggest a return to auteurism, but an acknowledgment from a poststructuralist perspective that both the author and the spectator are constructed in and through discourse and that for female spectators viewing this film there may be a recognition of their lived reality or a realization of others' lived realities.

Girlfight, like other female action hero texts, foregrounds women and violence. Whereas Buffy delivers her blows with a deft one-liner, there is little humor in Diana, the central character in *Girlfight*. Diana is true to her mythic namesake in that she, like the Roman goddess, is a protector of the weak and vulnerable. Diana's relationship with her brother, Tiny, resembles in an oblique way the goddess Diana's often uneasy relationship with her brother Apollo. A further comparison is that both women are portrayed as having unsatisfactory romantic relationships with men. Diana's journey to become a boxer traces a pattern that is familiar to the traditional romantic quest narrative from her beginning of a personal journey fraught with obstacles to her final exaltation as a hero. However, the plot's seemingly straightforward linear narrative and uncomplicated characterization are disrupted by the film's cinematic and embodied rhetoric which foregrounds a feminist tale of agential subjectivity.

Girlfight considers the psychological and social effects of both repressed and resistant femininity represented through Diana's dead mother and Diana respectively. Although Diana's mother is never an embodied presence in the film, her absent presence is felt in a number of ways. She is in Diana's thoughts and is (presumably) the reason for her determination to become a boxer. Her empty chair is always positioned in the foreground in the kitchen scenes, thus serving as an ever-present *memento mori* for the family and the viewer. Diana is her "double," as a friend of Diana's father remarks: "You are the living likeness of your mother." Further, Tiny has inherited his mother's artistic ability. By contrast, Diana appears as the antithesis to her mother. Whereas her mother suffered years of physical abuse before committing suicide, Diana actively seeks to use her physical strength as a means to fight against the dominance/submission paradigm of the patriarchal society in which she lives. Consequently, *Girlfight* attempts to resist patriarchal inscription of femininity as passive, weak, and vulnerable by offering a feminist alternative, which promotes a vision of female agency and power that fights against those elements of patriarchal society that limit women's life prospects and diminish female subjectivity.

Rather than dwell on the obstacles to female agency, the film depicts them as being overcome, ignored, or crushed by the female protagonist. In so doing, "space" becomes a recurrent motif in showing how Diana negotiates both alien and familiar territory. There are three key spaces which are sites of interaction in the film—the school, the kitchen, and the boxing gym (in particular, the boxing ring). Just as Buffy's movements across the different spaces of school, home, graveyard, and Hellmouth invert the traditional paradigm of the action genre which delineates masculine and feminine spaces as separate and exclusive, *Girlfight* disrupts the traditional spatial metaphors of the genre. While the school is ostensibly a gender-free space (though this is an arguable point), the kitchen is traditionally coded feminine, while the boxing gym is coded masculine. Diana unsettles the binary oppositional designation of these spaces through her actions which transgress "normal" gender-based protocols and conventions. For instance, she fights in the school corridors, she nearly kills her father in the family kitchen, and she invades the boxing gym and demands to train as a boxer. Consequently, the essentialist metaphors of these spaces as gender-specific or gender-neutral zones are no longer valid, and their espoused epistemological foundations, which serve to prefigure a static gender identity, are weakened.

As Diana moves into the boxing gym, she actively transgresses the female-forbidden male domain by becoming the one who looks and penetrates. Diana's look is not so much a desire to see, as is the masculine prerogative of the gaze, but a desire to know (Mulvey, *Fetishism*). In her desire to investigate the previously "secret" male world of the boxing gym, she becomes a transgressive and dangerous interloper. While the film never explicitly states why Diana wants to become a boxer, in the tradition of the quest story she is given a "sign" which foreshadows her journey. Rather than appear as a mystical portent, the sign Diana encounters in the subway is literally a handwritten sign pinned to a wall with the inscription: "When you're not training someone else is training to kick your ass." At the boxing gym, other signs appear and reappear throughout the various scenes, each an aphoristic commentary containing certain truths deemed important for life, survival, or for reaching goals. These signs, as part of the nondiegetic narration, are signifiers which alert the viewer (and Diana) to the secret men's business of the boxing world with its active promotion of a particular form of virile masculinity (for example, another sign reads: "Punches in Bunches"). Diana's invasion of this space threatens the very club membership of the gym with its systems of difference (male/female), rules, and rituals. She is told by Hector, who becomes her coach, "Girls don't have the same power as boys," but the veracity of this statement is overturned at several points by Diana as she physically defeats other male boxers.

Unlike Buffy, who epitomizes the all-American girl with her long blond hair and trendy clothes, Diana despises the artifice of femininity, and she is a member of a (growing) minority group. Her androgynous clothing (T-shirt, jeans, jacket, track pants) is an overt form of resistant femininity of which her father is critical: "Would it kill you to wear a skirt once in a while?" Although she disguises her sexuality to some extent by covering her body in loose and colorless clothing, Diana is, nevertheless, "Woman" and her power and toughness produce a fear in the males of what she can do to them—if not physically, at least psychologically. She is, in Barbara Creed's words, "the monstrous-feminine." Her monstrosity is further encoded in her Medusa-like stare, which the viewer first encounters in the opening scene and which is shown in close-up throughout the film. Within the patriarchal signifying practices of the boxing gym, Diana is reconstructed and represented as a phallic woman capable of castrating the men who come into contact with her. Their sexist jokes and admonishments ("You should act like a lady") are futile attempts to disguise their fear. Diana's physical strength, muscular body, and boxing prowess further ensure that her female body remains an enigma and threat. When Diana is fighting against a male boxer in her first real fight, he continually hits her below the belt. As the referee cautions him on this infringement, male members of the crowd of spectators call out in the boxer's defense:

"There's nothing below the belt."
"Ain't nothing but a pussy."

In psychoanalytic terms, the male boxer's punches to Diana's groin are a desperate attempt to make her benign while at the same time a defensive strategy to offset his own castration fears. Diana's strength and refusal to show vulnerability weaken the illusion of masculine power and supremacy. This is made clear when Diana's boyfriend and fellow boxer, Adrian, initially refuses to fight against her. Ostensibly his reason is that he doesn't want to fight his girlfriend, but more clearly it is because he fears the prospect of being defeated by a girl ("I don't want to be stuck in a ring with a girl"). Thus, Diana's body and her physical actions invert the familiar bodily imagos of femininity as soft, vulnerable, and penetrable, and her defeat of the male boxers similarly points to the folly of the hegemonic bodily imago of masculinity as hard, strong, and impermeable. In this sense, *Girlfight* challenges the naturalizing of these dominant bodily imagos. Furthermore, Diana is shown as a girl who has a goal. Whereas Adrian articulates on more than one occasion his desire to leave the Bronx and make a better life for himself, his desire is for flight to an unknown place, and unlike Diana he does not have a clear sense of his personal destiny. When Diana asks him directly, "What do you want?" he replies, "Fuck if I know." Adrian delivers this comment in a way that suggests confusion and disillusionment and in that way highlights the crisis of masculinity that the film underscores in its representation of Diana's virility in performance and usurpation of the phallic function of the boxer. While Diana's body is still the object-of-spectacle (which is literalized in her role as boxer), she is represented in a more positive way that tends to reverse the pejorative connotations of the woman-as-object of the masculine gaze. In this way, *Girlfight* illustrates Russo's notion of the female body being given "the opportunity to show off in a new way" (41), and in so doing creates "a revolutionary aesthetic of the body" (Bartky 43): One which does not rely on passive consumption.

Just as there is a reworking of the feminine body through Diana as phallic woman, there is a similar reworking of the hegemonic masculine body. Tiny is represented from the beginning as a young man who does not want the form of virile masculinity that is part of both the Latino and western cultural ideal. He boxes because his domineering father wants him to learn to defend himself against the violence of the community in which he lives. Furthermore, Tiny finds pleasure in passivity—he likes to draw, he finds confrontation difficult, and he readily accepts Diana's protective and dominant manner toward him. Thus, Tiny, with his infantilizing nickname, comes to represent a particular form of feminized masculinity. In contrast to Tiny's marginalized masculinity, his father is a man's man: He plays poker with his male friends, drinks heavily, and demands that Diana cook and clean for the male members of the family. However, Diana retaliates. In one of the key scenes in the film, father and daughter engage in a violent physical confrontation. Diana proves to be the more powerful; sitting astride her father's body as he lies choking on the kitchen floor, she berates him with accusations of his past violent treatment of her mother. The once powerful father is reduced to a gasping heap of vulnerability. This scene is a more forceful and convincing inversion of the dominance/submission paradigm of patriarchal culture (and its phallic order) than Buffy's choreographed kickboxing of male vampires could ever hope to achieve, as it speaks of deep-seated anxieties that Buffy can only play with. The fight can be seen as going beyond the narrative frame by giving a metaphorical expression to women's rage at male violence in general. While Tiny and the father represent two extremes of masculinity, they and the other male (Latino) characters, particularly Adrian and Hector, show the diversity within that community and hence disrupt notions of a unified masculinity for a particular ethnic group as if they were a natural, stable, and static unit.

FROM ABJECTION TO AGENCY

Like Buffy, Girlfight embraces aspects of the Gothic in its coloring and lighting, but particularly in its psychic configurations of the uncanny and the abject. Despite Girlfight's bleak color scheme, the film moves away from the more sensationalist Gothic imagery that Buffy blatantly exploits to focus on a feeling of Unheimlichkeit[3]: The restricted domestic interior space of the kitchen adds to the oppressive mood of Diana's family life. Furthermore, her aggressiveness and resistance to patriarchal domination stem from within the family and the home (Heim). Freud's notion of the uncanny contains a double fear—fear of repetition and fear of castration (Modleski 70). This aspect of doubling, which Modleski explains is an element of Gothic narratives, can be seen in Diana's fear of becoming her mother, of sharing the same fate (fear of repetition). There is also the fear of never developing an autonomy and separateness from her mother (fear of castration). Like the uncanny, the abject is also a psychic configuration that is related to the figure of the mother. Diana is thrown into abjection through two factors—her painful separation from her mother and by the failure or lack of her father as a parent. As Kristeva notes, the "bankruptcy of the fathers" (172) is the source of abjection. Diana's father's failure destabilizes and eventually collapses the Oedipal triangle: Daughter–mother–father. In a feminist twist to an otherwise tragic Oedipal tale, Diana is liberated from the law of the father (both literally and metaphorically). This point of liberation is realized in the fight between father and daughter when the father proves no match for his daughter's strength and physical superiority. She is also liberated from the mother and so breaks the legacy of victimization handed down from her. Consequently, *Girlfight* transforms the Oedipal narrative into a feminist (Gothic) tale of anger and resistance.

Both the male and female characters in *Girlfight* are enigmas, lacking individualization. The viewer is given only partial information about them and their motivations. Rather, narrative impetus is achieved mainly through non-focalized narration such as the actions of the characters. In order to fill in the gaps, the viewer must gain meaning from Diana's eyes (her look) which take in the world which she observes but rarely comments on. This form of internal focalization offers a more open text than that supplied by *Buffy*, where the characters' glib and continuous dialogue and banter leave no doubt about their feelings and desires.

From the opening scene in *Girlfight*, the camera acts as external focalizer by establishing Diana as both the narrative center and the marginalized other. (A similar contradictory image is made of Buffy, but she acts as the key focalizer.) As the bustling crowd of student bodies moves across the screen in the opening scene, the soundtrack of frenetic clapping matches the intense pace of the moving bodies. It is through a synchronization of soundtrack and camera shot that Diana is quickly revealed as the static figure in the background and the object of the camera's zooming. When sound and camera come to an abrupt stop, a close-up of Diana's face fills the frame: Her confrontational, Medusa-like look leaves no doubt that this is a young woman who demands our attention. Thus, the cinematic gaze is challenged by the image of autonomous and fearless femininity. Furthermore, Diana's presence disrupts psychoanalytic theories of identification and desire as her ethnicity and body shape and size resist the stereotype of white female beauty associated with visual pleasure with its implied universal white male spectator and reductionist approach to female subjectivity (or lack thereof). In a circularity of images, the final scene, showing Diana and Adrian in a parting embrace and kiss, reinforces female subjectivity and agency through a close-up of Diana's face; her look, which travels beyond the frame, suggests her life's trajectory away from Adrian and toward a destiny of her own making. While the image of the embracing couple visually encodes a romantic conclusion, Diana's look and brief dialogue leave no doubt that the film privileges female autonomy over heterosexual romance:

Adrian: "So you going to dump me now?"
Diana: "Probably."

YOUTH AUDIENCES: IDENTITIES, SPECTATORSHIP, AND PLEASURE

Both *Buffy, the Vampire Slayer* and *Girlfight* tell entertaining stories. A large part of their appeal could be attributed to their appropriation of the quest narrative as a popular persuasive discourse that works rhetorically to shape young people's identities, youth–adult relations, gender, and power. Embedded in the quest are the kinds of binary oppositions that are deeply rooted in western culture's political, social, and economic systems and structures. In this respect, one must question whether the popular female action genre can offer alternative possibilities for interpretation and negotiation other than relations of dominance and submission in everyday western societies. Or does the genre simply retain this same paradigm by way of an inverted gender representation? There is of course another possible response which refuses a political function by resting at the level of light and vicarious entertainment. No matter how adept Buffy's kickboxing skills, she can never be taken as a serious threat to "real" men while she continues to fight campy vampires with party tricks of morphing from American male to Gothic monster. However, *Girlfight*, in its rewriting of the romantic quest narrative from a feminist perspective, may offer a more political account of female agency and subjectivity for young people; one which does not simply reinscribe the status quo through the ludic postmodernist strategy of continual playfulness of signifiers such as vampires. It is because of this double-edged capacity of affect that spectators can be moved both emotionally and intellectually (Smelik 120). A further element of the quest narrative is the attention to difference, particularly in relation to the key protagonist. *Girlfight* and *Buffy* look at difference, but in the case of the former, difference is politicized by locating it within a social and historical dimension. *Buffy* collapses difference by privileging whiteness and valorizing "girl power" discourse while ignoring or marginalizing people of color (Ono 167). In this sense, Ono sees *Buffy* as serving a pedagogical function for youth audiences with respect to reaffirming social and racial inequalities. (Ono provides numerous examples of how people of color are humiliated, exterminated, or ridiculed in the series.)

With respect to youth audiences, one needs to consider whether they have access to (or a desire for) political discourses and a language that will allow them

to sufficiently critique and transform the existing cultural practices they encounter through the media and in their everyday social interactions (McLaren).
Alternatively, youth audiences may simply enjoy the kinds of vicarious and re-
flexive pleasures that texts like *Buffy* and *Girlfight* offer. Despite the part played
by the media in influencing young people's ideas of gender and other cultural
constructions, Anneke Smelik is convinced that "Female spectators want to be
able to identify with lifelike heroines without having to be annoyed by sexist
clichés or transported by hyperbolic stereotypes" (8). If Smelik's view has any validity among youth audiences, then perhaps films such as *Girlfight* offer an alternative and more "lifelike" account of female subjectivity. This kind of alternative
representation of action femininity, though uncommon to mainstream television
and film, manages to draw attention to the "transparency" of the white universal
female agent (see also the performances of Michelle Yeoh and Zhang Ziyi in
Crouching Tiger, Hidden Dragon as further examples of an alternative action
femininity: One which embodies an eastern aesthetic and athleticism).

McLaren makes the point that young people (indeed all people) are subjected
to a range of prevailing dominant discourses (for example, patriarchy, national-
ism, consumerism, and capitalism). Youth are, nevertheless, active subjects who
are capable of reimagining other possibilities for interactive agency and gender
relations that do not rely on the familiar dominance and submission binary.
However, to assume that the female action genre will guarantee "empowerment" for young women is to adopt a naïve position and to embrace a form of
liberatory politics that fails to acknowledge the fact that film and television are
cultural practices which actively construct images of, and meanings about, femininity and masculinity. To utilize a concept promoted by Homi Bhabha with
respect to cultural difference, the alternative female action texts alluded to
above may open up a "third space" (211) of possibilities for new forms of cultural identity and gender relations for youth audiences. In terms of the subject
of this chapter, action femininity, in its various media constructions, has the potential to open up such a space, but it needs to be mindful of not simply repack-
aging the same old story in new glossy wrapping.

NOTES

1. The early 1960s and 1970s television series *The Avengers, Charlie's Angels*, and
Wonder Woman, however, could be considered forerunners to the current list of female
action heroes.

2. Writer and director Karyn Kusama won the Sundance Best Director Award and
shared the Grand Jury Prize for best dramatic film.

3. A term used by Freud (in "The Uncanny") to give a sense of something we
thought was safe, homely, turning into something terrifying, uncanny.

WORKS CITED

Bartky, Sandra Lee. *Femininity and Domination: Studies in the Phenomenology of Oppression.* New York: Routledge, 1990.

Bhabha, Homi. "'Race,' Time, and the Revision of Modernity." *Oxford Literary Review* 131, 2 (1991): 193–219.

Buffy, the Vampire Slayer ("The Gift"). Dir. Joss Whedon. Warner, 2001.

———— ("Innocence"). Dir. Joss Whedon. Warner, 1998.

———— ("Invisible Girl"). Dir. Reza Badiyi. Warner, 1997.

———— ("Never Kill a Boy on the First Date"). Dir. David Semel. Warner, 1997.

———— ("Surprise"). Dir. Michael Lange. Warner, 1998.

———— ("Welcome to the Hellmouth"). Dir. Charles Martin Smith. Warner, 1997.

———— ("Witch"). Dir. Stephen Clegg. Warner, 1997.

Clover, Carol. *Men, Women, and Chain Saws. Gender in the Modern Horror Film.* London: British Film Institute, 1992.

Creed, Barbara. *The Monstrous-Feminine: Film, Psychoanalysis.* London: Routledge, 1993.

Crouching Tiger, Hidden Dragon. Dir. Ang Lee. Sony, 2000.

Freud, Sigmund. "The 'Uncanny.'" Trans. Alix Strachey. *Works,* vol.17, London: Hogarth Press, 1955. 217–52.

Kristeva, Julia. *Powers of Horror: An Essay on Abjection.* Trans. Leon S. Roudiez. New York: Columbia University Press, 1982.

Lara Croft: Tomb Raider. Dir. Simon West. Paramount, 2001.

McLaren, Peter. *Critical Pedagogy and Predatory Culture: Oppositional Politics in a Postmodern Era.* London: Routledge, 1995.

Modleski, Tania. *Loving with a Vengeance: Mass-Produced Fantasies for Women.* New York: Routledge, 1982.

Mulvey, Laura. "Visual Pleasure and the Narrative Cinema." *Screen* 16 (1975): 6–18.

————. *Fetishism and Curiosity.* Bloomington: Indiana University Press, 1996.

Ono, Kent. "To Be a Vampire on Buffy, the Vampire Slayer: Race and ('Other') Socially Marginalizing Positions on Horror TV." *Fantasy Girls: Gender in the New Universe of Science Fiction and Fantasy Television,* ed. Elyce R. Helford. Lanham, MD: Rowman & Littlefield, 2000. 163–86.

Owen, Susan. "Vampires, Postmodernity, and Postfeminism. *Buffy, the Vampire Slayer." Journal of Popular Film & Television* 27, 2 (Summer 1999): 24–31.

Reid-Walsh, Jacqueline. "Power Girl/Girl Power: The Female Action Hero Goes to High School (A Review of the Television Show *Buffy, the Vampire Slayer*)." *Journal of Adolescent & Adult Literacy* 42, 6 (Mar. 1999): 502–3.

Russo, Mary. *The Female Grotesque.* New York: Routledge, 1994.

Schick, Irvin. *The Erotic Margin: Sexuality and Spatiality in Alterist Discourse.* London: Verso, 1999.

Smelik, Anneke. *And the Mirror Cracked: Feminist Cinema and Film Theory.* Basingstoke, Eng.: Palgrave, 1998.

Tasker, Yvonne. *Working Girls: Gender and Sexuality in Popular Cinema.* London: Routledge, 1998.

Wilcox, Rhonda. "There Will Never Be a 'Very Special' Buffy." *Journal of Popular Film & Television* 27, 2 (Summer 1999): 16–23.

11

Game On:
Adolescent Texts to Read and Play

Lisa Sainsbury

The images of games were seen as a condensed formula of life and of the historic process: Fortune, misfortune, gain and loss, crowning and un-crowning.... [G]ames drew the players out of the bounds of everyday life, liberated them from the usual laws and regulations, and replaced established conventions by other lighter conventionalities. This was true not only of cards, dice and chess, but also of sports and children's games.... As yet there were not sharp divisions between them, as those that were later established.

Bakhtin 235

Within the bounds of the carnival square the fool becomes king, child becomes teacher and youth becomes conquering hero as hierarchies are turned topsy-turvy. As carnival law overcomes officialdom, Bakhtin's players adopt new and strange roles in a process that challenges notions of self and society. Ostensibly it is only a temporary release from the strictures of official law; nonetheless, the experience of carnival bleeds into the fabric of everyday life—the fool who has once been king will never again be the same fool.

In this chapter I examine a series of postmodern fantasies which, in the tradition of Bakhtin's carnival, invite their young readers to play out unfamiliar roles as narrative and game are combined. Perhaps the most innovative and controversial of these texts is *Myst* (1993), Cyan's demanding and germinal electronic adventure. The computer game industry is relatively new, but it has developed with awesome rapidity alongside the youthful audience it targets.[1] This is not to say, however (and, as we will see, this is where controversy begins), that electronic texts have no place in the history of narrative and literary development. Computer games are not simply part of the technological revolution. Many have a place in the evolution of literary history, a fact which becomes apparent when electronic texts are discussed alongside more conventional printed books. Consequently, I have chosen to juxtapose discussion of *Myst* with an overtly literary adolescent novel, *Hexwood* (1993) by Diana Wynne Jones, which constructs itself figuratively through game-play, and Ian Livingstone's *City of Thieves* (1983), an adventure gamebook which is the printed precursor to graphical adventures such as *Myst*.

ELECTIVE CARNIVALS

The emancipatory potential of Bakhtin's carnival seems particularly relevant to young people in contemporary society:

although adolescents undergo a rapid psychological maturation, society (especially a technologically advanced one) postpones their taking genuine adult roles by keeping them in school. So they have to work out a set of balances between their newfound sense of possibility and the restrictions with which adult society often appears to be threatening them. (Appleyard 97–98)

The hierarchical inversions of the carnival square could provide an opportunity to work out this "set of balances," but how might twenty-first-century adolescents gain access to Bakhtin's square? At least one answer to this question lies in the connection between carnival and postmodernism. The material forms generated by postmodernity, which frequently allow the individual to participate in the deconstruction of an authoritative, unified aesthetic, suggest that postmodernism might be described as carnivalesque. Indeed, the relativist ideals of postmodernity which espouse individual transformation of the social order clearly find an affinity with carnival transformation.

In more practical terms, young people might enter Bakhtin's carnival square through playful narrative structures which integrate narrative and game. The "call to play" presupposes interaction, since the text offers itself up to be played with; to be acted upon by the reader-player. This presupposed interactivity sets up complex narrative relationships, frequently involving the reader in the semiautonomous development of narrative. As I have suggested elsewhere ("Tales"), narrative can be classified—as elective or compulsive—by the extent to which it expects reader participation. Compulsive narratives, such as *Hexwood*, compel "the reader to move from one sentence, image or page to the next"; the reader is not overtly involved in the construction of plot ("Tales" 83). Elective narratives, such as the *City of Thieves* gamebook, involve the reader in a process of election which can affect both plot and story. However, it should be made clear that

this classification of texts merely serves to highlight the emphatic tendencies within individual narrative modes.... While both modes direct the reader to action through the

spaces left in the textual rendering of plot and story, the elective narrative also moti-
vates the reader through a *textual withdrawal* from the rendering of plot and story; the
reader of an elective narrative is overtly asked to make choices affecting narrative construction. ("Tales" 84)

This distinction helps to decide the nature and impact of a text's interactivity
and the extent to which the reader-player is constructed as an independent subject. Furthermore, I want to propose that texts which make effective use of elective structures can draw players out of the bounds of everyday life in a
carnivalesque challenge to prevailing notions of self and society.

FIGURATIVE GAMEPLAY

Diana Wynne Jones's fantasies for children and adolescents are currently en-
joying a renaissance in the wake of the hysteria surrounding the *Harry Potter*
series. Surely motivated by J. K. Rowling's success, Collins have recently
reprinted the back catalogue of Jones's complex, inventive, and challenging
novels which deserve equal success in their own right. Jones's novels reveal a
preoccupation with the conditions of reality and fantasy and a determination
actively to involve the reader in the text. This is best demonstrated by *Hexwood*, a postmodern fantasy for older readers which blends subtle elective qualities with dominant compulsive narrative structures.

In *Hexwood*, Jones constructs a fantastic universe controlled by hegemonic
rulers, the Reigners, who have control over numerous worlds. The Reigners
have the ability to distort reality as perceived by lesser beings, though they
have lost control of a machine called the Bannus, which "makes use of a field of
theta-space to give you live action scenarios of any set of facts and people you
care to feed into it" (11–12). This machine is located on earth, in a deserted estate called Hexwood Farm. Ann Stavely, apparently the book's protagonist,
lives close by and becomes subject to the distortions of Hexwood's "paratypical
field." However, midway through the narrative it is revealed that Ann is not
Ann, but rather an extraterrestrial named Vierran.

It is at this point of displacement, as identities become bewilderingly confused, that Jones's narrative shifts from compulsive to elective and that the adolescent reader's developing metacognitive capacity is truly tested. According to
Appleyard, adolescents are able to

think about thinking, to reflect critically about [their] own thoughts. This is the source
of adolescent self-consciousness and introspection, of the egocentricism of much adolescent thinking, of the sense of discrepancy between [their] authentic self and the roles
[they play] for an imagined audience. (97)

Once the text has been destabilized, so is the subject identified within and, thus,
the reader is likely to question her/his own narrative role. The reader is left to

decide whether Ann and Vierran coexist in parallel dimensions, whether they exist alternately in a series of spatial de/re-constructions, or whether Ann is simply extant in Vierran's mind. The fact that, linguistically, "Vierran" is an extension of the name "Ann"—in German "vier" means four, and consequently Vierran is Ann times four—could be figuratively applied to each theory in turn. It is difficult to accept Ann's nonexistence, since Jones is convincing in her portrayal of Ann and thus provides the key to her potential return. While Jones ostensibly closes the text with a denial of Ann's existence, she actually allows Ann to reenter the narrative at the reader's invitation. Jones leaves the question of Ann/Vierran's true identity, and the nature of narrative closure, to the reader, thus rendering these important aspects of her narrative elective.

Jones provides clues to this elective participation in the ubiquitous motif of adventure gaming. Ann reads her brother's books on role playing almost absentmindedly (19), though she is soon to learn that role play is far from trivial: "Yes, playing! Vierran told herself bitterly. The Bannus was not the only one who had played—and the Bannus at least played seriously" (199). Also, Sir Harrisoun, alias the meddling Harrison Scudamore, finally regrets his selfish desire to play at the expense of the safety of others, as a dragon threatens his own "life":

as far as everyone else in the hall could see, Sir Harrisoun appeared to go mad. He shook his fist at the ceiling. "You there!" he shouted. "Yes, *you!* You just stop this! All I did was ask you for a role-playing game. You never warned me I'd be pitched into it for real! *And* I asked you for hobbits on a Grail quest, and not one hobbit have I seen! Do you hear me?" (255–56)

Contained in this enraged attack is an important message for the reader: Gaming "pitches players in for real." That is, the reader's involvement in Jones's postmodern play is real, as s/he is actively involved in the furthering of narrative development. The final indication that reality, and therefore the "truth" of Ann's identity, is in the mind of the reader comes as Vierran ponders the existence of the voices she constantly hears in her head:

Damn it! Vierran thought.... Those four are good people. They *do* exist. It just shows you what this castle does. And, suddenly, as if her head had cleared, she was quite sure that wonderful things did indeed exist. Even if they're only in my own mind, she thought, they're *there* and worth fighting for. (213)

Vierran has no concrete evidence of these people's existence, but she is prepared to accept that existence is a state of mind; if she has the mental capacity to imagine their existence, then they exist. Similarly, the reader's conviction that Ann exists in some parallel world deconstructs Jones's suggestion that she never really existed; it is enough that she exists in the reader's mind.

Jones's playful closure resembles Linda Hutcheon's "anti-closure closure" (176), through which time, place, and identity cannot be fixed. Jones achieves her slippery closure through manipulation of narrative relationships and a complex play of theoretical relationships governing space and time. Thus, *Hexwood* reveals the potential for elective participation in ostensibly compulsive texts, providing a sophisticated challenge for its adolescent readership. However, the elective potential of *Hexwood* will only be realized by the most enthusiastic and astute reader; by the reader who, like Vierran, is prepared to question the conditions of reality and close/develop the narrative accordingly.

Hexwood certainly demands active, intellectual engagement with its narrative development, but elective play is finally limited by its primarily compulsive narrative structure. A radical challenge to this structure is needed to bring the reader a step closer to the playing out of roles figuratively explored by Diana Wynne Jones, a challenge realized by printed and electronic gamebooks.

ELECTIVE GAMEBOOKS

While the appeal of adventure gamebooks may have peaked in the mid-1990s, they nevertheless warrant consideration in a discussion of youth cultures, in that they were the predecessors of electronic adventures. Furthermore, gamebooks provide an evolutionary steppingstone between compulsive novels and elective electronic fiction. The following discussion will focus on Ian Livingstone's *City of Thieves*, an early, typical example of gamebooks. The most commercially successful British writers of gamebooks, Ian Livingstone and Steve Jackson, who often coproduce titles, started producing their Fighting Fantasy Gamebook series in 1982. By the mid-1990s they had sold more than 13 million copies worldwide and inspired a number of imitative titles, such as R. L. Stine's *Deep in the Jungle of Doom* (1996) and Morris's *Island of Adventure Gamebook* (1994), based on Enid Blyton's original text.

The hybridization of game and book is clear in the term "gamebook," terminology which implies interactivity and emphasizes the challenge to conventional narrative structure. Since these are constructed, authored texts, the level of actual control allowed to the reader is questionable. Although these books represent an interesting challenge to conventional narrative experience, I am going to suggest that their structural creativity is actually inhibited by their printed   format.

City of Thieves underlines the reader-player's role on the covers of the book, through the following statements:

- A thrilling fantasy adventure in which YOU are the hero!
- Part story, part game, this is a book with a difference—one in which YOU become the hero!
- YOU are an adventurer, and the merchants of Silverton turn to you in their hour of need.
- YOU decide which route to take, which creatures to fight and which dangers to risk.

Attention is drawn to the capitalized letters, which negotiate a central position for the reader in this text. Also, as demanded by postmodernist discourse, the supremacy of an identifiable author is not only undermined, but self-consciously denied. "YOU" is used as a kind of tag word, which seems to be a pivotal selling point for the entire series (and might be perceived as an extension of the thrust toward privatization in Britain which was central to "Thatcherism" in the 1980s). The potential for reader-player interactivity is emphatically guaranteed, but its implications are more significant than the rhetoric might suggest. In these four simple sentences the reader-player is identified as an active and centrally significant subject, is endowed with civic responsibility and heroic strength, and is portrayed as both author of, and actor in, an as yet unwritten adventure. These assertions, promising an emancipatory power over an almost tangible fantasy world, seem particularly relevant to socially marginalized adolescent readers. It may be that the appeal of gamebooks lies in a rare opportunity for adolescents to take control.

Close scrutiny of the text, however, reveals that "you" acts as a kind of smokescreen, obscuring the fact that the adventuring "you" is really no different from any other third- or first-person adventurer. Readers do not do anything different in processing the textual elements of *City of Thieves*; they simply read about the adventures of a warrior called "you." While the use of second person spins the illusion of interactive participation, it does not directly provide readers with an alternative means of engagement. In fact, Livingstone's employment of the second-person pronoun is often cumbersome:

An old woman standing next to you offers you two eggs to throw. Not wishing to appear to be an outsider, you take the eggs and hurl them. But as you do so, the old woman picks your pocket without you noticing. Lose 1 Gold Piece or any one item you may have. Unaware of your loss, you walk away from the crowd to look at the various stalls. (148)

The reader-player is invited to relate to this scene through three alternating perspectives: The passive narratee receives information about the theft from the narrator; the real reader-player must cross out a coin from her/his list of possessions; the reader "in character" must mentally feign the ignorance of the unknowing warrior. So, through awkward narrative construction, the reader is required to remain unaware of that which s/he does in fact know.

City of Thieves utilizes a distinctive elective structure in which the narrator guides the reader to action through a series of numbered chunks of prose. The numbered sections of text close, either with an imperative—"you" might be told to fight or to turn to another section—or, more frequently, with a number of options, one of which must be chosen by the reader. Livingstone narrates the bulk of the adventure and is ultimately responsible for the creation of the narrative maze. However, the aleatory element of the narrative, in terms of its unpredictable battles and confrontations, means that Livingstone frequently leaves the reader-player to act alone. As game play is introduced and dice are thrown, only the reader-player can propel the narrative forward as the narrator withdraws. Indeed, the mental sensation of active participation in, and creation of, a fictive world is rooted in this frequent movement between reading and playing. Structural trickery—in the use of the second-person pronoun, providing the reader with a false sense of self-fictionalization and the authorial withdrawal at the moment of dice play—is fortified by the necessity of actual play in the forward propulsion of narrative flow.

However, the scope of the reader-player's involvement in the elective development of the narrative is undermined for several reasons. First, although many character attributes and battle outcomes are decided by dice—which should mean that reader-players enter combat on different terms and experience situations variously—it is possible to cheat and fix scores. The overtly elective structure of such texts assumes a trust which is not necessarily realized. Also, the central place of chance in the narrative construction of *City of Thieves* means that the reader-player has only limited control over the field of play. Having said this, there are opportunities for reader-players to make informed decisions. For example, some choices rely on generic knowledge in which heroism is ultimately rewarded; the true "hero" knows that monsters should always be confronted. Alternatively, the dedicated reader-player will draw a map to chart progress through the narrative maze.

The temptation to cheat also affects the gamebook's multilinear structure. Livingstone explains that "there is one true way through the City of Thieves and it will take you several attempts to find it" (17). In order to distract the reader-player from this true way, Livingstone embellishes the narrative with numerous dead ends, unfolding an extensive narrative maze (consisting of 400 numbered sections of text). Potentially, then, adventurers achieve a greater sense of textual manipulation than most readers, as their negotiation of this maze contributes to a unique process of plotting. However, the printed form of gamebooks allows the reader-player to read each narrative option before progressing, thus ensuring that Livingstone's true way is discovered at the first attempt, effectively nullifying the text's multilinear structure.

If fantasy responds to the human desire for wish fulfillment, Fighting Fantasy Gamebooks might be perceived as an attempt, literally, to make wishes come true. Although problematic, their provision of a participatory role for the reader-player begins to destabilize the boundaries between fantasy and reality, revealing a postmodern affinity with Jones's more complex novel. In his shamelessly direct address to a youthful audience, Livingstone opens up the text to his young reader-players and therein lies its success.

City of Thieves does provide its reader-players with an alternative narrative experience which involves them in the construction of plot. However, this interactive experience is undermined by an awkward mode of reader address, a shallow storyline, and a printed format which cannot sustain the ingenuity of its elective structure. Livingstone offers the possibility of carnivalesque transformation, but having opened up the carnival square, fails to realize its potential. Ultimately, the printed text is too visible and accessible to support the gamebook's multilinear network, perhaps explaining its decline in popularity; a decline matched by the rise of computer games, which are able to support the playful structures introduced by gamebooks.

ELECTRONIC ADVENTURES

Electronic adventures are possibly the most controversial of the texts in this chapter, since ostensibly they bear no relation to the literary sphere and, for many adults, encapsulate some of the more purposeless and wasteful aspects of youth culture. This attitude to computer programs is exemplified by John Clare (the *Daily Telegraph*'s education editor) in a recent guide to education:

None ... is more offensive than those that claim to "lay the foundations for a life-long love of reading" by introducing children to books through what is essentially a distracting medium that discourages concentration. The worst offenders are publishers—including the Oxford University Press—who produce "interactive animated story books with sound effects, talking characters and music, which are far more likely to lay the foundations for a life-long love of trash video and television than literature.

Clare is confounded by the lowly descent of Oxford University Press to the netherworld of computer technology, but I wonder to what extent he has explored its domains. His disparaging comments do apply to the majority of electronic books that fruitlessly mimic their printed counterparts, making little use of multimedia tools. However, inventive electronic books, such as Oxford University Press's *Winnie the Witch*, deviate from their printed pretexts, using electronic gameplay to explore thematic content and to open up narrative structure. Such software is likely to enrich children's experience of the original book, and it seems narrow-minded and mean-spirited to deny them access to the electronic companion simply because printed literature is more highly valued by pedagogic authorities.

Even the most inventive electronic books, however, fail to explore narrative in a radical manner, because their formative starting point is the printed book. More exciting are electronic adventures which provide a viable alternative to printed narratives, making use of multilinear pathways which synthesize game and story in the construction of elective narrative. In a refinement of Livingstone's and Jackson's gamebooks, electronic adventures provide players with viable narrative roles, involving them in a constructive process of decision making. One of the most influential graphical role-playing adventures, *Myst*, also shares affinities with Jones's compulsive novels, while representing a convincing departure from them.

Where *Hexwood* becomes increasingly complex, culminating in an ambiguous closure, *Myst* confounds its player through a formidably opaque opening. Like most adventure games, *Myst* has a user's manual, but its bias is technical, providing only a limited narrative context:

You have just stumbled upon an intriguing book, titled *Myst*. You have no idea where it came from, who wrote it, or how old it is. Reading through its pages provides you with a superbly crafted description of an island world. But it's only a book ... isn't it? As you reach the end of the book, your own world suddenly dissolves into blackness, replaced by the island world the pages describe. Now you're here, wherever here is, with no option but to explore. (2)

This scenario provides little concrete information on which the player might act, but it is significant in textual terms. The figurative element of the game is introduced, as Myst is identified as both book and island. It is a story to be told and a place to be explored: Metaphors which develop as the narrative progresses. Also, the player's role is loosely addressed as "you." "You" is constructed as the explorer of an unknown environment; to explore this world is to understand it and your role in it. So this introductory narrative confirms that *Myst* is open to textual analysis, but as the following "message from Cyan" (*Myst*'s creators) suggests, its structure departs from conventional texts:

You are about to be drawn into an amazing alternative reality. The entire game was designed with little or no extraneous distractions on the screen to interfere with your feeling of being in another world. Myst is not linear, not flat, and not shallow. Myst is real. And like real life, you don't die every five minutes.... Pay attention to detail, collect information, and use logic because these are the pieces of the puzzle you'll use to reveal the secrets of Myst. Rely on information you've gathered from Myst and from life itself. (2)

Several key points are raised here, the first of which relates to *Myst*'s depth and multilinearity. As Lydia Plowman proposes, many electronic texts challenge the linear coherence of Aristotelian narrative through the multilinear pathways opened up at various "foci of interactivity;" points at which the player must act in order to progress ("Secret World" 92). Unlike gamebooks, which cannot help but expose their pathways, *Myst*'s secrets are hidden and can be revealed only as the explorer solves various puzzles. Following the imperative to explore—motivated perhaps by Cyan's directive, but more likely through the need to impose order or sense upon this uncharted world—leads to a process of exploratory mapping individual to each player. The player is encouraged to locate boundaries in order to gauge the limits of the field of play; and limited they must be, since they are constructed through a finite sequence of code. Once the general location has been marked out—a small island, housing a number of structures, central to which is a partially burnt-out library—then narrative details can be sought and pieced together. Indeed, this process is mirrored by the presence of "marker switches" on the island, which correspond to points on a map in the library. Throughout the game, geographical devices such as telescopes and rotating towers come into play, emphasizing the significance of mapping and claiming territory. Depth, however, is not simply a question of topography in *Myst*; it is also a measure of the metaphoric structure which gradually reveals itself as the player uncovers Myst's history.

The metaphoric play of *Myst* relates to the boundaries of fantasy and the impact of narrative on reality, concerns which are exposed by Cyan in its rhetoric as the developers construct the paradox which makes fantasy real: "Myst is real," but it is only "like real life." While Myst is not a real-life island, it is a tangible virtual landscape and can be explored through the tools used to navigate real life, such as logic and observation (enabling autonomous player involvement). Through metafictive sleight-of-hand, Cyan exposes the constructedness of *Myst* in order that its environments might seem natural.

Of course, it is more difficult to progress through *Myst* than Cyan's advice might suggest. While the authors have purposely refrained from "extraneous distractions on the screen," players may be daunted by the lack of direction. As the game opens, the player is confronted by a deserted dock, skillfully rendered in darkly realistic graphics. Unlike many virtual adventures, there are no characters to speak to and no obvious tasks to perform; the only option is to point, click, and explore. As Sherry Turkle confirms, "In video games, you soon realize that to learn to play you have to play to learn. You do not first read a rulebook, or get your terms straight" (70). *Myst* immediately demands emergent thinking of its player-reader, a process of bricolage that Turkle compares to the concrete thinking Jean Piaget recognizes in young children. Turkle maintains that postmodernism has validated contextual and situated reasoning as a widespread way of thinking, so that concrete reasoning is no longer relegated to early childhood (54–59). Furthermore, as I have previously argued ("Tales" 93), constructing narrative through emergent thinking requires that objects be acted upon and placed in a hypothetical relationship with other objects/events. Perhaps of relevance to adolescent players, this process reflects their newfound ability to "reason in terms of the formal or logical relationships that exist among propositions about objects" (97).

The player may flounder in the early stages of *Myst*, a result of lack of direction and purpose, but difficulty also lies in her/his narrative construction. Unlike most electronic adventures, *Myst* does not construct a virtual protagonist for the player to control; rather it addresses "you," occasionally directly (in contrast to the gamebooks, which make endless use of second-person address), but mostly through silent implication. Initially, it is unclear whether the player is expected to assume the role of an identified fictional character. However, it soon transpires that "your" experience of *Myst*, and of real life, is the key to its solution and, thus, when Achenar and Sirrus beg for "your" help, they do so literally. Bound up in the initial lack of discernible identity is the absence of obvious motivation and, thus, it seems that identity is established through the demarcation of territory and the uncovering of narrative. Finding home and purpose provides the player with a growing sense of self-awareness, eventually culminating in a narrative climax—one of a possible three, in fact, that depend on your actions—which finally involves you in the evolving history of Myst. In the manner of the carnival square, *Myst* is a space which encourages the exploration of self through the adoption of a new persona. Thus, as you become a lone traveler on the shores of *Myst,* so you look to yourself in order to move forward.

While the mapping of Myst island is largely a logical process, involving Bruner's (1986) paradigmatic mode of thinking, full comprehension of *Myst's* secrets involves piecing together various clues through the narrative mode. Thus, both Bruner's modes of thought (paradigmatic and narrative) are required if the player is to complete the game successfully. This is not the clumsy bridge between education and entertainment manifest in many examples of multimedia edutainment. Like Bruner, Cyan seems to recognize that human experience is conveyed through a combination of logical argument and story and, therefore, a convincing simulacrum of a human environment must marry the two convincingly. The structuring of narrative is truly elective as its evolution and sequence depend on the actions of the player-reader.

Narrative, then, plays a significant role in *Myst,* and the player frequently becomes reader in the gathering of story elements. One of the first clues provided is a note on the path from the dock to the library, immediately proposing a connection between travel and books. This note, along with a number of journals in the library, introduces Atrius as the author of these texts and the creator of Myst. Clearly something terrible has happened to Atrius, a mystery which is uncovered gradually. The journals suggest that Myst exists in several "ages," which potentially are accessible to the player-reader. Alongside Atrius's journals lie two more books, apparently containing distorted recorded messages from his sons. Each son begs for the delivery of further pages, finally providing the player-reader with a concrete task. It eventually is revealed that Sirrus and Achenar have been trapped in these books by their father and that these pages will secure their freedom.

In an inversion of *Hexwood's* figurative use of game-play, literature becomes a complex metaphor in *Myst,* representative of freedom and incarceration. Story has the power to create and allow entry into other worlds, but as is true of all sources of power, it can be abused and corrupted. Unharnessed imagination is destructive and must be tempered with the routine structures of daily life; as Atrius observes: "I gave them free reign to the books—perhaps it was not wise.... [T]heir imaginations went wild." However, Cyan does not seem to be suggesting that books are in themselves dangerous; after all, the library is central to the solution of the game. Perhaps these books are representative of new technologies, of a new medium for narrative, still being nursed by the father while abused by the son. In self-reflexive mode, it seems possible that Cyan is aware of the role-play enthusiasts who relinquish real-life (referred to acronymically by dedicated players as RL) while inhabiting virtual domains on the Internet. Accordingly, it seems that Sirrus and Achenar relinquish home life as the fantastic places realized in the "ages of Myst" consume their attention. However, the metaphoric play of Myst is finally positive, signaled by an endgame which celebrates the freedom to explore. Indeed, Cyan is careful to distance their game from those which meet with death at every corner, as the notes say, "you don't die every five minutes." This is not another "shoot 'em up" to be thrown on John Clare's heap of derivative rubbish.

It seems to me that *Myst* represents an exciting development in the evolution of narrative structure and should not be dismissed because it dares not to be a book. In carnivalesque fashion it requires the adoption of a new identity (as you become the lone explorer of Myst's shores), which nonetheless relies on self-knowledge reaped from everyday life. Furthermore, in the manner of Bakhtin's carnival square, its opaque presentation gives the impression of a world to be discovered anew, of a world within our own which, while obeying its own rules and laws, draws on the conventions of real life for its construction. In many ways, *Myst*'s game-play offers its player-reader the constructive time-out allowed by carnival and so the opportunity for a similar analysis of self and society.

LOOKING TO THE FUTURE

Many games and rituals, it is true, merely socialize us to the culture we live in, but in genuinely playful activity we negate the ordinary and open up novel frames of reference and innovative alternatives to our conventional ideas and behaviors (Appleyard 55).

If adolescent readers are willing to engage with new literacies as their texts cross the divide between book and game, then we should be prepared to follow them across the bridge that brings ideas and action together. The texts in this chapter represent an experimental challenge to conventional forms of narrative, and so it is not surprising that there are problems in the execution of elective play. However, if we consequently refuse to accept these texts, then we are guilty of a regressive intolerance which is likely to alienate young people. I am not suggesting that even the most inventive of electronic narratives should replace books; indeed it should not be a question of ousting one format with another as, evidently, different formats can work side by side.

The inherent danger in my selection of texts is that discussion becomes dominated and even distorted by qualitative issues of literary content. The intricate plotting and thematic agility of *Hexwood* might be superior to that of *City of Thieves* and *Myst*, but such an assertion misses the point of this chapter. Each of these texts is representative of a distinct narrative structure, and it is the elective nature of these structures which is of central concern. *Myst* represents the most effective elective structure, for its multimedia platform is able to support the invisible pathways of its authorship, blurring the boundaries between author and player-reader, reality and fantasy.

Of course, the elective potential of *Myst* could be realized in much more exciting ways. Imagine an electronic narrative which, making use of AI technology, could adapt itself to the player-reader's individual response, or consider a collaboration between such authors as Diana Wynne Jones or Philip Pullman and software developers such as Cyan. The possibilities are endless. Consequently, we need to welcome these hybrid texts as part of the evolutionary narrative and supratextual landscape and to embrace them for the "timeout" pleasures they offer youth in a world characterized by seriousness and relentless reality.

NOTE

1. David Perry, a game developer for Shiney Entertainment, states that eight- to sixteen-year-old children constitute the company's best target market (quoted in *Edge* editorial 29).

WORKS CITED

Appleyard, Joseph. *Becoming a Reader.* Cambridge, Eng.: Cambridge University Press, 1994.

"An Audience with Dave Perry." *Edge: UK Edition* 33 (June 1996): 26–29.

Bakhtin, Mikhail. *Rabelais and His World.* Trans. H. Iswolsky. Bloomington: Indiana University Press, 1984.

Bruner, Jerome. *Actual Minds, Possible Worlds.* Cambridge, MA: Harvard University Press, 1986.

Clare, John. "The Role of Computers." *The Best for Your Children: Part I. Ages 0–5 Pre-School,* ed. John Clare and Chris Woodhead. London: Telegraph Group, 2001. 18.

Cyan, Inc. *Myst.* Hartlepool, Eng.: Broderbund Software, 1993.

Erikson, Erik. *Toys and Reasons: Stages in the Ritualization of Experience.* New York: Norton, 1977.

Hutcheon, Linda. *A Poetics of Postmodernism: History, Theory, Fiction.* London: Routledge, 1988.

Jones, Diana Wynne. *Hexwood.* London: Mammoth, 1994.

Korky, Paul, and Valerie Thomas. *Winnie the Witch.* Oxford: Oxford University Press, 1987.

Livingstone, Ian. *City of Thieves.* Harmondsworth, Eng.: Puffin, 1983.

Morris, Dave. *The Island of Adventure Gamebook.* London: Macmillan, 1994.

Plowman, Lydia. "Narrative, Interactivity and the Secret World of Multimedia." *English and Media Magazine* 35 (Autumn 1996): 44–48.

———. "Narrative, Linearity and Interactivity: Making Sense of Interactive Multimedia." *British Journal of Educational Technology* 27, 2 (1996): 92–105

Sainsbury, Lisa. "Tales from the Mouse House: Playing with Reading on CD-ROM." *Where Texts and Readers Meet,* ed. Eve Beaume and Victor Watson. London: Routledge, 2000. 82–97.

Stine, R. L. *Deep in the Jungle of Doom.* Goosebumps series. London: Scholastic, 1999.

Turkle, Sherry. *Life on the Screen.* London: Weidenfeld & Nicolson, 1996.

12

The Orangutan in the Library:
The Comfort of Strangeness in Terry Pratchett's Discworld Novels

David Buchbinder

Terry Pratchett is certainly a popular writer—of that there can be no question. His Discworld novels now number twenty-eight, including *The Amazing Maurice and His Educated Rodents*, the first work intended for children in the series, and another novel is scheduled to appear in early 2002. The books have been translated into several languages (an interesting phenomenon, given the rather English world and customs depicted in the series). There is an electronic game based on the fantasy narratives, and animated film versions of some of the novels have also been produced.

Moreover, a sort of support-and-publicity industry has grown up around the Discworld series. These include the publication of maps (for instance, *The Streets of Ankh-Morpork*), cookbooks (*Nanny Ogg's Cookbook*) and annual diaries (the *Discworld Fools' Guild Yearbook*, which offers an eight-day week, Octeday following Sunday). There is a *Discworld Companion*, as well as a guide to the ways things work in the Discworld, *The Science of Discworld*, both with Pratchett as coauthor. The final pages of several of the novels advertise figurines based on characters in the Discworld series, as well as at least one international convention centered on the Discworld *oeuvre*. There are numerous Web sites in several languages dedicated to Pratchett, the L-Space Web site being perhaps the most informative—certainly the most ambitious, including the electronic version of an M.A. thesis on Pratchett's work and identifications of the many intertexts and intertextual jokes embedded in the individual novels.

While for some time most of the serious, nonfan material on Pratchett's output has consisted largely of reviews of new titles in the series, gradually a body of scholarly commentary on Pratchett's Discworld novels is emerging, as evidenced, for instance, by the recent appearance of a collection of essays, *Terry Pratchett: Guilty of Literature*, edited by Andrew M. Butler and others. The present chapter is, of course, a further instance of the gradual movement of Pratchett's work into the arena of scholarly analysis, commentary, and criticism.

In this way, readers of Pratchett's Discworld participate actively in its creation and re-creation in different forms. Yet there is also a tendency in such participation to seek a certain fixing of both the spatial and temporal coordinates and other "facts" of the Discworld. Of this desire for consistency Pratchett has remarked, "sometimes even I forget who was who, and where things are. Readers don't like that sort of thing. They write me letters" (quoted in Pratchett & Briggs 8–9).

Yet this occasional writerly amnesia has not been a generic trait of fantasy fiction. Indeed, most fantasy authors have been extremely careful to maintain the consistency of the worlds they create, even when—as in J. R. R. Tolkien's *Lord of the Rings*—the imagined world is enormously complicated by a detailed attention to racial or ethnic histories as well as to a general history anterior to the events unfolded in the actual narrative, to various linguistic groups, to mythologies, and so on. This is signaled, for instance, by the provision of maps of the fictional world as part of the text, not, as in the case of the Discworld series, as a series of belated additions and supplements to the text (though of course any such map is, in some sense, a supplement to the written narrative). One effect of this punctilious observation by the fantasy author of the cosmological "facts" of the world that she or he creates, of course, has been to condition readers to *anticipate* that consistency: No wonder, therefore, that Pratchett receives letters from disgruntled or merely puzzled readers.

Should we assume therefore that Pratchett's is a slapdash sort of art of fantasy fiction writing? He himself has observed

I don't think ... even the most rabid fan expects complete consistency within Discworld, because in Ankh-Morpork you have what is apparently a Renaissance city, but with elements of early Victorian England, and the medieval world is still hanging on. It's in a permanent state of turmoil, which is very interesting for the author. (quoted in Hills 130)

The interest for the author aside, I suggest that this latter comment points to a pronounced characteristic of the Discworld series, namely, its tendency to satirize, ridicule, or deconstruct (these activities are not, of course, mutually contradictory) the traditional fantasy fiction narrative, and in particular that genre's epic form.

Space does not allow a thoroughgoing comparative analysis between Pratchett's version of the fantasy world and narrative and that of the genre's more traditional, even conservative, exponents. If we take Tolkien's epic as the domi-

nant example of twentieth-century modernist fantasy narrative, certain characteristics can be enumerated that will be found in many other fantasy narratives: For instance, a predilection for an archaized, cadenced language; the motif
of the quest to attain something, discover some knowledge, or destroy some object; the reinscription of traditional gender roles, by which women may be represented as beautiful and desirable, but not sexualized, men as brave and chaste
(those characters violating these narrative requirements often stigmatized as
immoral or, worse, as villainous); nobility of motive and heroism of deed; willingness to sacrifice oneself or one's object of love and desire to the greater good;
and a valorization of military codes of honor and the concomitant foregrounding of a masculine cult of comradeship and close male bonding. Above all, there
is often the sense of a closed universe, however akin to our own actual physical
or social world it might be.

Pratchett's Discworld series systematically disrupts such traditional features of classical fantasy writing. The Discworld itself is literally a disc, not a
sphere, transported through space on the backs of four elephants that stand in
turn upon the carapace of Great A'Tuin, a gigantic cosmic turtle (or astroche-
lonian, as Pratchett periodically calls it) swimming slowly through space toward a mysterious destination and destiny—in *The Light Fantastic* it is to
hatch a brood of eight eggs (274–75). A disc-shaped world is in itself something of a novelty in fantasy fiction, though versions of it can be found in science fiction (for instance, Larry Niven's Ringworld series, or the torus-shaped
worlds in Iain M. Banks's Culture series). In addition, Pratchett's imaginary
universe is porous, leaky—it allows various aspects of our own social and cultural world to intrude. Hollywood and filmmaking (*Moving Pictures*), rock
music (*Soul Music*), journalism and newspapers (*The Truth*)—these and other
elements create powerful connections between the fictional fantasy world and
the reader's social reality that subvert fantasy's traditionally closed universes.
Moreover, intertextual allusions also function to redirect the reader's attention to the sociocultural world with which she or he is familiar, problematiz-
ing any simple immersion in the fantasy world at hand. Thus, for instance,
Moving Pictures begins

Watch …
This is space. It's sometimes called the final frontier. (9)

The second line reworks the famous portentous voiceover opening to each
episode of the television series *Star Trek*—"Space—the final frontier"—
thereby reminding the reader of the world outside the text.

Nor does Pratchett indulge in the fondness for archaic language often found
in narratives of the fantasy genre. However, just as Tolkien was careful to construct different linguistic habits for the various races or ethnicities in his imagined world, so Pratchett also creates registers of linguistic difference, whether

the precise, ironic elegance of the speech of Lord Vetinari, the patrician of Ankh-Morpork, the demotic language of such lower-class characters as Nobby Nobbs of the Ankh-Morpork Night Watch, or the earthy provincial vulgarities of Nanny Ogg, one of the witches of the Kingdom of Lancre.

The quest motif in the Discworld series is largely focused on a search for information, knowledge, even the truth. At the simplest and most literal level, in the narratives centered on the Watch this theme resolves itself as the process of detection of the culprits responsible for nefarious activities. But it is also the theme, for instance, in *Hogfather*, where Susan, Duchess of Sto Helit, finds herself having to solve the riddle of the vanishing tooth fairies and, indeed, of children's lost teeth.[1] A more complex example of this motif is to be found in one subplot in *The Truth*, which likewise focuses on the discovery of "the truth," though initially from the perspective of journalistic interrogation of events. This plot resumes a motif to be found elsewhere in the Pratchett *oeuvre*, namely, the sinister forces of conservatism. William de Worde[2] discovers that his father is plotting with a cartel of noblemen to do away with the Patrician Vetinari, in order to reinstate the nobility as the ruling class of Ankh-Morpork. Similarly, in *Men at Arms* the assassin Edward d'Eath, last scion of one of Ankh-Morpork's oldest families, attempts to restore monarchy in the city (there are clear indications that Carrot, a human raised by dwarves, is the rightful king—a plot device straight out of traditional melodrama, except that Carrot, who seems, in this novel at least, to be aware of his ancestry, declines to take up his birthright). In *Feet of Clay*, there is an attempt, again by a clique of noblemen, to set up Nobby Nobbs, the most disreputable of the members of the Night Watch, as a puppet king. And there are other examples in the Discworld series.[3] Such examples suggest that a theme that underlies the series itself is that epistemological quests can be only *provisionally* successful: As the sequence continues to unfold, Pratchett's refusal to fix the details and make them consistent means that the "truth" remains always *to be* uncovered and only *temporarily* recognized. Given the traditional marking of fantasy as purely escapist literature, this motif places the Discworld series apart from the conventional fantasy narrative.

Political issues in the real world also find expression in the Discworld novels. For instance, in *Equal Rites*, Esk's right, as a female, to study wizardry at Unseen University, an institution hitherto with an exclusively male student body, raises questions of equity and civil rights. The nonchalant acceptance of Nobby's penchant for cross-dressing as part of his quest to find his inner woman—a process that begins in *Jingo*—together with the wizard Rincewind's encounter, in a parody of the Sydney Gay and Lesbian Mardi Gras, with the drag queens on the continent of Ecksecksecksecks[4] (*The Last Continent* 319 ff.) indicate Pratchett's awareness of social issues to do with nonnormative gender constructions and sexual orientations.

On the Discworld, honor and pragmatism go hand in hand—even Samuel Vimes's sense of duty and honor are combined with a strong sense of territorialism and professionalism, so that several impulses are served in the way that he keeps law and order (such as it is) in Ankh-Morpork. By contrast, Lord Vetinari's ruthless Machiavellian autocracy may be read as the complement of Vimes's commitment to uphold the law: It is clear that Vetinari's political activities and motivations are subtle and deeply complex—as one would expect of someone who has licensed the Thieves' Guild to contract with the people of the city for a certain number of thefts, burglaries, and muggings and who has permitted the Thieves' Guild itself to attend (with a certain rapid finality) to infractions of this arrangement by overzealous "professional" members of the guild or by rank amateurs and interlopers. Vetinari is quite capable of swiftly and acutely analyzing situations and even of setting them up, as is demonstrated in *Feet of Clay* by his early realization that he is being poisoned by fumes from his candle (401); or, in *Guards! Guards!*, by the revelation that, having anticipated being imprisoned in one of his own cells, he has had the cell door designed in such a way as both to protect him from any danger outside the cell and to allow him to leave the cell whenever he chooses to do so (254–59).[5]

As to sexual relationships, we know that Mrs. Palm runs a brothel in the seedier part of Ankh-Morpork, with a reference to the old joke redefining the act of masturbation as a visit to Mrs. Palm and her five daughters—in *Guards! Guards!* Carrot lodges with Mrs. Palm, whom he mistakenly understands to be running a "boarding house" (41) rather than the more probable "bawdy house"—and there are continual references to sexuality, as well as eroticized descriptions of some of the female characters, such as Conina (*Sourcery*) or Ptraci (*Pyramids*). However, in the developing relationship of Carrot with the she-werewolf Angua, commencing in *Men at Arms*, we find the representation of a sexualized partnership: "And shortly after that, for Corporal Carrot, the Discworld moved" (*Men at Arms* 311). The announcement by Lady Sybil Vimes, née Ramkin, that she is pregnant (*The Fifth Elephant* 288) may come as something of a surprise to the reader, since not only are Sir Samuel and Lady Sybil apparently middle-aged, but their relationship seems to be companionate rather than sexual: Yet this is precisely the point—even the middle-aged, often represented in fantasy fiction as beyond the pull of desire, are permitted to engage in sex in Pratchett's reworking of the genre.

The subversion of traditional fantasy narrative suggests another reason for the popularity of the Discworld series among younger readers. Pratchett's novels, taken simply as narratives in the genre, are fast-paced, intriguing, and full of surprising turns. Moreover, they belong to a comparatively new subgenre in fantasy fiction, namely, comic fantasy. In the Discworld series, humor operates at various levels, from the worst sort of pun to high comedy, and is very self-aware: The occasional laboriously contrived setup thus reads as deliberate, rather than the result of incompetence or inexperience on the author's part.

Pratchett participates in a British tradition of satiric comic fiction that reaches back at least as far as Jonathan Swift and Henry Fielding, in the eighteenth century. He targets the shibboleths and sacred cows of late-twentieth-century culture—for instance, its entrepreneurial greed (symbolized in Ankh-Morpork by Cut-Me-Own-Throat Dibbler and in other places on the Discworld by his various avatars); its obsession with celebrity and fame (lampooned, for instance, in the rise from obscurity to stardom of Victor Tugelbend and Theda Withel in *Moving Pictures*); its fascination with technology (embodied in Ponder Stibbons, archetypal postgraduate student and techno-geek, who first appears in *Moving Pictures*, and whose bizarre invention Hex, reminiscent of a Heath Robinson/Rube Goldberg mechanical contraption, is Unseen University's equivalent to the computer—and uses a real mouse); and the late twentieth century's romance with managerialism (sent up in, among others, *Eric*, in which the bureaucratic Astfgl, the demon king of Hades—and there are intertextual references to the demon king of traditional English pantomime—is finessed by Lord Vassenego into becoming an ineffectual president, with an office, a desk, and endless opportunities to issue memos). In its satirizing of various and very familiar aspects of the world that its readers inhabit, the Discworld series invites us all to recognize our own social, historical, and cultural context and therefore to invest to some degree in individual novels, if not also in the series as a whole.

I am interested, however, in the younger readership of these works, for anecdotal evidence suggests that the Discworld series finds enthusiastic readers as young as twelve or thirteen years of age. Certainly the cartoonlike cover designs by Josh Kirby might suggest that the books are aimed chiefly at an adolescent audience (and is probably the reason that one finds from time to time some of the Discworld titles in the children's literature section of bookshops). However, the profusion of intertextual, historical, and other allusions scattered throughout the novels suggests that Pratchett aims at a wider audience than simply a youth audience. Many of those references—for instance, as Penelope Hill points out, *Moving Pictures* includes parodic allusions to many classic films, for example, *Singin' in the Rain, Gone with the Wind,* and *King Kong* (59)—are unlikely to be recognized by adolescents attuned chiefly to the most recent and contemporary of cultural outputs. Nevertheless, the novels are replete with cultural references that younger readers *are* likely to pick up. These include women's rights (*Equal Rites*); racial prejudice and chauvinistic patriotism (*Jingo*); religious fundamentalism and prejudice (*Small Gods*); the media that have come to dominate our lives—rock music (or "music with rocks in," as it is called in *Soul Music*), cinema (*Moving Pictures*), and print journalism (*The Truth*); and the fantasy of the island getaway vacation and Australia as a holiday destination (*The Last Continent*). Broader cultural concerns are also targeted, for instance, the presence and fear of death (a personified Death stalks through many of the novels, but some, for example, *Mort* and *Reaper Man*, feature him as a central character).

The youthful desire for savvy or "street cred" often results in the appearance, at least, if not also the reality, of a world-weariness and cynicism about their culture, its values, and its actions; and the relentless parody and often sardonic humor that run throughout the Discworld series no doubt appeal to such a readership. Indeed, the first of the series, *The Colour of Magic*, a collection of related short stories, opens with a parody of Fritz Leiber's classic Lankhmar series of fantasy novels, which ranks high with youthful *cognoscenti* of the genre. The names alone echo Leiber's: His heroes Fafhrd and the Gray Mouser become Bravd and the Weasel under Pratchett's parodically transformative hand, while the latter's city of Ankh-Morpork seems to be a partial anagram of Leiber's Lankhmar.

In this book, too, we first make the acquaintance of the Luggage. Fashioned of magical sapient pearwood and provided with a myriad of legs, it is a chest that functions not only as luggage normally does (though, unlike one's suitcases in the real world, the Luggage miraculously cannot be lost, for it always finds its owner, no matter in which country or plane of reality the latter may be), but also as a sort of companion and pet, on the one hand,[6] and menacing bodyguard on the other—it will protect its owner, and its open lid is often likened to a gaping maw ready to swallow any opponent. And, to get its way, it is just as likely to turn on its friends. However, in its magical capacity to open and produce almost any item one might require or desire—from fresh linen to gold—it is reminiscent of the magical chests and boxes that feature in children's fantasy stories like those by Enid Blyton, a genre revived recently in J. K. Rowling's Harry Potter series, though perhaps a little removed from the childhood reading experiences of many youngsters today.

In *The Light Fantastic* we meet another parody of another hero from another fantasy series: Cohen the Barbarian, a wizened elderly hero whose name suggests Jewishness, and who serves to ridicule Robert E. Howard's jutting-jawed, muscle-bound, taciturn, and definitely pagan hero Conan the Barbarian. Pratchett's Discworld narratives thus may be understood as a form of meta-fantasy fiction, in that it is fantasy self-consciously speaking about and lampooning itself; and this is certainly a type of narrative that a youthful audience, cynical about the practices and ideology of its culture, is likely to appreciate.

As John Clute points out, several narrative sequences can be identified in the series:

The first two titles in the sequence—*The Colour of Magic*, which is a series of linked novellas, and *The Light Fantastic*, which is a proper novel—go together to make one long introductory tale, which comprises a kind of guided tour of the Discworld. The remaining volumes are grouped into several sequences—the main three deal with Granny Weatherwax and her world, with Grimes [sic] and Carrot of the Ankh-Morpork police or Watch, and with Death. Each sequence follows a rough internal chronology, though it shows no clear chronological relationship to the other Discworld stories. (15)

These three sequences are certainly dominant ones. However, there are other ways to group the novels, and Clute himself goes on to indicate some of these, though largely by way of indicating Pratchett's development as a writer and, especially, as a writer of comedy. For instance, he describes the middle period novels as belonging to the Cinderella type, in which we learn "the story of an adolescent boy or girl who must achieve some goal, usually that of gaining proper employment in one or another of the countries spread across the disc" (15).

While this is—as the applied sobriquet of Cinderella suggests—both a traditional and very familiar theme (and one that has no doubt featured in many of the private fantasies of young people, as a way to escape current family circumstances), it may also have special significance to a young readership facing a future of uncertain stability of employment and disillusioned by the history of exploitative commercialism and economic greed of immediately antecedent generations. For another thread running through the Discworld narratives is that of the control and oppression of the young by the old. In the witch sequence, for instance, the neophyte witches Magrat Garlick and, later, Agnes Nitt are controlled and managed by the more powerful Granny (Esme) Weatherwax and Nanny (Gytha) Ogg (*Wyrd Sisters, Witches Abroad, Lords and Ladies, Maskerade, Carpe Jugulum*)—indeed, Agnes has to be manipulated into accepting her witch status. In *Equal Rites*, the as-yet-unborn girl infant Esk in the village of Bad Ass in the Kingdom of Lancre, erroneously taken by the dying wizard Drum Billet to be the eighth son of an eighth son (the smith, somewhat redundantly named Gordo Smith), inherits the wizard's staff, and thus becomes a wizard herself. However, she must first face the reluctance of Granny Weatherwax to allow a female to become a wizard—whose magic generically is understood to be masculine—rather than a witch; and then Esk must confront the accumulated prejudice and conservatism of Unseen University when she seeks training there as a wizard. Upon the death of his father, Teppic, in *Pyramids*, reluctantly must give up his training at the Assassins' Guild in Ankh-Morpork to return to Egypt-like Djelibeybi (one of Pratchett's many puns) to take up his throne and scepter and submit himself to the endless routine of kingship under the authority of the high priest Dios. In *Sourcery*, the boy Coin, a powerful "sourcerer" (that is, one who draws on but also becomes the source of magic itself), is controlled by his malevolent and only putatively deceased father Ipslore, whose soul inhabits the wizard's staff that he has bequeathed to his son. Even the appalling offspring of the vampire Count de Magpyr in *Carpe Jugulum* chafe beneath the yoke of their progressive father, yearning to exercise their own power as vampires and do as they like.[7] And in the sequence centered on Susan Sto Helit, the daughter of Death's erstwhile apprentice Mort and Ysabell, Death's adopted daughter, the heroine finds herself drawn into her adoptive grandfather's activities in the world of humans, and especially his recurring battle with the gray Auditors of the universe, who seek to bring life and all its vibrancy, muddle, and unpredictability into stasis because it is so much easier to manage and account for (*Reaper Man, Hog-father, Thief of Time*).

The tyranny of the older generation is felt also in *The Fifth Elephant* by Angua, a member of the City Watch but also a werewolf, daughter of the Baron von Uberwald. Her werewolf heritage means that she can never take her place fully as a human being in the Watch, though Carrot ignores this aspect of Angua, preferring to accept her as she is.[8] Paternalistic control and manipulation, which we have already seen in the attempts by conservative forces in Ankh-Morpork to control the city's fortunes, are to be found also in the way the patrician's secretary Lupine Wonse seeks to use his rabble, constituted as an arcane society, the Elucidated Brethren of the Ebon Night, to summon forth the magical dragon that will give him the power to "cleanse" and control Ankh-Morpork (*Guards! Guards!*). And the symbolic parental influence of Ankh-Morpork's aristocracy, manifesting itself in various ways—the calm certainty of Lord Vetinari, the patrician, as well as the snobbery, moral blindness, and outright stupidity of many of the landed class—causes Captain Samuel Vimes (the descendant of a republican regicide) irritation similar to that felt by the young toward their elders, even when he marries Lady Sybil Ramkin and is himself ennobled as a knight, becoming Commander Sir Samuel Vimes (in *Men at Arms*).

This sort of parental control magnified institutionally and socially is to be found also in the sequence of novels centered on the hapless wizard (or, as he spells it on his hat, "Wizzard") Rincewind. He appears in the first story in *The Colour of Magic* and reappears periodically through the series, the most recent novel so far in which he features being *The Last Continent.* A consummate coward, Rincewind's greatest talent is survival, and even Death becomes fascinated by Rincewind's ability to evade his reach: He drops in for a courtesy visit to Rincewind when the wizard is imprisoned and faces hanging in the morning. He remarks to Rincewind, "I shall look forward to hearing how you escaped" (*The Last Continent* 278). In almost all cases, Rincewind's predicaments are not of his making but are rather imposed upon him by circumstances created by the will or desire of others.

The theme of control by parental or quasi-parental figures and institutions coincides in places with another, still more sinister, theme, namely, that of the possession of another's body or soul or mental faculties. I have already mentioned Coin's submission to his father Ipslore's cruel tutelage in *Sourcery*, which may be counted in this category, as may the more benign possession of Agnes Nitt by her alter ego Perdita.[9] Agnes is also mind-controlled by the vampire Vlad, the son of Count de Magpyr in *Carpe Jugulum;* and the clay golems in *Feet of Clay* may be understood also as functioning under a form of possession, caused by the script placed in their hollow heads—the liberation of the golem Dorfl from *his* script (by the insertion of another script that makes him his own owner) makes this clear. In *Witches Abroad*, Granny Weatherwax confronts her evil sister, who seeks to control the process of narrative itself, while the forms of possession exercised, first, by Holy Wood, in *Moving Pictures*, over both those involved in producing films and those consuming them, and second, in *Soul Music*, by Imp's guitar or, more abstractly, the music of the universe over audiences, might be regarded as barely veiled warnings against the unquestioning acceptance of the popular culture in which young readers are always-already immersed.

In the context of the theme of control over others, Pratchett is capable of creating characters who strike an extremely sinister chord. In *Hogfather*, the mad Mister Teatime (pronounced "Tay-ah-tim-ay," 30 and *passim*), described by Lord Downey, the head of the Guild of Assassins, as possessing a "corkscrew of a mind" (29), exhibits both a coolness about and a relish for his work as an Assassin that must surely appall most readers. Mr. Clete, secretary of the Guild of Musicians in *Soul Music*, is simply a thuggish union executive who does not balk at employing strong-arm tactics. His mirthless laugh—"Hat. Hat. Hat" (33 and *passim*)—is as chilling as Teatime's polite social conversation. In a fine multiple irony, his soul is taken not by Death but by the Death of Rats, whose snigger echoes Clete's:

> He looked down at what he'd thought was his body, and realized that he could see through it, and that it was fading away.
> "Oh, dear," he said, "Hat. Hat. Hat."
> The figure grinned, and swung its tiny scythe.
> SNH, SNH, SNH. (369)

The motif of control, though it has many ramifications, may especially appeal to adolescent readers of the Discworld novel as they seek to establish their own presence in the social world. The figure of the librarian of Unseen University perhaps best represents such a reader's social fears and fantasies. Transformed by a magical accident into an orangutan (*The Light Fantastic* 15), the librarian insists on retaining his new form, even going so far as to prevent any of his wizard colleagues from finding out his real name, lest they forcibly return him to human shape (see *The Last Continent* 33 ff.). We may read this as articulating a desire to retain control over his own identity and, hence, destiny.

In *The Last Continent*, the librarian succumbs to an illness that affects his morphic field, so that, as he sneezes, he changes shape. He is last seen—both in this novel and the series as a whole—as a baby orangutan on the shores of the lost continent of the title (342). Read across the span of the series, the librarian's physical identity may thus be understood as bridging childhood to adulthood, the insistent references to his size, strength, and hairiness suggesting perhaps some of the effects of puberty on a male. That is, the librarian may be understood as representing the process of adolescence itself; and, I suggest, specifically of *male* adolescence.

This idea is strengthened by certain other details in the narratives concerned with the librarian, who, while not so far the central character in any of the narratives, does play important roles in a number of the novels. As a librarian, he is privy to certain arcane knowledges, such as the existence of L-Space (that is, Library Space). These knowledges allow him to go back in time to identify the book of dragon lore stolen from the library (*Guards! Guards!* 201); they allow him, moreover, to cross space, to rescue volumes from the burning library at Ephebe and to relocate them in the library at Unseen University (*Small Gods* 216). He alone appears capable of controlling the magical books of the library, which have minds and wills of their own; and he protects them when they are threatened by the return of sorcery (*Sourcery* 151 ff.). His knowledge of out-of-the-way information enables him to identify and interpret the strange glyphs warning of the forces from another plane of reality that seek to dominate the minds of the inhabitants of the Discworld through film (*Moving Pictures* 164–65) and to consult the most dangerous of the magical books in the library, the *Necrotelicomnicon* (168–70, 174–77). This sort of specialized knowledge is not reserved only for professionals like librarians—or doctors or lawyers, if it comes to that: With the advent of the Internet, which L-Space closely resembles in its rhizomatous connecting of different spaces and knowledges, young people have also the potential to develop arcane specialties, thanks to the Information Superhighway.

In *Soul Music* the librarian, himself a musician of some talent, is overcome by his exposure to rock music and is inspired to try playing the Unseen University organ in this mode (115–16), which wakes up the entire university staff and results in the organ's explosion: I imagine that many a reader with a teenage would-be guitarist in the house feels a twinge of recognition and sympathy at this point in this particular novel. But worse—and equally recognizable—is to follow: As though tracing the evolution of a juvenile delinquent, the narrative represents the librarian once more seeking specialized knowledge, here the notebooks of Leonard of Quirm (the Discworld's equivalent of Leonardo da Vinci, of course), in order to build the Discworld's version of the first motorbike (132–33, 346–49). In addition, he frequents the Mended Drum, where he plays Barbarian Invaders, a mechanical version of the electronic Space Invaders of our own world. The librarian screams "with rage every time he lost a penny" (259).

Like a teenage male, the librarian is replete with contradictions. Though originally human, he prefers to remain an ape and thinks of himself as separate from humans (see, for instance, *Guards! Guards!* 264–65; *Maskerade* 283). Outwardly an animal, he is intelligent and resourceful in human ways, yet he builds a nest for himself in the library out of blankets and rags (see, for instance, *Guards! Guards!* 9)—which must bear, to a reader with adolescent children, a strong resemblance to a teenage son's bedroom. Capable of rage at being called a monkey instead of an ape, the librarian nonetheless is able to control himself and behave in a kindly and gentlemanly manner, as when he prevents Agnes from finishing the word "monkey": "The orangutan raised its other hand and waved a finger politely in front of Agnes's face" (*Maskerade* 255–56). He is thus positioned at the nexus of various oppositions, the chief of which are articulated in his physical appearance and his professional function: The ape who is nonetheless a librarian. In this, Pratchett neatly encapsulates and ironizes the idea that ontogeny recapitulates phylogeny, for while the librarian's physical form seems to represent human regression back to an earlier evolutionary phase, his intellectual and emotional capacities far exceed those of most of the humans on the Discworld, including the wizards of Unseen University itself. He is thus an endearing figure whose several contradictions are likely to recommend themselves to adolescent readers—especially males—still trying to find their own social identities in an eventful world.

NOTES

1. This novel also engagingly introduces us to Bilious, the Oh God of Hangovers: Just as Dorian Gray's portrait in Oscar Wilde's novel becomes the receptacle of its original's decline into old age and descent into immorality, so poor Bilious is the recipient of the headaches and nausea that properly belong to the merry-making and carefree God of Wine.

2. His name echoes that of Wynkyn de Worde, originally Jan van Wynkyn, the fifteenth-century Alsace-born printer who became Caxton's assistant in England and, upon his master's death in 1491, inherited the press.

3. On occasion, however, Pratchett ironically and humorously reverses this theme of a return to an anterior, oppressive state of things: In *Carpe Jugulum*, for instance, the old Count de Magpyr awakens from his cataleptic sleep to find that his descendants, in their drive to become modern vampires (ruling by forced consent, no longer allergic to daylight or to garlic, and so on), have violated the family's traditional code of conduct (which includes impeccable manners), and he dispatches them.

4. For which read "Australia"—the name is a reference is to a certain brand of Australian beer.

5. He has also trained the magic-affected rats in the prison to act as his servants, messengers, and retainers while he remains incarcerated.

6. In *Interesting Times*, the Luggage finds an apparently female Luggage and sires "four little chests, the smallest being about the size of a lady's handbag" (345).

7. As so often in Pratchett's work, a great deal of subtle meaning as well as a complex joke may be packed into the title of this novel. *Carpe jugulum*, "seize the throat," at once encapsulates the fabled activity of the vampire while reminding us at the same time, through its twisting of the original, of the Roman poet Horace's ode (I, 11) which ends with the lines "Carpe diem, quam minimum credula postero": "Seize today, and put as little trust as you can in the morrow," precisely the motto of the Magpyr offspring. The same poem contains the line "Tu ne quaesieris, scire nefas": "Do not ask, such knowledge is not for us," an idea that has its own resonance in this novel. At the same time, however, *jugulum*, "throat," may also be intended as a punning diminutive of *jugum*, "yoke." Hence, *carpe jugulum* may mean "seize the little yoke," a theme that runs through the narrative, as various characters—the King, Verence; Magrat, his wife;

Agnes Nitt (and her *alter ego* Perdita); the Omnian cleric Mightily Oats; even Granny Weatherwax—are each made to confront and accept his or her own individual limitations.

8. The fact that Wolfgang, her brother in Uberwald, has an attitude toward nonwerewolf kind that echoes Nazi master-race ideology (complete with a cult of exercise and nudity) suggests that Angua fears the influence not only of her physical identity as werewolf but also of her ideological heritage, as daughter of an aggressive, cunning, and tyrannically ambitious lineage.

9. Perdita X Nitt is her chosen *nom de sorcière* in *Lords and Ladies*, but becomes Perdita X Dream as Agnes's stage name in *Maskerade*, narratively a parody of Andrew Lloyd Weber's *Phantom of the Opera*. It is in this novel that Perdita comes into her own as the alter ego, acting heroically later in *Carpe Jugulum*.

WORKS CITED

Butler, Andrew M., Edward James, and Farah Mendlesohn, eds. *Terry Pratchett: Guilty of Literature*. Foundation Studies in Science Fiction, vol. 2. Reading, Eng.: Science Fiction Foundation, n.d.

Clute, John. "Coming of Age." *Terry Pratchett: Guilty of Literature*, ed. Andrew M. Butler, Edward James, and Farah Mendlesohn. Foundation Studies in Science Fiction, vol. 2. Reading: Science Fiction Foundation, n.d. 7–19.

Hill, Penelope. "Unseen University." *Terry Pratchett: Guilty of Literature*, ed. Andrew M. Butler, Edward James, and Farah Mendlesohn. Foundation Studies in Science Fiction, vol. 2. Reading: Science Fiction Foundation, n.d. 51–65.

Hills, Matthew. "Mapping Narrative Spaces." *Terry Pratchett: Guilty of Literature*, ed. Andrew M. Butler, Edward James, and Farah Mendlesohn. Foundation Studies in Science Fiction, vol. 2. Reading: Science Fiction Foundation, n.d. 129–44.

The L-Space Web. 14 Oct. 2001 http://www.lspace.org.

Pratchett, Terry. *The Amazing Maurice and His Educated Rodents*. London: Doubleday, 2001.

———. *Carpe Jugulum*. London: Corgi, 1999.

———. *The Colour of Magic*. London: Corgi, 1998.

———. *Equal Rites*. London: Corgi, 1987.

———. *Eric*. London: Corgi/Vista, 1996.

———. *Feet of Clay*. London: Corgi, 1997.

———. *The Fifth Elephant*. London: Doubleday, 1999.

———. *Guards! Guards!*. London: Corgi, 1990.

———. *Hogfather*. London: Corgi, 1997.

———. *Interesting Times*. London: Corgi, 1995.

———. *Jingo*. London: Corgi, 1998.

———. *The Last Continent*. London: Corgi, 1999.

———. *The Light Fantastic*. London: Corgi, 1996.

———. *Lords and Ladies*. London: Corgi, 1995.

———. *Maskerade*. London: Corgi, 1996.

———. *Men at Arms*. London: Corgi, 1998.

———. *Mort*. London: Corgi, 1997.

———. *Moving Pictures*. London: Corgi, 1991.

————. *Pyramids*. London: Corgi, 1997.

————. *Reaper Man*. London: Corgi, 1992.

————. *Small Gods*. London: Corgi, 1998.

————. *Soul Music*. London: Corgi, 1995.

————. *Sourcery*. London: Corgi, 1999.

————. *The Streets of Ankh-Morpork*. London: Corgi, 1993.

————. *Thief of Time*. London: Doubleday, 2001.

————. *The Truth*. London: Doubleday, 2000.

————. *Witches Abroad*. London: Corgi, 1998.

————. *Wyrd Sisters*. London: Corgi, 1998.

Pratchett, Terry, and Stephen Briggs. *The Discworld Companion*. London: Millennium-Gollancz, 2000.

Pratchett, Terry, Stephen Briggs, and Tina Hannan. *Nanny Ogg's Cookbook*. London: Transworld, 1999.

Pratchett, Terry, Lyn Pratchett, and Stephen Briggs. *Discworld Fool's Guild Yearbook Diary 2001*. London: Gollancz-Orion, 2000.

Pratchett, Terry, Ian Stewart, and Jack Cohen. *The Science of Discworld*. London: Ebury, 2000.

Tolkien, J. R. R. *The Fellowship of the Ring, Being the First Part of the Lord of the Rings*. New York: Ballantine, 1965.

————. *The Return of the King, Being the Third Part of the Lord of the Rings*. New York: Ballantine, 1965.

————. *The Two Towers, Being the Second Part of the Lord of the Rings*. New York: Ballantine, 1965.

13

Coprophilia for Kids:
The Culture of Grossness

Roderick McGillis

Caveat lector: The subject is unsavoury
The role of the lower intestine in the efforts to build a better nation is one
that is often neglected by historians.

Terry Pratchett, *Carpe Jugulum*

This chapter is neither a mere listing of the instances of the gross and disgusting in kids' culture today, nor a jeremiad. To list examples of the gross is easy:
What the books in Bantam's short-lived "Barf-O-Rama" series refer to as the
"five regrettable fluids" (defined as "pukus, mukus, waximus auriculas, numero
uno, and numero dos" [Pollari, *To Wee* 115]) appear regularly in films, television programs, toys, and books for the young. Even commercials and advertisements display the splatter of food and disgusting acts. Here's a quick and
very slim list: Mr. Hankey the Christmas poo in *South Park*, Robert Munsch's
I Have to Go! (1987) and *Good Families Don't* (1990), the Meanie Babies toys
such as Hurley the Pukin Toucan and Boris the Mucousaurus, the "Gooflumps"
books supposedly written by one R. U. Slime, chewing gum in the form of poop
pellets that come inside a small plastic toilet, pooping cow and pig key chains,
television commercials for beer, Pizza Pops, and even catsup that delight in presenting displays of stupidity and uncouth behavior, and various computer
games and Web sites that display images of the gross and vulgar. For the six- to
nine-year-old reader, we have the "Captain Underpants" series by Dav Pilkey.
For adolescent moviegoers, we may add a sixth "regrettable fluid" to the list, as
viewers of *Scary Movie* (2000) or *Something About Mary* (1998) well know.
But, as I say, this chapter does not offer mere listing.

Nor do I wish to argue that such instances of the gross and uncouth are a sign of the deterioration or degeneration of culture, a sort of *fin de siècle* breakdown of civility and politeness or an indication of the dumbing down we hear so much about these days. Plenty of other people decry the vulgarity of kids' culture and what Jon Pareles refers to as our "grotesque cultural moment" in which the "governing intelligence seems to belong to a hormone-addled 15-year-old boy who can't tell whether he's horny or furious" (1–3). And so what I essay here is an understanding of what the current delight in the impolite might signify. Accordingly, I offer a series of observations held together by the proposition that what we are experiencing, from one point of view, is not new, and from another point of view is simply the workings of the so-called free market.

The market works on the principle of demand and supply: Ask for it and someone will produce it. But the relationship between the asking and producing is not that simple. First, the producer needs to know who is asking for what and to make the answer to this question less unpredictable than it might otherwise be, the producer makes assumptions about what it is the purchaser wishes to buy. To support these assumptions, the producer primes the purchasing pump by promoting certain products which the purchaser then assumes she or he wants to buy; indeed, the purchaser may even believe that he or she wanted to buy such a product before that product was available for purchase. ("Gee, I've always wanted something like that.") In other words, the purchaser feels free to buy that which s/he wants to buy; the purchaser feels s/he is in control of economic exchange. As Stephen Kline puts it, faith in the marketplace leads consumers to believe that they "will be sovereign because their choice determines what will be produced for that market" (2). The invisible hand of competition guides the working of this system of production and consumption and keeps the purchaser from knowing that the true "sovereign" here is money, exchange, the market itself. The trick is for producers to meet the choices of those who consume. Lately, children have become independent consumers (and in a big way), and the trick is to offer them what they are most likely to choose. We have run the gamut of products until now we find an array of the gross and vulgar available for consumption.

Someone somehow and at some time got the impression that children liked to play with things gross, and perhaps they do. If Freud's account is correct, then an antipathy to disgusting bodily effluvia is something we learn as part of the civilizing process. We learn, after a few years of training, not to play with our shit, and even to revile the stuff. As we grow into social beings, we put the gross and impolite behind us, so to speak. We can see such a civilizing process at work in, for example, the medieval book of courtesy, *The Babees Book* (c. 1475), in which the young reader is exhorted not to pick his nose or eat with his mouth full so bits fall out and disgrace the table. In a state of nature, perhaps we'd all be indulging in coprophagia. But, as I say, we learn not to do disgusting things and to avoid these things in others. Dominique Laporte in *The History of Shit* chronicles the effort to put the disgusting into its proper place and remove it from the lady's cosmetic table where fecal matter and urine found themselves useful as beauty aids until well into the eighteenth century (106–7). Earlier, in the fifteenth century, it was common practice "to use urine for the cleansing of draperies and clothes" (32). Once the nineteenth century discovered niceties of hygiene, feces and other material of the disgusting became taboo by the time we left the cradle.

And so why does contemporary culture carry on a distasteful love affair with the disgusting? Are the Meanie Babies and the Barf-O-Rama books signs of cultural decline? Delight in the disgusting may be such a sign; it may be the reduction of the "culture of Gothic" described by Mark Edmundson in *Nightmare on Main Street*, or it may be business as usual as Mark Caldwell judiciously suggests (without the pun) in *A Short History of Rudeness*. But then again it may be the continuing extension of the "feast of fools" or the spirit of carnival, that breaking out from conventions in order to maintain those very conventions. Carnival mimics a return to nature; it is, as Bataille suggests, "the cessation of work, the unrestrained consumption of its products and the deliberate violation of the most hallowed laws" (90). It is a release from that which humanizes us. Again, I draw upon Bataille: Carnival (what Bataille calls "festival") is "a return by man to his vomit" (90). The return to nature is necessarily a return to the body, an acceptance of that which is "accidental, natural, perishable" (91).

Carnival, as Bakhtin and Ashraf Rushdy after him, have argued, is a celebration of the "material bodily lower stratum" (*Rabelais*, title of chapter 6; Rushdy 2), a celebration intended "as the covert political statement of the people against oppressive hegemony" (Rushdy 2). However, this very "covert statement" is itself orchestrated by those forces the "people" think they are protesting against. The carnival works to contain as much as to release dangerous energies. In other words, carnival is an aspect of repression worked variously by state or market or whatever system is most powerful at any time. We might see this mechanism at work within the family when a parent works his or her will upon a child by carefully satisfying that child's desire. Satisfy and in doing so repress.

For the mechanism of repression to work, we need to feel that we have the reins of instinct in our own control and that we control the beast that desires to gallop free. That which disgusts has always served both a psychological and social purpose: Essentially the purpose of repression. That which disgusts us disgusts us precisely in order that we both receive sly pleasure and maintain order and civility (Miller). For children—I think given the context, I should switch to the colloquial "kids"—for kids, to delight in the gross and gruesome is to transgress. They have learned that adults disapprove of anything that smacks of the smutty and scatological, and so they enjoy the fun of shocking both themselves and those adults who represent the staid and perhaps stodgy politeness that wishes to keep itself clean, both bodily and mentally. Dav Pilkey's Captain Underpants books thrive on the shock-value of the gross. In the most recent volume, *Captain Underpants and the Perilous Plot of Professor Poopypants* (2000), the two young heroes, George and Harold, change the letters around in a school sign so that the sign reads "Please Don't Fart in a Diaper." When the principal, Mr. Krupp, catches them, they explain that what they have done is only a joke. Here's the dialogue:

> "Heh-heh," laughed Harold. "Th–this is just a little joke."
> "A JOKE?!!?" yelled Mr. Krupp. "Do you boys think that's funny???"
> George and Harold thought for a moment. "Well … *yeah*," said George.
> "Don't *you?*" asked Harold.
> "NO, I don't think it's funny!" yelled Mr. Krupp. "I think it's rude and offensive!"
> "That's why it's funny," said George. (28–29)

George and Harold understand that what they do is harmless and that the outrage of their elders is also harmless. And funny. Kids who read the Captain Underpants books learn in the first few pages of every book that George and Harold, despite being inveterate cut-ups responsible for all sorts of mischief, are "actually very nice boys. No matter what everybody else thought, they were good, sweet, and lovable.… Well, OK, maybe they weren't so sweet and lovable, but they were good nonetheless" (*Adventures* 3). These are the good bad boys Leslie Fiedler described forty years ago (254–87); we might call them artists of the unclean and the unacceptable. They triumph over adults who are pretty much a confining and stodgy lot, and they delight in the rude and off-color as a strategy to defeat the boredom of school. In *Captain Underpants and the Invasion of the Incredibly Naughty Cafeteria Ladies from Outer Space (and the Subsequent Assault of the Equally Evil Lunchroom Zombie Nerds)* (1999)—how could I resist including this richly allusive title?—we learn that the two boys are "very clever and good-hearted.… Their only problem is that they're fourth graders. And at George and Harold's school, fourth graders are expected to sit still and pay attention for *seven hours a day!*" (15). Obviously, we are to conclude that no one should be asked to sit still and pay attention for seven italicized hours a day. To deal with such purgatory, George and Harold delight in shocking their teachers. They also create comic books about Captain Underpants. These two are talented.

Kids like George and Harold know that adult politeness is a veneer. The adults who produce gross cultural products for kids also know pretensions to politeness are a veneer. In exposing what lies beneath the veneer, children and their complicit adult partners (here Dav Pilkey) make those who wish to maintain standards of politeness nervous, irritated, and sometimes even outraged (hence the loud capitalized exclamatory speech of the punningly named Mr. Krupp). Exposing adult hypocrisy takes the form of play, a messing about with things sticky, unstable, and fetid.

This exposition is, however, a duplicitous form of play. Perhaps because the exposing of the human being's necessary connection to the five (or six) regrettable fluids appears outside the norms of socially sanctioned behavior, it can cannily serve socially sanctioned behavior. Like the medieval carnival that Bakhtin so fulsomely discusses, the Captain Underpants books and other manifestations of the grotesque body in kids' culture serve as a release of instinctive urges to the naughty and perverse, harmless release that allows civilized behavior to carry on where it counts, in the institutional contexts of human interaction. Why not humor the kids if to do so means the kids will fall into line complacently once the giggle fit has run its course? And why not humor kids if to do so means greasing the sprockets of the market machine with spondulicks? Incorporate the gross into the system and it no longer threatens civility; rather, it becomes yet another aspect of order and civility.

Order and civility, however, come at a cost. And it is the cost that interests me here. What cost civility and order? For Freud, of course, the cost is repression of certain basic instincts. And repression serves a social good since those certain basic instincts, if allowed to have their way, would topple the intricate web of social interaction that civilization has laboriously constructed these past few millennia. Yet civilization has its discontents, as Freud noted; it chafes at the repressive supervision of what it perceives as superego forces, sometimes figured in the person of teacher, parent, police, CEO, or whoever has a position of influence and control. To delight in the disgusting is one way of demonstrating freedom from control. In-your-face "fartillery," a word I appropriate from the Barf-O-Rama books to indicate generally disgusting behavior, gives the propounder of the barrage of disgust the illusion of transgression, while he or she conforms to the consumerist ethic, if we can use the word *ethic* for market practices. Join the "Barf-O-Rama Club" (now defunct, I believe) or the Meanie Babies set, or participate in the Captain Underpants Contest (final page of *Captain Underpants and the Attack of the Talking Toilets*) and feel like a rebel, someone who spurns convention and all those stodgy, stiff-necked rituals of politeness perpetrated upon us by the guardians of civility and protectors from misrule. Join and spend your coin.

Disgust has entered the marketplace, as the Meanie Babies and poop pellet gum illustrate. Obviously, those who consider the economy consider kids, as well they might when preteens and teens together spend some $65.6 billion a year on consumer goods and influence their parents to the tune of another $168 billion (Minow & Lamay 56). Even if these figures are not fully reliable, they tell a story of child power the like of which was not on Mordecai Richler's mind in 1975 when he published *Jacob Two-Two Meets the Hooded Fang*, a book that championed "child power." But what kind of power do we have here? What connection does the power to spend have with the power to control one's own destiny? The child power Richler posited in *Jacob Two-Two* was akin to the array of "power" (flower power, black power, gray power, for example) that the 1960s spawned. This power promised what Michael Ignatieff has recently called "the ideal of authenticity" (99). The authentic life is the life freely chosen from among a plethora of possibilities. However, as Jack Zipes and others have argued, choice is an illusion. Zipes puts the situation this way:

Whatever healthy differences in perspective and identities that are fostered by the family, school or church in heterogeneous communities are leveled by homogeneous market forces that confuse the issue of freedom and choice and equate the power to buy with the power to determine one's identity and culture. (12)

To put this another way, we might note that the marketplace has taken advantage of play. Child power has become "wedgie power" (see the Captain Underpants books). The products children may purchase invite them to play with the gross and vulgar. Play defuses transgression; it becomes the child's form of carnival, a safe outlet for antisocial energies. When adults are outraged at the rudeness and vulgarity of children's culture, they play right into the hands of both the children who hope to get a rise out of their elders and the captains of industry who hope to make a lot of bucks from these same elders who prove complicit when they buy the books and toys and videos that trade in the gross and unpleasant. Transgression becomes an accepted form of behavior, and its acceptance effectively transforms transgression into conformity. This sleight-of-hand is what Herbert Marcuse spotted years ago in *One-Dimensional Man*: The market satisfies while it represses. Today this sleight garners the term *homogenizing* (Zipes 1–23). Of course, satisfaction is only half the story, since in order to keep things moving, to keep the exchange of cash for product moving, the market must not only satisfy but also dissatisfy.

Dissatisfaction is a result of an overload of false choice. The number of toys, books, videos, games, items of sportswear, trading cards, and other stuff for kids to buy is staggering. Everything produces a spinoff, at least everything that is successful. In children's books, first we had a few titles by the likes of Christopher Pike, Diane Hoh, and R. L. Stine. Then came the series Fear Street, Nightmare Hall, Spooksville, and so on. The most popular was Goosebumps, which itself produced at least two spinoff series, Barf-O-Rama and Gooflumps, the latter consisting of two titles: *Stay Out of the Bathroom* and *Eat Cheese and Barf!* (both 1995). The move was from horror to gross-out. With Barf-O-Rama we reached the nadir of the offensive and objectionable. All the while, the message these books conveyed had something to do with accumulation and consumption. As Perry Nodelman noted in his analysis of the Goosebumps series:

Goosebumps encourage the most widely held values of contemporary consumer culture. Their marketing supports self-indulgence and the importance of gratifying desire; the belief that adult concerns are authoritarian and the encouragement of rebellion against them; the importance of status with other children, and the lack of importance of pleasing or agreeing with conventional adults and with conventional adult ideas about behavior or morality or literary excellence. (119)

Self-indulgence is perhaps what most needs glossing here. *Narcissism* is the word Douglas Kellner uses to describe culture today. He includes in this characterization everything from Rush Limbaugh and Howard Stern to the focus of his essay, Beavis and Butt-Head, the cartoon duo who are obsessed with "excrement ... nose-picking, farting and other activities previously taboo on television" (92–97). Certainly, the current obsession with bodily fluids fits with our culture's intense focus on the body. The question is whether play with the five regrettable fluids serves a parodic and perhaps then a useful function or whether it is simply another instance of "the tradition of American anti-intellectualism" (Kellner 92). Could such aggressive attention seeking by the kids who indulge in this vulgarity be a call for more authority rather than less? Well, I doubt it.

The indulgence in the gross on the part of kids is not something newly invented by them. Kids' oral culture has a long history of delight in the unsavory and impolite, and if we forget our own childhood play with such impoliteness then we need only check compendia of children's lore such as those compiled by the Opies or Mary and Herbert Knapp's *One Potato, Two Potato*, or Josepha Sherman and T. K. F. Weisskopf's *Greasy Grimy Gopher Guts: The Subversive Folklore of Childhood*. I doubt whether kids have eagerly resorted to gross humor as a ploy to encourage their parents to exert more authority over them. The market has merely recognized the gross as a source of revenue. What we are experiencing in the market's pandering to kids' delight in the shock value of the lower bodily strata and orificial deposits of a variety of kinds is a socializing in the ways of consumer society. Good young entrepreneurs can sell anything, even shit. And they can sell anything, even shit, to kids as well as adults. Indulge potential shoppers and they will buy.

I think my emphasis on the cynicism of the marketplace, although probably legitimate enough, is not the whole story. If we trace the current interest in the five regrettable fluids to its source in children's literature, we will most likely find Raymond Briggs's *Fungus the Bogeyman*, which appeared in 1977. Briggs created the world of Bogeydom in which Bogeys drink slime, use cow dung for face cream and food coloring, eat watercress grown in cesspools, flaked corns from the feet, and earwax. The five regrettable fluids make their contemporary debut in this story of one Bogey's quest for meaning in life. The characters in this book literally roll in filth. Clearly, Briggs was having fun with our notions of high art, propriety, social convention, and obsession with the body. His creation is truly carnivalesque in that it punctures the pretensions of our culture. Whereas we have the theater and the cinema, Bogeys have the Odeum where they go to enjoy the odor of strong flatulence; Bogey literature boasts such masterpieces as *Anne of Green Bogeys, Charlie and the Chocolate Bogeys,* and *A la Recherche de Bogeys Perdus*; Bogey art galleries proudly display paintings of rotting fruit, dead flowers, dead animals, black stagnant lakes, sewers, and the deaths of children. In short, Bogeydom turns our society and its conventions upside down. Briggs's interest is in exposing the hypocrisy and artificiality of the world we inhabit. His work has a social purpose; it attempts to liberate the reader from false pretensions and unnecessary fastidiousness. The anger that is clear in other work by Briggs, *Gentleman Jim* (1980), *When the Wind Blows* (1982), and *The Tin-Pot Foreign General and the Old Iron Woman* (1984), for example, is not far below the surface in *Fungus*.

The anger connects Briggs with the carnivalesque. This is an anger that expresses itself through laughter, laughter at the grotesque body. The Bogey is the body grotesque, the dirty side of the human being. And the laughter elicited by this book is ambivalent. On the one hand, it is the laughter of a misanthrope out to expose the crudities of human life; on the other, it is the laughter of healthy regeneration, a healing and equalizing laughter (Bakhtin, 66–73). Laughter, like everything else human, is of the body. What Briggs taps in *Fungus* is the essential nature of the body in all human activity. Briggs, like all great writers and illustrators for children, knows what the child knows, and what the child knows is that life is of the body. Here is Norman O. Brown on this very point:

What the child knows consciously, and the adult unconsciously, is that we are nothing but body. However much the repressed and sublimating adult may consciously deny it, the fact remains that life is of the body and only life creates values; all values are bodily values. (293)

Brown calls for a release of the body from sublimation, and Rushdy follows him in calling for an "emetics of interpretation" (Rushdy 4). Release, resurrection, pleasure, carnival, heterology, polymorphous: These are terms relevant to such an emetics. For Rushdy, the concern is with a critical practice that allows for free flow, for dialogue one with another, for difference and for open-endedness. Metaphors insist on returning us to what Rushdy refers to as the "alimentary canal" (2). What I am moving toward is a reading of kids' culture as such an open-ended play with all things bodily. What some see as the vulgarization of the child's world may instead be an expression of utopian desire. Take, for example, the Belgian writer Wally de Doncker's *Ahum* (2000), which is about a group of people called Toesjepans. Among other rather dull things, they love "farting very loud" (n.p.).[1] This is not very rewarding, but acceptance of the body and the human capacity to use this body for making love is rewarding.

Acceptance of the body in all its beauty and ugliness may be a way out of the impasse of an economic imperative that perceives human life as sustainable only through mechanisms of sublimation. I say "may be a way" because I am not at all certain of this. I am at something of an impasse myself. Is the culture of grossness simply vulgar both in itself and as an economic ploy or does it give us access to genuine transgression? To approach an answer to this question, I'll close this chapter with a look at children's books, both the popular and the canonical. And I shall begin with the most recent and the popular—the Barf-O-Rama books.

As I mentioned earlier, the Barf-O-Rama series was short-lived. Nary a trace of it exists on Bantam Books' Web site. It does, however, take the culture of grossness to an extreme and this may explain its short life. Whether the publishers were being cynical in producing these books or whether they had a more radical purpose in mind hardly matters. The books exhibit a grossness that may have offended by virtue of their very success in transgression. Your average citizen, trained in the conventions of social intercourse, does not gladly suffer the gross and disgusting. For this citizen, that which disgusts does so precisely to remind us of the necessity for inoffensive behavior; the disgusting is not something to savor, relish, or generally revel in. And so the Barf-O-Rama books' descent into disgust for the sake of disgust was most likely too much for potential buyers of these books to take.

No matter what we think about the Barf-O-Rama books as literature, it is difficult to ignore their self-consciousness. We might label them "postmodern" in their parodic exuberance, using postmodern in the sense of a work that is "bound up ... with its own complicity with power and domination, one that acknowledges that it cannot escape implication in that which it still wants to analyze and maybe even undermine" (Hutcheon 4). To suggest that these books "want to analyze" anything, aside from the five regrettable fluids, is perhaps a stretch. But their excessive disgustingness does serve the purpose of helping us analyze the cultural interest in the gross and impolite. Make no mistake, these books are disgusting in that they both deal with that which pollutes and they threaten to pollute young minds with the belief that play with such polluting subject is acceptable. The crucial question is, Does the disgust in which these books traffic liberate their readers in a positive or negative direction? Do they serve social conventions or do they threaten social conventions? Are they acceptable reading for the young or are they execrable trash?

Number 6 in the series is *To Wee or Not to Wee* (Pollari), the title giving a clue to both the naughty content of the book and to its intertextual connection with the theater, high art, and Shakespeare. To make its point about the soiling of high art in the parodic culture of children, the book uses epigraphs for each chapter drawn from the work of one Shakespew. For example, chapter 1 begins with "But soft! What whiff through yonder hinder breaks?" (1). Chapter 12 begins with this epigraph "What's in a name? That which we call vomit or gumbo or puke or stomach contents or heave or hurl, by any other name would smell as morbific" (79). Aside from the play with Shakespeare (the messing with an icon, as it were), this epigraph also illustrates the Barf-O-Rama series' interest in the language of disgust. Not only do these books describe familiar instances of disgust, but they do so in a language that strains to test the limits of inventive crassness. We get such neologisms as "morbific," "gack dance," "buttnado," "barficane," "fettucine al snotto," "boogaroni," "buttwurst," "pooptonium," and so on. The writer of these books, Pat Pollari, knows that much of the joy kids might take in the gross and disgusting is linguistic. When parody strikes it takes everything, even language, as its target.

The plot of *To Wee or Not to Wee* is simple to a degree: Two friends, Alonzo and Bryan, are interested in a girl, Kelly Armstrong. Kelly is to play Juliet in the school production of *Romeo and Juliet,* and both boys want the part of Romeo so they can kiss the girl they admire. Bryan, however, is a bully and he sabotages Alonzo's every move—that is, until after the two boys attend a performance of a hypnotist, Zaraband the Magnificent. Bryan is his usual obnoxious self during Zaraband's performance, and so Zaraband challenges him to come on stage, where he hypnotizes Bryan and plants five deadly words in Bryan's mind. Each word when uttered within Bryan's hearing will activate in dramatic and excessive volume of one of the five regrettable fluids. This doesn't make much sense, but it does offer a pretend rationale for lava flows of ear wax, rivers of urine, avalanches of snot, and the threat of an explosion of numero dos. We get a series of scenes in which one or more of the five regrettable fluids makes an appearance in such volume as to gross out the kids nearby—on the school bus, in the gym, at home, wherever.

The catch is that all this over-the-top disgust serves a purpose over and above the simple gross-out. Bryan, remember, is a bully. He needs a comeuppance. This he gets in heaps, as it were, of humiliation. Alonzo quickly realizes the power he now has over the person who has tormented him for years, and he uses this power to his advantage. The book tries to make light of its "moral" by having Alonzo, the story's narrator, list two morals as he finishes his narrative. He delivers these morals whimsically, but they have their serious edge: "Don't play hooky" and "stand up for yourself. Don't let anyone push you around" (113). Another book in this series, *Party Pooper* (Pollari), is perhaps even more disgusting (if this is possible; one character actually blows snot through a straw so that it lands on other people's faces). It centers on Aisha Vaughn, a young girl obsessed with cleanliness and neatness. Her friends refer to her as "retentive," by which they mean "clean to the point of being truly nauseating" (118). Aisha has two problems: She has to baby-sit for an extremely disgusting family with three children, the youngest of whom is a baby with the largest and stinkiest "diaper gravy" imaginable (the book's glossary defines this "gravy" as "one of the most deadly substances known to man," 116) and she has a friend Karen who is trying to drive her around the bend so that she can replace Aisha as the leader of the "pep squad" (the book avoids the term "cheerleaders"). And so this book also has its morals: Don't be overly fastidious and treat your friends with honesty and respect.

What conclusion might we draw from Barf-O-Rama, the series that was? Its short life is clearly an indication that it did not sell. If I may be blunt, shit sells unless it smells too ripe. Seeing a good suburban family splattered with spray and bits from a septic tank apparently draws a laugh in the film *Meet the Parents,* as does a gigantic turd in *Dogma;* however, I guess you can have too much of a dirty thing, and Barf-O-Rama was too much. A little bit of dirt makes the world seem okay (this is one lesson we can draw from *Party Pooper*). Or a little bit of poop makes the lessons go down in the most delightful way, but too much poop and it's a different story. Older viewers of films such as *Dogma* and *Meet the Parents*, the comic book crowd perhaps, may enjoy the whiff of the privy, but younger viewers (and readers) require a more delicate handling. Lesson or no lesson, eschew the toilet jokes and avoid the gross-out when these flow too freely. A lot of poop is either carnivalesque, in which case only those poor oppressed souls in need of respite from the constipation of enforced convention will appreciate it, or downright disgusting, in which case no one except the barbarian could take any interest at all in it. But I return to that inevitable bottom line: If it sells, it's okay; if it languishes on store shelves, it's done for. Barf-O-Rama is done for.

But we need not stop here. Despite my theme of market influence in the lives of children and in the current shitload of things offensive to the polite and pure, I keep Norman O. Brown, Ashraf Rushdy, and Georges Bataille in mind. Can we find something positive after all in this deluge of the gross and unsavory? I think the answer is yes. Take for example, the recent (2001) film version of William Steig's picture book *Shrek!* The book, about a repulsive creature who sells some of his "rare lice" to a witch in return for his fortune, ends with Shrek finding his true love, a princess who is even uglier than he is. Steig clearly delights in creating a creature who is all body, smells and lumpy nose, pointy head, green skin with stubby hair, and ears like tiny trumpets. The filmmakers go further and show Shrek showering in mud, killing fish with his flatulence, using his earwax for a candle, and eating the grossest things imaginable. He uses pages from a fairy tale book for his stercoraceous business. And he saves a princess. This inversion of the familiar story of the brave knight who saves the beautiful princess turns on the assumption of bodily pleasure in its most grotesque manifestations. The reader of Steig's book and the viewer of the film cannot but be enthralled by the character's acceptance of the body—warts and all. Here is an example of the gross as a love of life that scrambles beneath the veneer of polite convention and embraces the world.

Another example of what I mean is available in Wally de Doncker's *Wolken in het Zand*. In this book, a small bird named for the "little heap of crap" that she emits from her body after eating wonders why she lives. What purpose does she serve? She comes close to despair when she cannot find an answer to the question. All she can do is eat flower seeds and then deposit little heaps of crap. She feels that she wants to die. Then, miraculously, she sees growing from the little piles of excrement she has left a host of flowers. The book ends with a vision of flowers everywhere.

One of the most popular and enduring of children's books may have something to add to this scrutiny of the scatological. I refer to *Charlotte's Web*. E. B. White's classic takes delight in life as an alimentary canal, with a beginning, a middle, and an end that takes us back to the beginning in a joy of all things bright and beautiful as well as dark and dubious. *Charlotte's Web* expresses in a deeply moving manner, I think, Bataille's assertion that "life is a product of putrefaction, and it depends on both death and the dungheap" (80). The Zuckermans' barnyard is a place where all things grow and die and serve a purpose. A rotten egg may be disgusting to one but desirable to another. Here rats and spiders have their use as well as horses and cows. Muck and slops feed some, while milk and honey feed others.

The fullest and nicest expression of White's embrace of life's open-ended cycle that contains the pure and the impure is the beginning of chapter 3, the paragraph that in White's first version of his story began the book. This is the description of the barn:

The barn was very large. It was very old. It smelled of hay and it smelled of manure. It smelled of the perspiration of tired horses and the wonderful sweet breath of patient cows. It often had a sort of peaceful smell—as though nothing bad could happen ever again in the world. It smelled of grain and of harness dressing and of axle grease and of rubber boots and of new rope. And whenever the cat was given a fish-head to eat, the barn would smell of fish. But mostly it smelled of hay, for there was always hay in the great lift up overhead. And there was always hay being pitched down to the cows and the horses and the sheep. (13)

The sense of smell is keenly associated with disgust, and here White raises smells we associate with unpleasant olfactory sensation: Manure, dead fish, sweat, breath, and so on. William Ian Miller notes that such smells conjure up beginnings and endings, the sweat of labor, the results of completed digestion, and death itself, and that with such reminders of beginnings and endings desire can find no purchase. "Desire," he says, "requires that we suppress entirely thoughts of beginnings and endings" (69). Miller writes, perhaps, not of the Lacanian desire that is a function of the very process of change and movement, a restless failure to adjust to beginnings and endings. The desire Miller refers to is the desire for satisfaction of the bodily senses, and we cannot be satisfied if we are constantly reminded of mortality and decay. We remember Snow White's stepmother's anxiety on this matter of mortality and decay.

But White has a different take on the smells of decay. The manure, perspiration, and dead fish in the barn combine with the hay and breath of cows and rubber boots and axle grease to make a satisfying aroma. Hay goes in one end and nourishes; then having nourished, it comes out the other end to begin another cycle. The dead fish too may stink, but it will nourish the cat and then reappear as something else. The alchemy of the alimentary canal will work its way. The barn is a place of richly experienced life. Here life and death connect as they inevitably must, but they do so not in ways that disturb or disgust. Quite the reverse is true. The barn is a place of comfort and reassurance precisely because here everything is acceptable and satisfying. Here we find White occupying the same revisionary Freudian territory as Brown and Rushdy. To embrace life fully means to embrace all that it has to offer, the pure and the impure. White puts this succinctly near the end of *Charlotte's Web* when he reasserts the goodness of the barn as a place of life in all its manifestations. The barn with its garrulous geese and changing seasons and heat and swallows and rats and sheep and spiders and "smell of manure" is "the best place to be" because here one experiences "the glory of everything" (183).

NOTE

I thank my friend and colleague Jan Susina, who obliged me with some references for this chapter, and I also thank Ashraf Rushdy, whose silence will not allow me to forget that he encouraged me to write on a similar topic ten years ago.

1. Wally de Doncker has kindly sent me translations of two of this books, *Ahum* (2000; translated by Ineke Debels) and *Wolken in het Zand (Clouds in the Sand,* 1998; translated by Wally de Doncker).

WORKS CITED

Bakhtin, Mikhail. *Rabelais and His World.* Trans. Helene Iswolsky. Bloomington: Indiana University Press, 1984.

Bataille, Georges. *The Accursed Share,* vols. 2 and 3. Trans. Robert Hurley. New York: Zone, 1993.

Briggs, Raymond. *Fungus the Bogeyman.* London: Hamish Hamilton, 1977.

———. *Gentleman Jim.* London: Hamish Hamilton, 1980.

———. *The Tin-Pot Foreign General and the Old Iron Lady.* London: Hamish Hamilton, 1984.

———. *When the Wind Blows.* London: Hamish Hamilton, 1982.

Brown, Norman O. *Life Against Death: The Psychoanalytical Meaning of History.* Middletown, CT: Wesleyan University Press, 1959.

Caldwell, Mark. *A Short History of Rudeness.* New York: Picador, 1999.

"Crass Act: Popular Culture Has Really Hit the Deck As Everything from TV to Toys Gets Yucky." *New York Daily News,* 25 Jan. 1998, 3–4.

de Doncker, Wally. *Ahum.* Leuven, Belg.: Davidsfonds/Infodok, 2000.

———. *Wolken in het Zand.* Leuven, Belg.: Davidsfonds/Infodok, 1998.

Dogma. Dir. Kevin Smith. Lions Gate, 1999.

Edmundson, Mark. *Nightmare on Main Street: Angels, Sadomasochism and the Culture of Gothic.* Cambridge, MA: Harvard University Press, 1997.

Fiedler, Leslie A. *Love and Death in the American Novel.* 1960. New York: Dell, 1966.

Freud, Sigmund. *Civilization and Its Discontents.* Vol. 12 of *The Penguin Freud Library,* ed. Albert Dickson. London: Penguin, 1991. 245–340.

Hutcheon, Linda. *The Politics of Postmodernism.* London: Routledge, 1989.

Ignatieff, Michael. *The Rights Revolution.* Toronto: Anansi, 2000.

Kellner, Douglas. "*Beavis and Butt-Head:* No Future for Postmodern Youth." *Kinder-Culture: The Corporate Construction of Childhood,* eds. Shirley R. Steinberg and Joe L. Kincheloe. Boulder, CO: Westview Press, 1998. 85–101.

Kimmelman, Michael. "What's This About Cultural Pollution?" *New York Times on the Web,* 5 Nov. 2000. http://www.nytmes.com/2000/11/05/arts.

Kline, Stephen. *Out of the Garden: Toys and Children's Culture in the Age of TV Marketing.* Toronto: Garamond, 1993.

Knapp, Mary, and Herbert Knapp. *One Potato, Two Potato: The Folklore of American Children.* New York: Norton, 1976.

Laporte, Dominique. *History of Shit.* Trans. Nadia Benabid and Rodolphe el-Khoury. Cambridge, MA: MIT Press, 1993.

Marcuse, Herbert. *One-Dimensional Man.* Boston: Beacon, 1964.

Meet the Parents. Dir. Jay Roach. Universal, 2000.

Miller, William Ian. *The Anatomy of Disgust.* Cambridge, MA: Harvard University Press, 1997.

Minow, Newton N., and Craig L. Lamay. *Abandoned in the Wasteland: Children, Television, and the First Amendment.* New York: Hill & Wang, 1995.

Munsch, Robert. *Good Families Don't.* Toronto: Doubleday, 1990.

——. *I Have to Go.* Toronto: Annick, 1987.

Nodelman, Perry. "Ordinary Monstrosity: The World of Goosebumps," *Children's Literature Association Quarterly* 22 (1997): 118–25.

Opie, Iona, and Peter Opie. *The Lore and Language of Schoolchildren.* London: Oxford University Press, 1959.

Pareles, Jon. "Worked Up Again over Gross-outs," *New York Times on the Web,* 20 Aug. 2000. http://www.nytimes.com/2000/08/20/arts.

Pilkey, Dav. *The Adventures of Captain Underpants.* New York, Toronto: Scholastic, 1997.

——. *Captain Underpants and the Attack of the Talking Toilets.* New York: Scholastic, 1999.

——. *Captain Underpants and the Invasion of the Incredibly Naughty Cafeteria Ladies from Outer Space (and the Subsequent Assault of the Equally Evil Lunchroom Zombie Nerds).* New York: Scholastic, 1999.

——. *Captain Underpants and the Perilous Plot of Professor Poopypants.* New York: Scholastic, 2000.

Pollari, Pat. *Party Pooper.* New York: Bantam, 1996.

——. *To Wee or Not to Wee.* New York: Bantam, 1996.

Pratchett, Terry. *Carpe Jugulum.* London: Corgi, 1998.

Richler, Mordecai. *Jacob Two-Two Meets the Hooded Fang.* Toronto: McLelland, 1975.

Rushdy, Ashraf H. A. "A New Emetics of Interpretation: Swift, His Critics and the Alimentary Canal," *Mosaic* 24 (1991): 1–32.

Scary Movie. Dir. Keenen Ivory Wayans. Miramax, 2000.

Sherman, Josepha, and T. K. F. Weisskopf. *Greasy Grimy Gopher Guts: The Subversive Folklore of Childhood.* New York: August House, 1995.

Shrek. Dir. Andrew Adamson and Vicky Jenson. Dream Works, 2001.

Steig, William. *Shrek!* New York: Farrar, 1990.

There's Something About Mary. Dir. Bobby Farrelly. Twentieth Century–Fox, 1998.

White, E. B. *Charlotte's Web.* 1952. New York: Dell, 1973.

Zipes, Jack. *Sticks and Stones: The Troublesome Success of Children's Literature from Slovenly Peter to Harry Potter.* New York: Routledge, 2001.

Index

About the Contributors

CLARE BRADFORD is an associate professor in literature at Deakin University, Melbourne, Australia, where she teaches literary studies and children's literature. She researches and publishes mainly in children's literature, with an emphasis on colonial and postcolonial theory and visual texts. Her most recent book is *Reading Race: Aboriginality in Australian Children's Literature*.

KAREN BROOKS is a lecturer in popular culture at the University of the Sunshine Coast, Queensland, Australia, as well as a fantasy author and radio talk show host.

DAVID BUCHBINDER is an associate professor in the School of Communication and Cultural Studies at Curtin University of Technology, Perth, Western Australia. He teaches in the areas of cultural, gender, and literary studies and his particular field of research is the cultural representation and construction of masculinity. In addition to a number of journal articles and book chapters, some of his other publications are *Contemporary Literary Theory and the Reading of Poetry* (1992), *Masculinities and Identities* (1994), and *Performance Anxieties: Re-producing Masculinity* (1998).

DAVID BUCKINGHAM is professor of education at the Institute of Education, University of London, where he directs the Centre for the Study of Children, Youth and Media (www.ccsonline.org.uk/mediacentre). He has written numerous books, including *Children Talking Television* (1993), *Moving Images* (1996), and *After the Death of Childhood* (2000). He is currently directing research projects on the uses of new media by refugee/migrant children, young people's responses to sexual material on television, and the textual characteristics of computer games.

JOHN HARTLEY is dean of Creative Industries at Queensland University of Technology, Brisbane, Australia. His research interests are popular media and journalism. He has written a dozen books, translated into ten languages, and is founding editor of the *International Journal of Cultural Studies*. Recent books are *Popular Reality* (1996), *Uses of Television* (1999), *American Cultural Studies: A Reader* (2000), and *The Indigenous Public Sphere* (2001).

MARY CELESTE KEARNEY is an assistant professor in critical and cultural studies and gender and sexuality in the Department of Radio-Television-Film at the University of Texas at Austin. She is also the founder and director of Cinemakids, a program devoted to youth filmmaking that is part of the Cinematexas International Short Film Festival. Her recent publications are "Girlfriends and Girl Power: Female Adolescence in Contemporary U.S. Cinema," in *Sugar, Spice, and Everything Nice: Cinemas of Girlhood* (2001); "Producing Girls: Rethinking the Study of Female Youth Culture," in *Delinquents and Debutantes: Twentieth-Century American Girls' Culture* (1998); and "The Missing Links: Riot Grrrl—Feminism—Lesbian Culture," in *Sexing the Groove: Gender and Popular Music* (1997).

CATHARINE LUMBY is an associate professor and director of media and communication studies at the University of Sydney, Australia. Her most recent book is *Gotcha: Life in a Tabloid World* (1999). She is also a widely published journalist who currently writes a regular column for the *Bulletin* magazine.

KERRY MALLAN is a senior lecturer in the School of Cultural and Language Studies in Education at Queensland University of Technology, Brisbane, Australia. Her main teaching and research interests are in children's literature. Her recent publications have focused on aspects of gender, sexuality, and visual representation in youth literature, picture books, and film for young people.

RODERICK McGILLIS is a professor of English at the University of Calgary, Canada. Publications in press are on masculinity, the B western film, identity politics, George MacDonald and queer fantasy, and the IRSCL/Greenwood volume of essays titled *Children's Literature and the Fin de Siècle*.

CLAUDIA NELSON is an associate professor of English at Southwest Texas State University. She wrote *Boys Will Be Girls: The Feminine Ethic and British Children's Fiction 1850–1910* and the forthcoming *Homeward Bound: Representations of Adoption and Foster Care in America, 1850–1929*.

SHARYN PEARCE is a senior lecturer in the Faculty of Creative Industries at Queensland University of Technology in Brisbane, Australia. She has published extensively, mostly on Australian studies and children's literature. Recent publications are *Shameless Scribblers: Australian Women's Journalism 1890–1995* (1998) and *Strange Journeys: The Works of Gary Crew* (1999). Most recently she has edited a series of essays on masculinities, entitled *Manning the Next Millennium* (2002).

LISA SAINSBURY is a lecturer in children's literature at the National Centre for Research in Children's Literature at University of Surrey Roehampton, United Kingdom. Some of her previous publications are articles on postmodern adolescent literature and narrative development in children's multimedia.

JOHN STEPHENS is professor in English at Macquarie University, Sydney, Australia, where he teaches and supervises postgraduate research in children's literature, as well as in other literatures. He wrote *Language and Ideology in Children's Fiction; Retelling Stories, Framing Culture* (cowritten with Robyn McCallum); two books about discourse analysis; and around sixty articles about children's (and other) literature. More recently, he has edited *Ways of Being Male: Representing Masculinities in Children's Literature and Film*. His primary research focus is on the relationships between texts produced for children and young adults (especially literature and film) and cultural formations and practices.

GORDON TAIT is a senior lecturer in the School of Cultural and Language Studies in Education, at the Queensland University of Technology, Brisbane, Australia. His research interests are Youth, Sexuality, Education, and Humor.